Cross-Curricular Learning 3–14

Cross-Curricular Learning 3–14

Jonathan Barnes

Paul Chapman
Publishing

Paul Chapman Publishing
A SAGE Publications Company
1 Oliver's Yard
55 City Road
London EC1Y 1SP

SAGE Publications Inc
2455 Teller Road
Thousand Oaks, California 91320

SAGE Publications India Pvt Ltd
B-42, Panchsheel Enclave
Post Box 4109
New Delhi 110 017

A catalogue record for this book is available from
the British Library

ISBN-10 1-4129-2057-4   ISBN-13 978-1-4129-2057-5
ISBN-10 1-4129-2058-2   ISBN-13 978-1-4129-2058-2 (pbk)

Library of Congress Control Number: 2006930261

Typeset by C&M Digitals (P) Ltd, Chennai, India
Printed in Great Britain by Athenaeum Press, Gateshead, Tyne and Wear
Printed on paper from sustainable resources

'…just help them find where they can be creative and fulfilment will follow.'

To

Gerry Tewfik who said these words and inspired many of the principles which underpin this book and to Kay and Bill Barnes my parents, who have tirelessly encouraged my creativity.

Contents

About the Author

Jonathan Barnes

Lives in Canterbury with his wife, potter, Cherry Tewfik and fluctuating numbers of their children and grandchildren. He is senior lecturer in Education at Canterbury Christ Church University. He teaches music and geography to primary teacher trainees. He has wide experience of further, secondary and primary teaching and worked as education officer for English Heritage. From 1992 to 2000 he was head teacher of a primary school.

He has taught in: Kenya, Tanzania, Malaysia, Indonesia, and India as well as England. He has worked closely on education policy for local and national museums including the Victoria and Albert Museum and the National Maritime Museum.

In writing and research he has specialized in creative and cross-curricular approaches to teaching, and the development of creative thinking. Books for teachers and children include titles on: Music, Kenya (for the BBC), Castles, cross-cultural environments, Design Technology, and citizenship. Four of his guides for teachers on using the historic environment to promote creative learning have been published by English Heritage.

His keen interests in language, art, music, geography, history, RE and citizenship resulted in the implementation of cross-curricular modules which have now become a feature of all primary courses at his university.

Acknowledgements

There is no doubt that my chief thanks go to my wife Cherry who has loved, sustained, inspired and encouraged me throughout a difficult year so crammed with important family events that writing a book seemed impossible. Similarly, my children Ben, Naomi, Esther and Jacob have contributed in ways they are not always fully aware of. They have tolerated my divided attention and listened, always with love and patience, to my overexcited conversation on the topics raised in this book.

Many friends and colleagues have been generous with their time and attention. Stephen Scoffham, particularly, has courageously read chapters and generously commented in fine, informed and intelligent detail. But I must also thank Vanessa Young, Linden West, William Stow, Glen Sharp, Jane Stamps (my inspiring sister), Paul Thompson, Ian Shirley, Robert McCrea, Ken and Matt Miles, Andrew Lambirth, Robert Jarvis, Bryan Hawkins, Grenville Hancox, Teresa Cremin, Tony Booth and Judy Baker who met my fervour for curriculum reform with enthusiasm and added their own wisdom to my thinking. I owe a great deal to them.

I have attempted not to identify individual schools who have helped, because the messages they give can apply across schools in many different locations and settings. The following schools, without their town or county, will know who they are when I thank them for accommodating me on my research. I admire them all for their immense energy, inspiration and hope: Astor Arts College, Bethersden Primary School, Bodsham C of E Primary School, Brockhill Performing Arts College, Brompton Westbrook School, Fonthill Primary School, Goodwill Primary School, Hythe Community Infants School, St Nicholas School, St Peter's Methodist School, St Stephen's Junior School, The Churchill School, The Coram School and The Priory School.

Organizations and individuals have also helped in many ways and I have been grateful for moral support and photographic materials from The Scottish Children's Parliament, Room 13, Creative Partnerships, Kent, North London and Bristol, The HEARTS project, Siemens, Canterbury Christ Church University, Simon Adams, Cherry Tewfik, Robert Jarvis, Jane Heyes, Tony Ling, Dorothee Thyssen and Priory Sue.

Finally, I thank Helen Fairlie and Jeanette Graham for their patient and wise editorial and organizational support.

Introduction

I wrote this book to make a twenty-first century case for placing cross-curricular experience at the heart of the school curriculum. I attempt to steer a path between the heavy emphasis on separate 'core' and 'foundation' subject disciplines which has characterized primary and secondary education since 1990 and the overgeneralizing and usually adult-led tendencies of 1970s-style 'topic work'. The book is intended for head teachers and coordinating teachers planning a securely based, cross-curricular approach to children's learning, those engaged in teacher education, educationalists and education tutors. I put forward practical suggestions, planning formats, carefully chosen case studies, research evidence and a guiding rationale for a new and informed look at cross-curricular teaching and learning.

Innocence and experience

And Priests in black gowns, were walking their rounds,
And binding with briars, my joys and desires. (Blake, 1789 [1967])

Our experience of the world is cross-curricular. Everything which surrounds us in the physical world can be seen and understood from multiple perspectives. As adults we tend to see each aspect of the perceptible and imagined universe from a variety of more or less 'experienced' viewpoints, but the 'innocent' eyes of the child have probably always seen a different world to that of their parents and elders. When, as experienced adults, we look at the tree or bramble outside our window, depending on our education and experience we will each 'see' it in slightly different ways; we may 'know' something of its biology or its geographical implications – the part it plays in reducing the impact of pollution or releasing oxygen. We may, like Blake, think of the poetic or symbolic resonances of our bramble, its potential as an art object or the way it enhances or spoils a view. It is unlikely that a child of 6 or 7 would perceive this part of the natural world in the same ways as an adult. Perhaps a child is more likely to see the same tree as a quiet place for talking, a hiding place, a threat, a magical mine of fascinating moving things, a den or simply one side of a goal. Perhaps the bramble will represent an uncomfortable memory of scratches, a threat or a source of tasty blackberries – the possible associations are endless.

Children need liberating from an adult dominated curriculum. One of the threads which bind this book will be the suggestion that it is important for the child to enjoy being a child, to enjoy learning *now* for its own sake and not primarily for some future role they may or may not take on in the adult world. This emphasis on the child's 'here' and 'now' will involve the examination of various research and curricular attempts to discover what is important to children in today's school classes. The concentration on children's lives will result in considering how we as teachers might help to use children's distinctly different viewpoints, as motivation, method and model for their learning. It seems from all we know about children learning, that motivation, self-esteem, personal relevance, authentic challenge and a sense of achievement are all crucial. At the same time current thinking on emotional well-being and children, would suggest that an inner sense of personal happiness is not just a key motivator for now, but also central to future good health and security. What experiences, attitudes, and resources can we weave into our curricula that make the generation of positive feelings more likely for each child?

Research

This book is underpinned by a range of research projects involving teachers, student teachers and children aged 3–14. My own research was conducted in five recent projects:

- the Higher Education Arts and Schools (HEARTS) projects funded jointly by the Esmee Fairbairne Trust and the Gulbenkian Foundation (Barnes and Shirley, 2005
- the Creative Teaching for Tomorrow (CTFT) project funded by Creative Partnerships Kent (Grainger, Barnes and Scoffham, 2006)
- the Spaces for Sports and the Arts Report funded by the Arts Council and Sport England (Dismore et al., 2006)
- a series of observations in case study schools between July 2005 and June 2006, followed up by email and telephone interviews with key members of staff
- my own PhD thesis on the impact of autobiography on teachers' values (Barnes, 2006b).

In addition to this empirically grounded work which I draw upon throughout the text, include themed reviews of recent research by others, from which I draw tentative conclusions relevant to the classroom. The research has employed mixed methods, in particular interviews, observations and filed notes, and *autoethnography* – thinking about the influence of my own history and character in the development of the values and educational practice I propose.

Interviews

I interviewed school heads and/or heads of curriculum in the six case study schools about their views on curricula in general and their own school curriculum in detail. In each semi-structured interview I asked about principles, views on creativity, cross-curricular links and the organization of principles into a curriculum. I also held a series of group interviews with children engaged in cross-curricular activity. Some children were given cameras, and in two cases a video, to capture key moments in their work at school. These images were used to guide conversations which were recorded and transcribed. I also made dated research notes on informal interviews or informal comments from children whilst engaged in cross-curricular activities in school. I interviewed teachers in 10 different schools, teaching 3–14 year olds in cross-curricular settings. Some of these interviews were fully transcribed and analysed as part of a research study for Creative Partnerships Kent (Grainger, Barnes and Scoffham, 2006) and in field notes in my research journal. These schools are acknowledged at the beginning of this book.

Many interviews were followed up with email conversations and enquiries, which also formed part of the evidence base for this book.

Observations

I had the privilege of observing many lessons in many different indoor and outdoor settings (Barnes, 1994; Barnes and Hancox, 2004). Observations were, with permission, supplemented by photographs, many of which you will see in the text. Notes taken in observations were again analysed for themes and salient examples, which illustrated theoretical positions. Approximately 50 hours were devoted to these observations

Autoethnography

The interpretations and viewpoints taken are my own. I come from a particular and unique history, like all of us. Take for example one moment in my life:

> I am in St Paul's Cathedral, an 11-year-old school choirboy temporarily covering the services for the 'real' choir. Standing at the foot of the odd and fascinating monument to John Donne, I am waiting to process into the choir of the vast cathedral. The light is streaming in through gold-coloured windows to my right and the overpowering organ music of Olivier Messiaen is crashing and echoing around the colourfully mosaic-ed walls. I am fully aware and proud that minutes later I am to be altering the environment by my sounds and my presence in a daily ceremony once central to my culture.

The experience of joy was so positive, affirming, overpowering, almost transcendental that I have struggled ever since to re-create it in other forms for myself and the children I work with. That moment and many others profoundly influenced my attitude to the combining of subjects in interpreting experience.

Equally powerful was my experience 40 years later as a head teacher: I am in a meeting with a school inspector who tells me that our creative and cross-curricular ideas are 'too risky' and I should only consider continuing them after the Standard Assessment Tests (SATs) results have achieved well above the expectations for our particular school. This painful and unnerving experience galvanized me to action. I decided I was in the wrong job and moved to teacher education.

I cannot fail to keep both (and many, many more) examples in mind as I examine the curricula of schools, read prospectuses, learned papers and government proposals. The stories in my life profoundly influence the views I take. The views I take have been shaped into some coherence by the very mind that holds those views. My mind is also part of a culture, indeed many cultures, part of a profession and part of a team of professionals who deeply impact upon my thinking. In writing several versions of my own autobiography for my doctoral thesis I have become very aware of such layers of influence. Reflexive study for a PhD has shown that this book is an attempt to make sense of the aspects of my own life which might have a bearing on the curriculum. In research terms, therefore, I have used my fully written out autobiographies as a further source of research data. This data has been used to maintain an awareness of the sources of my assumptions and sometimes to challenge or seek corroboration of them.

The chapters

Chapter 1 briefly explores some relevant aspects of the twenty-first century world into which our children have been born. These aspects are highly selective, but chosen because of their implications for education and, particularly, potential plans for the curriculum that children will follow. There can be no escape from the fact that, currently, adults make the decisions, produce the plans and control the direction of learning. That this is as things should be does not seem unreasonable. The experienced adult perhaps might have the advantage of a wiser, longer and wider perspective. But the second thread running through this book is the proposition that adults in school should be easy with a more complex set of roles than simply planner, imparter and assessor of knowledge and 'standards'. Perhaps a key distinction between a trainer and a teacher is that the teacher allows space for individual learners to be different from one another; indeed, such individual differences could be seen as the chief resource of the teacher. There may be times when power relationships in a class are more appropriately shifted towards the children. In a cross-curricular setting, conscious of the child's cultural, spiritual, social, physical, personal and intellectual needs, the teacher may at different times be follower, co-learner, instructor, coach, observer, adviser, assistant, mentor, conscience, Master of Ceremonies (MC) servant or inspiration.

Chapter 2 consists of a fairly detailed set of case studies in ordinary schools which show some of the variety and range of cross-curricular approaches. Chapters 3, 4 and 5 consider the classroom implications of some recent neurological, psychological and pedagogical research.

The remainder of the book is devoted to practical guides on implementing a cross-curriculum in your school. The issue of the role of the individual subject disciplines must be discussed, however, before we begin to address the idea of teaching across them.

Discipline or not?

Howard Gardner, educationalist, psychologist and neurologist, and argued by some to be amongst the most influential of western thinkers on education, said recently that the 'scholarly disciplines' were the most significant invention of the last two millennia. The subject disciplines represent for Gardner, 'the most advanced and best ways to think about issues consequential to human beings' (Gardner, 2004, p. 138). Yet it is clear from other areas of his writing and research that he also believes, 'any topic of significance can, and should, be represented in a number of different ways in the mind' (Gardner, 2004, p. 141). Some of the 'intelligences' Gardner postulates (see Chapter 3) correspond closely to particular subject disciplines (musical, naturalistic, linguistic, logical-mathematical), some are closer to what we might call character traits (interpersonal, existential, intra-personal) and some to more physical capabilities (spatial, bodily kinaesthetic) but all are ways in which we make sense of real-life experience (Gardner, 1999a). Gardner is a great defender of subject skills and subject knowledge but sees twenty-first century education as providing: 'the basis for enhanced understanding of our several worlds – the physical world, the biological world, the world of human beings, the world of human artefacts and the world of the self' (Gardner, 1999b, p. 158). He follows this by a revealing statement about the relative importance of disciplined knowledge and skills:

> the acquisition of literacy, the learning of basic facts, the cultivation of basic skills, or the mastery of the ways of thinking of the disciplines – ... should be seen as means, not ends in themselves ... literacies, skills and disciplines ought to be pursued as tools that allow us to enhance our understanding of important questions, topics and themes. (Gardner, 1999b, p. 159)

Gardner's theory of multiple intelligences and his qualification to make judgements on the curriculum may be contested but, regardless of opinions on the science and language of his theory, his work and the research of many of his contemporaries has seriously opened out definitions of intelligence and shifted the debate towards more democratic, inclusive and humane approaches to the curriculum. The fact that he recently (2004) gained a professorship at one of the largest universities in China (East China Normal University) is testimony to the continuing impact of his thinking beyond 'western liberal' cultures.

British writers (for example, Robinson, 2001; Wrigley, 2005) argue with equal passion for the breakdown of subject boundaries Some argue for a competencies-based curriculum to 'open minds' (RSA, 2003), some the development of a curriculum which engenders 'a creative and critical orientation towards experience' (Abbs, 2003, p. 15), a curriculum which makes sense to pupils rather than teachers (Halpin, 2003, p. 113), more opportunities for play (David, 1999), less curricular prescription (Alexander, 1998) or an emotionally literate curriculum (Morris, 2002). The sum of educational advice grows daily.

There are principles, however, which may well reach beyond specific cultural and institutional contexts, and these are examined in Chapter 6. There is no shortage of educational research and general advice on how to enhance the learning experience of a child, but few publications offer usable models within which the ideals of cross-curricular and creative learning may be realized in practice. This book hopes to address such a need in Chapters 7, 8, 9 and 10.

Organization

You will read here an argument for a balance between the unique skills, knowledge and attitudes of each 'traditional' subject and the uniquely motivating effects of cross-curricular and child-centred learning. This book is written now because of the rapidly growing interest in topic-based, thematic and cross-curricular approaches in primary schools and increasingly in Years 7 and 8 classes in secondary. A practical guide for teachers in service and student teachers seems necessary because of the current paucity of direct guidance and out of a concern that guiding principles should be debated and established. It is probably already clear that it is also written out of a belief that the curriculum should be packed with opportunities for each child to find his or her strengths and activities which provide genuine challenge and multiple prospects for individual achievement. It is hoped that you will find workable examples of how such activities and experiences can be successfully planned and delivered.

The book is divided into chapters with clear foci. You do not have to read the chapters in any particular sequence, but can read them in order of their relevance to you. Most chapters are headed by a question which points to the chapter's theme:

- Chapter 1: What should schooling in the twenty-first century look like?
- Chapter 2: What does good cross-curricular practice look like?

- Chapter 3: What is the contribution of neuroscience to ideas about cross-curricular learning?
- Chapter 4: What are the contributions of modern psychology?
- Chapter 5: The view of the pedagog: 'We learn according to how we are taught'.
- Chapter 6: What principles should we apply?
- Chapter 7: What themes are suitable for cross-curricular learning?
- Chapter 8: How should we plan for cross-curricular activity?
- Chapter 9: How can we assess cross-curricular and creative learning?
- Chapter 10: Key issues for debate.

There are summaries and key questions at the end of each chapter and full lists of references and websites at the end of the book.

You may already have noticed that this book is well illustrated. Most illustrations come from the schools consulted and researched in writing this book. If information, principles, examples and issues are shown visually as well as in text, a different, perhaps deeper and more personal, level of understanding may be gained. There seems little doubt that visual images form an increasingly important part in the world of communication and knowledge, and every advertiser knows that images and objects have a powerful effect upon our minds and imaginations. I argue that we also learn through the feelings and associations that images generate in us. I believe we vastly underestimate the power of the visual in our teaching and learning. By more fully exploiting our species' ability to make fine and wide-ranging visual discriminations, we access areas of knowing beyond words. Each chapter is therefore illustrated with examples of children's work and children working in a variety of contexts. Photographs and diagrams are used as models too, but names of individuals are changed and schools only identified by their region.

Definitions

It is fairly easy to define the unique qualities of each National Curriculum subject; the National Curriculum document (DfEE/QCA, 1999b) provides a clear lead on this for each of the nine subjects of the curriculum, Information and Communications Technology, and Modern Foreign Languages. The various Special Advisory Councils on Religious Education in Schools (SACREs) in each education authority have made their own definitions of Religious Education. However, definitions of the terminology used in discussions on cross-curricular approaches are often vague and used interchangeably. In this book the following definitions apply:

The curriculum: the narrow definition is the subjects, topics and emphases chosen (usually by adults) to be the focus of learning in a school. In the context of this book, however, a broader definition, which also includes the 'hidden curriculum' of attitudes, assumptions, relationships and school ethos is used.

A discipline: a domain of knowledge generally held to be of importance by a culture. It has its own ways of thinking, its own rules, language and symbols, and has to be intentionally passed on (usually in education) to survive; it is not transferred in the genes.

Cross-curricular learning: when the skills, knowledge and attitudes of a number different disciplines are applied to a single experience, theme or idea, we are working in a cross-curricular way. We are looking at the experience of learning on a macro level and with the *curriculum* as the focus.

Disciplinary understanding: when students are able to use the knowledge and 'ways of thinking of a particular subject discipline, appropriately in novel situations' (Boix Mansilla, Miller and Gardner, in Wineburg, S. and Grossman, P., 2000).

Interdisciplinary: the interaction between two disciplines applied to a single problem, issue or environment. When we are looking at the learning experience on a micro level with the *discipline* as the focus, we are working in an interdisciplinary way.

Topic-based or thematic curriculum: these terms are used interchangeably to mean a curriculum where at least part of the week is devoted to the study of a particular theme or topic (like water, 'beauty', India or the microscopic life in the school pond) through the eyes of several curriculum subjects. The *stimulus* is the focus.

Thinking: the skilled use of intelligence. Good thinking can be considered as the process in which people are engaged, to attempt to solve a difficult or challenging task and which results in improvement in a person's intellectual power (Shayer and Adey, 2002).

Creativity: the ability in all humans imaginatively or practically to put two or more ideas together to make a valued new idea.

Creative teaching: teaching which uses the teacher's own inherent and learned creativity to make learning accessible.

Teaching for creativity: the intention of the teacher is to stimulate and develop the creativity inherent in every child in any subject or experiential context.

Assumptions

It is impossible to write a book on aspects of the school curriculum without making many assumptions. You will become aware of many as you read this book and should apply a critical mind to them. Certain assumptions must be brought into the open from the outset, however. The previous definitions make it clear that, along with many other educationalists, I believe *all children and teachers are potentially creative in some aspect* (see Craft, 2000; Csikszentmihalyi, 1997; Perkins, 1992; Sternberg, 1997b). This is an important assumption because cross-curricular work is often seen as a way of stimulating and nurturing creative thinking. I also believe that *creativity is best stimulated in cross-curricular and authentic contexts.*

It is assumed that *generating thinking is an important role of education.* Professor David Perkins, summarized 20 years of research into children's learning in the following memorable phrase 'Learning is a consequence of thinking' (Perkins, 1992, p. 34). Although this statement can sound blindingly obvious, when reflected upon in the light of much current practice, it provokes a number of key questions: do schools generally put children's *thinking* at the centre of the learning experience? Is there a difference between politely sitting, listening and following instructions (or not!) and thinking? Are trainee teachers taught to generate thinking in their classes or to pass on a body of knowledge and skills?

This book also assumes that *intelligence is not a single and measurable entity* that in different times, cultures and settings different behaviours seem to be intelligent. Each psychologist and educationalist will have a slightly or dramatically varying view of intelligence, but few today hold the early twentieth-century view that it is something measured in intelligence tests alone. However we see intelligence – a combined working of several mental processors, our intellectual faculties, our natural mental and physical dispositions, a combination of memory, inherited 'g' factor and individualized creative, practical and analytical strengths – it is only a meaningful concept when it is applied in a relevant cultural setting. We use it when we attend, engage, think or act.

It is assumed that *not all children respond positively to the same style of teaching or the same stimulus*; it is therefore understood that cross-curricular approaches will not suit all children. The good teacher hopes to engage all children but in Robert Sternberg's words, 'he or she needs the flexibility to teach to different styles of thinking, which means varying teaching style to suit different styles of [student] thought, (Sternberg, 1997(a), p. 115). Engagement *may* for some individuals, be gained in setting up periods of solitary, academic, convergent and purely cerebral activity, but experience and research (Abbs, 2003; Barnes and Shirley, 2005; Csikszentmihalyi, 2000) suggests it comes more often from a mix of social, practical, personally relevant and creative activity.

The final assumption is more contentious, it is that *education is at least partly about helping children appreciate, enjoy and understand their lives and worlds now.* Geographer, Simon Catling has written persuasively of the 'marginalisation' of children in both their school environments and their neighbourhoods he sees a 'discontinuity between their real lives and the school curriculum' (Catling, 2005a, 325). A child's world is clearly very different from an adult's. A western child's world, which might well include iPods, 'blue tooth' connections, satellite television, the World Wide Web, video and computer games, Internet chat rooms, mobile phones and digital versatile discs (DVDs), is technologically and geographically more sophisticated than most of their parents' and many of their teachers'. There are other worlds of the child too: of play, fantasy, playground morality, safe and unsafe places, people or products, unarticulated barriers, taboos, fashion, fast food, loud music, cheap drugs and earlier sexual maturity. These worlds are little seen or understood by many of the adults surrounding them. Indeed, such worlds of children may not even be acknowledged in some primary classrooms. This book is written to suggest ways in which adults can adjust the curriculum so that children's worlds are represented and widened, and their views, concerns and interests allowed for, celebrated and developed. It is suggested that a major route towards a more child-centred education is through creative and cross-curricular responses to real experience.

The history

Cross-curricular learning has a long pedigree. Educators since the beginnings of formal education have been conscious that combined perspectives were required in order to understand aspects of the physical, social or personal world. More than two millennia ago, Plato promoted a mix of story, physical education and music in an early version of Personal, Social and Health Education (PSHE) and citizenship. In his curriculum Plato combined subjects to serve a higher goal than simple disciplinary instruction: 'Anyone who can produce the best blend of the physical and intellectual sides of education and apply them to the training of character is producing harmony in a far more important sense than any mere musician' (Plato, *Republic*, p. 155).

Cross-curricular pedagogies infer a particular set of values and attitudes. These are often liberal, inclusive, constructivist and perhaps more recently also relativist and intercultural. Plato, who despite many elitist and exclusive ideas on education, called it: 'the initial acquisition of virtue by the child, when the feelings of pleasure and affection, pain and hatred that well up in his soul are channelled in the right courses before he can understand the reason why' (Plato, *The Laws*, 1970).

Seventeenth- and eighteenth-century pioneers: nature and meaning

Unlike Plato, the seventeenth-century Czech philosopher, Jan Comenius, believed that education was for *all* people and that nature was herself the great teacher. Comenius was an early champion of physical and outdoor education, and saw physical education, playing with ideas, artefacts and materials, and learning by easy stages as essential foundations for education. Sometimes known as the 'father of modern education', he was probably the first to illustrate children's textbooks. But his views on internationalism in education, his belief that teachers should understand the developing mind of the child and his insistence on teaching 'with the greatest enjoyment' and *thoroughly*, put him at the forefront of influences on modern educational thought in Europe. His eloquent and humane approach to learning is captured by the following paragraph from his book *The Great Didactic* published in 1649:

> The proper education of the young does not consist in stuffing their heads with a mass of words, sentences, and ideas dragged together out of various authors, but in opening up their understanding to the outer world, so that a living stream may flow from their own minds, just as leaves, flowers, and fruit spring from the bud on a tree.

> (Comenius, 1967, p. 82)

Jean Jacques Rousseau (1712–78) was also deeply inspired by the natural world. The eighteenth-century 'enlightenment' brought forth, and to an extent rested upon, powerful and romantic philosophies like his. Rousseau was a believer in the inborn good of humanity and was the originator of the idea of the 'the noble savage'. Typical of the intellectuals and artists of his time, he was awed and fascinated by nature. He believed that education was needed in order to learn how to live and that the best learning was accomplished very near to the natural world. Rousseau felt that experience was the starting point for learning. He used very physical and sensory images throughout his writing; the metaphor of education as plunging into the cold waters of the Styx, or feeling the warts on the back of the toad to illustrate natural learning. He saw education as a meeting of the natural, the practical and the cultural; as he put it in his education treatise *Émile ou de l'éducation*, of 1762:

> This education comes from nature, from men or from things. The inner growth of our organs and faculties is the education of nature, the use we learn to make of our growth is the education of men, what we gain by our experience of our surroundings is the education of things. (p. 15) (Rousseau, 1762, website para. 15)

> We are each taught by three masters. If their teaching conflicts, the scholar is ill-educated and will never be at peace with himself; if their teaching agrees, he goes straight to his goal, he lives at peace with himself, he is well-educated.

> (Rousseau, para. 16)

First by using the senses, then by making and using artefacts and, finally, by seeking truth in arts, science and religion, Rousseau expressed a progression which was much later taken up by Piaget. But he also had strong views about the adult domination of the curriculum: 'We never know how to put ourselves in the place of children; we do not enter into their ideas; we lend them ours, and, always following our own reasonings, with chains of truths we heap up only follies and error in their heads' (Rousseau, Para. 577).

Comenius and Rousseau among many thinkers of the seventeenth and eighteenth centuries suggested that education was lifelong, very much aligned with nature and, by implication, cross-curricular because it relied upon helping the child interpret and understand their day-to-day *experience* of the world. They argued that children should be allowed to be children before they were 'men' and accepted philosopher Locke's view that children were rational beings. Such thoughts on the meaning and purpose of education still underpin many of the arguments of those who defend cross-curricular, experiential and child-centred approaches to learning.

Nineteenth-century pedagogs: play, purpose and perfection

As formal and eventually state-run education developed throughout the western world in the nineteenth century, Rossueau's educational philosophies were added to by thinkers and teachers such as Johann Pestalozzi (1746–1827) and Friedrich Froebel (1782–1852). Pestalozzi wanted children to learn through activity and arrive at their own answers. The personality was all important and each child needed to be taught with love in the context of direct concrete experience and observation. Froebel's major contribution was the foundation of the 'kindergarten' and his powerful arguments for the importance of play. These early nineteenth-century progressives advocated primary education through practical activity, objects, 'natural' interest and spontaneity. Contemporary traditionalists, on the other hand, encouraged pragmatic and efficient mass education techniques of textbook and rote learning required by religiously conservative and rapidly industrializing countries. In line with the times, however, even the radical pioneers maintained a religious justification for their ideas:

> I wish to wrest education from the outworn order of doddering old teaching hacks as well as from the new-fangled order of cheap, artificial teaching tricks, and entrust it to the eternal powers of nature herself, to the light which God has kindled and kept alive in the hearts of fathers and mothers, to the interests of parents who desire their children grow up in favour with God and with men. (Pestalozzi, quoted in Silber, 1965, p. 134)

> The purpose of education is to encourage and guide man as a conscious, thinking and perceiving being in such a way that he becomes a pure and perfect representation of that divine inner law through his own personal choice; education must show him the ways and meanings of attaining that goal. (Froebel, 1826, *Die Menschenerziehung*, p. 2)

Twentieth-century child-centred education

The concept of 'child-centred' education spread with the ideas of John Dewey (1859–1952) and Rudolf Steiner (1861–1925) in the first half of the twentieth century. Dewey's philosophical approach to education is based in the concepts of democracy, freedom and the provisional nature of knowledge. He argued that children should be deeply and personally involved in the creation of knowledge through problem-solving and experiment, and that community would be enriched by individuals whose personal experience had been enlarged through education. Education was rarely seen as an individualistic activity; Dewey was often at pains to stress the importance of the group:

> I believe that the only true education comes through the stimulation of the child's powers by the demands of the social situations in which he finds himself. Through these demands he is stimulated to act as a member of a unity, to emerge from his original narrowness of action and feeling, and to conceive of himself from the standpoint of the welfare of the group to which he belongs. Through the responses which others make to his own activities he comes to know what these mean in social terms. The value which they have is reflected back into them. (Dewey, J., My Pedagogic Creed in *The School Journal*, vol. LIV, no. 3 (16 January 1897), pp. 77–80)

Steiner's ideas were more spiritual and personal, he believed like Rousseau in the innate wisdom of the human. In proposals for his 'Waldorf schools' (Steiner, 1919) he gave a detailed outline of a developmentally based curriculum strongly infused with the arts. The Waldorf curriculum is, at different periods, subject-based or thematic and designed to mirror and guide the child's unfolding consciousness, creativity and imagination. Its classical aims – to cultivate responsibility for the earth and other people and prepare children for the challenges of the future – are met through a curriculum designed to be personally engaging, spiritually conscious, experience based and in the context of the physical world of nature.

By 1931 the Hadow Report (UK Board of Education, 1931) clearly reflected the progressive child-centred, philosophies of preceding centuries in suggesting that learning in the primary curriculum should be seen 'in terms of activity and experience rather than knowledge to be acquired and facts to be stored'. *Knowing* and *doing* were in some ways seen as synonymous with each other, and purposeful activity suited to the child's specific environment needed to be planned in accordance with the varying nature of children. To this end, distinctive styles of education were recommended for those aged 5–7 and 7–11 years old.

Although the Hadow Report was hailed as a triumph for progressive education, the spirit of its recommendations were not fully advanced until the Plowden Report (DES, 1967). This influential report gave government and professional support for cross-curricular and child-centred approaches, arguing that: 'Rigid division of the curriculum into subjects tends to interrupt children's trains of thought and of interest and to hinder them from realising the common elements in problem solving ... some work at least, should cut across subject divisions at all stages of the primary school' (DES, 1967, Para. 535, p. 197).

In its chapter on 'Children learning in school' (DES, 1967, para. 202, p. 189) the Plowden Report includes a roll-call of eighteenth-, nineteenth- and twentieth-century educational writers and thinkers to support its case. In addition to the educationalists already mentioned, Maria Montessori, Rachel Macmillan, Susan Isaacs, Jean Piaget, Jerome Bruner – names which still feature in the education debate today – are cited in defence of the 'child-centred', 'active learning', experience-led, 'discovery' approach.

Much of the 'discovery' approach was underpinned by the work of Jean Piaget(for example, Piaget, 1954). He and his followers suggested, from the 1920s, that humans go through distinct stages of learning. We pass through periods of sensori-motor exercise and reflex actions, to exploratory activity consisting of either pre-conceptual or intuitive experimentation with tangible things, and finally arrive at a state of 'formal operations', which relies upon reason, imagination and abstract thinking. At each stage the child is said to be learning through accommodation and assimilation – essentially through making and understanding errors. Piaget likened the developing child to a scientist constantly making, testing and revising hypotheses. Piaget's theories still underpin much of our educational and curriculum decision-making, though many have recognized that the developmental stages he described need not be tightly ascribed to particular ages but apparently need to be passed through in sequence at *any* age if a new concept is to be fully learned.

Lev Vygotsky's and, later, Jerome Bruner's work on the centrality of social intercourse in helping children make sense of the world has had profound impacts upon classroom organization (Bruner, 1968, 1996). Under their influence, many school sessions have introduced forms of 'scaffolded learning', where 'more knowledgeable others' support the concept formation of the rest. Learning is seen by these psychologists as primarily a social activity: 'making sense is a social process; it is an activity that is always situated in a cultural and historical context' (Bruner and Haste, 1987, p. 4).

Vygotsky was also clear that the discovery, construction and solving of problems, usually within a social situation, was a crucial part of concept formation (Vygotsky, 1962). Concepts are more easily formed and understood; learning is more permanent if the learner thinks about their learning with others. Bruner also argues for learning 'scaffolded' by others. He and many psychologists since the 1970s have argued that thinking about learning or 'metacognition' is facilitated by relaxed and warm teacher–pupil and pupil–pupil relationships where questions such as 'What if ... ?', 'How can we ... ?', 'How did we ... ?', 'Tell us how ... ', 'Why don't we ... ?' are part of the everyday currency of classroom language (Bruner, 1996; Perkins, 1992; Pollard, 1996; Smith and Call, 2000). Such questions imply a 'real-world', integrated approach to the curriculum, which concurs with Plowden.

Only nine years after Lady Plowden's recommendations, British Prime Minister James Callaghan made his Ruskin College speech (Callaghan, 1976) where he called for a 'Great Debate' on education and raised the issue of the unease felt by parents and employers regarding: 'the new informal methods of teaching, which seem to produce excellent results when they are in well-qualified hands but are much more dubious when they are not'. This speech and the rapid progress in the next 10 years towards a national curriculum of separated subjects effectively stifled the development of creative and cross-curricular teaching and learning in all but the most courageous British schools.

The National Curriculum

The history of the National Curriculum is well known, but its effect on the cross-curriculum have not often been considered. Not only was the curriculum subdivided into 10 separate areas but some areas were allotted differing degrees of status, depending upon whether they were *core* or *foundation* subjects. Core subjects were to be given more time, especially after 1997 when the National Literacy Strategy (NLS) and the National Numeracy Strategy (NNS) were put into place. Time was made available for these new strategies by relaxing the requirement to report on the Foundation Subjects by the Office for Standards in Education (OFSTED) in 1998. The Qualifications and Curriculum Agency (QCA) later bolstered subject divisions by publishing detailed schemes of work (QCA, 1998(a)) for Key Stage, 1 and 2 for each subject. Whilst only intended as guidance, the QCA schemes quickly became seen as an alternative national curriculum for many schools.

The National Advisory Council on Creative and Cultural Education (NAC-CCE, 1999) responded to this situation by recommending parity of all subjects in the curriculum. This recommendation has so far been overlooked by goverenment. Indeed, the term 'foundation subjects' was even replaced in some official documents by the somewhat demeaning term, 'non-core' in 2000. From 1999 onwards Physical Education (PE) hours were reduced, school fields sold, school concerts and plays became less frequent and the arts were said to be 'disappearing' from school and college curricula (Rogers, 1999). The subsequent Standards for Qualified Teacher Status (QTS) (TTA, 2003) only require trainee teachers to 'have *sufficient* understanding of a *range* of work' *across* history *or* geography, art/design *or* design/technology and the *performing* arts (surreptitiously replacing music as a requirement for QTS). As a result, most local authority foundation subject courses have declined, subject advisers have either lost their jobs or been forced to combine subject roles, and out-of-school visits, field trips and other activities have dwindled (Barnes, 2001; Bell, 2004; Rogers, 2003). Opportunities for quality cross-curricular work could be argued to have been squeezed out for lack of developed curriculum subject expertise.

The current context

It has become almost a truism of educational criticism that in these times of perhaps unprecedented change we need to develop a flexible and learning society. The lifelong learning lobby is well accepted and strong, and organizations such a the Campaign for Learning (2006, website) have much support from a broad spectrum including education, politics and industry. However *what* is to be learned is very much more debatable. Homespun American philosopher, Eric Hoffer, noted in the middle of the twentieth century that current education may not be relevant: *'In times of change learners inherit the earth, while the learned find themselves beautifully equipped to deal with a world that no longer exists'* (Hoffer, website). But late in the same century some of Britain's educated elite applauded heartily when Sir Roy Strong argued for a distinctly narrow and culturally exclusive definition of the curriculum:

> It is more important for a young person to be made to wonder at the architecture of something like the Palace of Versailles or glimpse what underlies ... a single scene in a Mozart opera than to paint another bad picture or bang a drum in the false interests of self expression. (SCAA, 1997)

This debate rumbles on against a background of massive social, political and technological change, as you will read in Chapter 1, but it is an essential debate. What we teach, what we require children to know and understand, and how we teach it will without doubt significantly change the minds of the generations that will shape the twenty-first century.

How we teach is equally important. Governments have became newly concerned about individual well-being, partly as a result of alarming statistics on depression (Layard, 2006). The new interest in well-being has sparked a number of government initiatives directed at a more holistic view of health (see, for example, DHSS, 2004, DH/DFES, 2005). Late in the day education is now seen to play a key role in the physical and mental health of all nations – the curricular implications are huge.

CHAPTER 1

What Should Schooling in the Twenty-First Century Look Like?

What you do is question everything they say do,

every goal, ideal, or value they keep pushin' on you,

if they ask you to believe then question whether it's true

and if they ask you to achieve – is it for them or for you? (Williams, 2005)

What you think a school should be like depends on the values you hold. What a school *is* like is dependent on its values. A school's values are reflected in the curriculum it offers. *Curriculum,* as it is used throughout this book, is therefore defined very broadly to include the subjects a school teaches, the choices it makes within those subjects, the means it chooses to deliver them, but also the attitudes, relationships and beliefs which pervade the school. In putting forward an argument for greater cross-curricular and creative elements in our primary and secondary curricula, it is suggested that many current curricula are unfit for twenty-first century purpose.

We are constantly being reminded of the unprecedented rates of change we will experience as we travel through the twenty-first century (see, for example, Greenfield, 2003; Robinson, 2001). It has been suggested that 75 per cent of the scientific knowledge we will need in order to address life in the middle of this century has not even been invented yet (Joubert, 2001). Such illustrations of the exponential growth of knowledge, the development of technology, nanotechnology, micro-biology, artificial intelligence and the rest, pepper most books about the future. This is not the place to comment on such predictions, but it is safe to say, even on the basis of our own experience of change in the past 20 years, that the world today's children inherit will be very, very different from our present world. Almost undoubtedly our children will have to face the realities of global warming, rising sea levels, pandemics, human cloning, increasing terrorism and extremism, water, oil and food shortages, frequent job change and, perhaps, economic meltdown. Taking a more optimistic view, they may witness the more concerted use of international cooperation, good

Illustration 1.1   *Teachers can have a major influence on children's futures. School children from a village in south India*

government, a more equitable sharing of the earth's resources and the science and technology to address such challenges. Either way, today's children are already living in a century of unparalleled, rapid and global transformations which will quite literally change our minds. What is our education system doing to address this? How can we establish a curriculum of Hope?

Preparing for an uncertain future

The education we currently offer our children was not really designed to help children thrive in, and live fulfilling lives through, times of unimaginable change. Aside from Information and Communications Technology (ICT), most National Curriculum subjects we teach in UK schools would have been recognizable in a late nineteenth-century school. Some 'new' subjects have been introduced such as Design and Technology, a foreign language, and the non-statutory Citizenship and PSHE, but even these subjects were hardly revolutionary activities for any liberal-minded teacher of the twentieth-century. A statutory consideration of the future itself has not yet been considered necessary for those under 11, except for a few minor references within the geography curriculum.

Various teachers and writers have taken the opportunity offered by the recent guidance on Citizenship, to propose a curriculum intended to address the personal, local and global futures which young people clearly care about (see Alexander and Potter, 2005; Hicks, 2001; Page, 2000; Slaughter, 1996; Wrigley, 2005). Geographers and others interested in 'futures education' (the study of views about probable, possible and preferable futures) have championed curricula aimed at helping children think more critically and creatively about the future. They are motivated by the need to empower children to be able to do something about addressing the pressing issues facing their future world.

Young people contemplating the future in this century seem to expect a very much less utopian prospect than the 'baby boomers' of the 1950s foresaw. Research amongst children in the USA, UK, Sweden and Canada, shows children to be very serious and very worried about the future (Hicks, 2001). They are concerned about future health, wealth, security, poverty and relationships but, paradoxically, remain generally hopeful about their *own* futures. They are much more pessimistic about the future for the world and are particularly worried about issues currently headlined in the news. This shift from the general optimism of the 1990s to a much more gloomy view of the 2000s (see Bentley, 2006) is evidenced in government directives on well-being, health, sustainability conservation, safety as well as in newspaper headlines.

Children also seem less positive about the future. Contrary to youthful optimism for their personal future, boys' views about the *world's* future tend towards the gender-stereotypically violent and destructive, with wars, terrorism, natural disasters and disease dominant. It seems that girls more often imagine a generalized peaceful and idealistic future, but continue to be worried about disease and pollution.

Children and all of us live very much in the present but decisions within our present society deeply impact upon our futures. Tom Bentley, a government 'think tank' adviser, expresses new aims for education this dilemma in the following terms: 'we are searching for means through which individuals can transform themselves through a process of internal discovery and self actualisation, by participating in the reshaping of the shared context in which they live out their individual lives' (Bentley, 2006). Both the concept of self-actualization or a sense of personal meaning and thoughts about our influence on the future are such big and important subjects that they are generally not tackled at all by schools. Liberation of the unique attributes of the child and an intention to help them make their world a better place have been central themes of education philosophy and the highest values of education for millennia yet their systematic study remains the exception in most curricula. Reference to the twin aims of nurturing individuality and fostering better social and global relationships are among several themes running through this book.

Daily and in every school the unique and (often fragile) personality comes face to face with all the complex and messy issues of wider society. Children are often highly informed and aware of these issues. In addition to their keen interest in aspects of the future, a number of topics seem to have become particularly, even pressingly, relevant to the twenty-first century child. Key preoccupations are:

- information and communications technology
- global politics
- relationships
- individualism and the sense of self.

These powerfully motivating interests might profitably form the starting point of a new look at our school curricula. Until very recently, none of these topics could be said to form a central part of national or school-based curricula in the vast majority of schools.

Illustration 1.2   *Year 2 boy's view of the future: guns, army, bang bang, bullets, dried up river, dried up stones*

Illustration 1.3　*Year 2 girl's view of the future: wind, fallen trees and bushes, shattered houses*

Harnessing children's interest in information and communications technology

Nowhere are the rapid changes in the developed and developing world more evident than in the area of ICT. Growing numbers of people in all societies have access to powerful and sophisticated technologies which two decades ago were the stuff of science fiction. In 2002 in England 93 per cent of 11-year-old children reported having at least one computer at home, in the USA the figure was 89.4 per cent (WHO, 2004, website).

Illustration 1.4 *Children gather enthusiastically around a computer screen in a village school in south India*

Home computers and the Internet are heavily used by children aged 9–16. Twice as many boys as girls use the Internet in all 35 countries studied by the World Health Organization (WHO, 2004, website). The Internet has rapidly become a preferred source of information for the young, with 50 per cent of parents admitting to little idea of what their children do on the Internet (Pew, 2005). Large numbers of children regularly use Internet 'chat rooms' to contact and make new friends. Some of the worst implications of these easy, anonymous and sometimes unpoliced contacts are well known. Adults' lack of control over the medium is exemplified by a recent finding from the USA that 95 per cent of parents could not identify common US chat-room language such as 'POS' (parent over shoulder) or 'P911' (parent alert) (Pew, 2005, website).

Year 11 pupils at a Dover school were given a free choice of fairy story to update and perform within a single session. They chose to rewrite 'Little Red Riding Hood'. After starting their play at the end, but in traditional manner with Red Riding Hood quizzing a wolf disguised as grandma about her big teeth and hairy arms, the students did a 'time warp' sequence and the audience was catapulted to the beginning of the story. The scene was the chilling context of a twenty-first century Red Riding Hood sitting alone at her bedroom computer. She was in an Internet chat room talking to a paedophile 'wolf' pretending to be her grandmother. (Robert McCrea, 2005)

Currently over 50 per cent of northern European children aged between 5 and 11 have a mobile phone (cell phone), rising to well over 90 per cent for those between 12 and 16. To children, the advantages of mobile phones over other ICT are privacy and control. Children report that for their mobiles, they need no permission, have little supervision and they appreciate the possibilities of constant communication (Childnet International, 2003, website). Some estimates suggest teenagers average up to four hours a week text messaging their friends.

Children today say they like the Internet and mobiles because these give them the greatest independence over what they see and find out. Children like the ways ICT helps them discover and connect to friends, and they appreciate the way it can help them create and communicate visually and in sound. Fifty-five per cent of 13-year-old Canadian girls, for example, use the Internet or mobiles to communicate with friends *every day* (WHO, 2004 website). Through the Internet and mobile technology children have access to music, sports and world news, advertising and powerful new games, they can communicate with television and film stars, vote out an unpopular *Big Brother* resident or catapult an unknown pop idol to stardom. They are also increasingly aware of the dangers of new technologies. Most have already dealt with text bullies, unwanted pornography, salespeople and crackpots well before their parents find out about it (Children's use of the Internet, 2006). Sadly, some do not have the personal resources to cope with such onslaughts and the ghastly results of the abuses of ICT are all too evident from news reports and investigative journalism. There are, however, interesting and positive uses of mobile phone technology which suggest it is an underused feature in our current school curricula:

> A primary school in Harrow maintains their link with a school in Uganda through mobile phone and texting links with the teachers in the Ugandan school. The head teacher reported, 'Rather than holding one-off cultural events, I wanted to promote a deeper understanding of global issues such as interdependence, global citizenship and rights and responsibilities'. Therefore children write regular letters to their partner school, but significantly they and their teachers now send regular texts with questions which are instantly answered and relevant to the moment. (*TES*, website, 2005)

Television has been with us rather longer than mobile phones, but its influence too has grown ever more dominant in the lives of children. In 2001, about 40 per cent of *pre-school* children in the USA had a television set in their bedroom (Pediatrics, 2002, website). In 2004, 90 per cent of UK children between 7 and 14 reported watching television every day, and 93 per cent of the same age group reported watching a video or DVD 'at least once a month' (UK Film Council, 2004, website). There are various estimates regarding television watching but most place the average USA or British child as watching about four hours of television per day, 61 per cent of them in their own bedroom. The suggestion of large numbers of children alone in their rooms watching televisions, computer monitors and videos for more than 28 hours a week conjures up perhaps a rather lonely image. Susan Greenfield, an

Illustration 1.5   *Teacher introducing the video camera to 8 year olds in a class project on the future of the school local environment.*

eminent scientist with a strong interest in future studies, has suggested we may already have reached a situation where for some children many of the traditional roles of the parent – imparting culture, providing a role model, resolving conflict, telling stories, sharing knowledge, passing on morals, sayings, advice and wisdom, showing how conflicts are resolved – have been unintentionally delegated to the monitor screen (Greenfield, 2003).

In Romania a recent study demonstrated the influence of TV. By far the chief role models of school-aged children were film stars and television personalities (Popenici, 2006). A stirring judgement on the profession was that teachers were amongst the least likely adults to be considered role models scoring lower than terrorists. There is little to suggest that figures would be startlingly different in the UK, USA, Japan or other 'developed' countries.

Even the subject of children's toys is not without its implications for education. Aside from the plethora of toys linked to video, television and computer game characters, the new generation of interactive cyber toys respond 'intelligently' to particular types of treatment or 'grow' or change with time or display 'real' facial expressions. The toy 'Robosapiens'® is sold as 'truly a fusion of technology and personality'. Such toys may be argued to create new kinds of moral and ethical dilemma. Do such toys and their descendants teach particular values and attitudes to children? Do they come with 'hidden agendas'? If so what are they and who decides?

Any web search will deliver large numbers of statistics and studies about ICT use amongst children and young people. Some findings should be interpreted with care because of the social/political agendas of their sponsors. But a thorough reading of research in these areas tells a consistent story of large numbers of children spending significantly more hours with ICT than they do at school. The fact that much of this activity may well be solitary or unsupervised is an issue largely for parents, but there are serious implications for schools too. Currently, and perhaps understandably, mobile phones are rarely welcome in

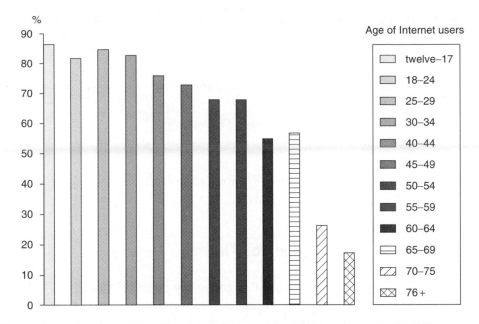

Figure 1.1 Graph to show the age and percentage of Internet use in the US

the classroom. The use of the Internet is still in its infancy in many primary classrooms and the school digital camera or video may not be used much because of lack of time. Television is probably less used now in school than 25 years ago. But these technologies form central parts of most children's home and social life. Perhaps schools should consider more systematically their use as motivators for formal education. Signs of such a change are already apparent. Information and communications technology is argued to deepen understanding and promote new learning more effectively than traditional methods. As a result, many of the new city Academies make the provision of individual computers or tablets a priority. Additionally in January 2006 the BBC launched its 'Digital Curriculum' (BBC, 2005, website) covering half the 7–14 curriculum. Even the power of the mobile phone can be used for educational purposes – texting a précis description, contacting another school following the same theme, permission to 'phone a friend' in the playground for help in a class quiz or voting for a school council member by text message might all be used to enliven school learning.

A rural primary school in Suffolk asked groups of six children on fieldwork near the school, to cooperate in using a mobile phone to text succinct (they could only send one message) descriptions concerning a range of contrasting environments near their school to a central group back in the classroom 'headquarters'. The 'HQ team' plotted the incoming summaries against appropriate locations on a base map so that the descriptive journey was already recorded as the 'environmental' teams returned to class.

In opening up the subject of the power of various types of ICT to influence the lives and thinking of children we are immediately confronted with questions of value.

- How might we use these technologies to the good, to develop good and wholesome attitudes?
- How do we decide what good and wholesome is?
- *Should* schools be extending the time children spend with ICT?

Chapter 2 includes some examples of how schools are beginning to address such issues in a cross-curricular context.

Supporting children's interest in global themes

Some schools have for centuries allowed and encouraged political debate. Easily available and global communications have now resulted in almost instant awareness of major events anywhere. Dramatic, violent or tense international situations, disturbing threats, images and moral issues which in the past would confront an unlucky individual only once or twice in a lifetime, are now an almost daily experience for most in the developed countries of the world. There are surprisingly few guidelines or exemplars however, on how to address current events, especially disturbing ones, within the curriculum. Timetables have become too inflexible. Tightly packed daily schedules rarely allow time for debate, discussion or questions on real issues from the television news or parents' newspaper. How many British schools, for example, had the time or courage to follow the example of an international school in Dar es Salaam which encouraged civilized and informed debate between the children of Christian and Islamic diplomats, aid workers and business people within days of the attacks of 11 September 2001 in the USA? If our curriculum is too crowded for such important matters then perhaps decisions need to be taken on the relative priority of current events and other opportunities for unplanned discussion and teaching within the normal school week.

We have seen (p. 19) that world issues, particularly emotive subjects such as terrorism, war, poverty, HIV/AIDS, pollution, disasters or peace treaties, are as important to many children as they are to adults, yet there is a feeling among some adults that these are concerns too complex for children to deal with. Successful current events programmes like Children's British Broadcasting Corporation's (CBBC) daily *Newsround* and its associated website cast doubt on this attitude. Such programmes are increasingly popular with children; the latest viewer figures (BBC, 26 August, 2005) show that between 2 and 3 million British children watch *Newsround* every evening. The success of the Live 8 initiative in July 2005 and the related 'Make Poverty History' campaign used the medium of television and Internet rapidly to raise consciousness of possible solutions to world poverty.

Illustration 1.6   *Children interviewing a local Member of the European Parliament and the Scottish Children's Commissioner on matters of global importance.* Courtesy of Scottish Children's Parliament

It caught the imagination of schools and children perhaps because it demonstrated that ordinary voices could influence seemingly impersonal trends in the global economy (One Org, 2005, website).

Television is not the only source of information about world events however; in the USA today 76 per cent of Internet users between the ages of 12 and 17 reported using the Internet to access news and current events (Pew, 2005, website). Increasing numbers have an automatic function on their mobile phones informing them instantly of key cricket or football scores or 'breaking news'. Video, Internet and television channel facilities on mobiles, Mp3s and iPods are rapidly becoming cheap enough for children in developed countries to covet and own. Each new technology brings the world closer into the child's life, but perhaps in ways which make the events they portray seem less and less real.

As a result of media coverage and successful campaigns, primary and secondary schools have been particularly successful in raising children's awareness of issues such as poverty, pollution, deforestation and climate change. Such topics regularly catch children's interest and passion, and their responses to appeals such as Comedy Relief, Children in Need, the World Wide Fund for Nature's 'Save the rain forest' or the *Blue Peter* 2002 'Clean water' campaign for unpolluted drinking water for communities in Tanzania and Uganda regularly reach ambitious targets from school and individual children's donations. Children are equally interested in 'green' issues closer to home.

This apparent interest in global issues is not a straightforward business, however; children's concern with aspects of the world seems very dependent upon what has been highlighted by the television and tabloid news editors. Very few American children knew where Iraq or Afghanistan were before the wars there, and the word 'tsunami' meant very little to most British people before 26 December 2004. Whilst relatively successful in raising consciousness on 'green' themes such as pollution and aspects of climate change, and despite compulsory geography on the curriculum, place knowledge and general geographical knowledge is often poor. A recent study of world 'place knowledge' amongst 18–20-year-old prospective teachers on a UK teacher education course, showed a serious lack of general knowledge about the location of many foreign countries outside western Europe (Catling, 2004). But the same lack of knowledge can apply even for the more emotive subjects such as environmental or development issues. Unless a child attends a school which has followed up leads such as the United Nations' (UN's) millennium goals (UN, 2000, website) or an individual teacher shares an interest in a particular place or issue, then children's exposure to these crucial aspects of their changing world remains a lottery.

It does not appear too difficult to fire children's interest in the health and future of the environment. They can see signs of environmental ill-health all around them in dying trees, polluted rivers, fly-tipping, disappearing countryside and asthma. Concerns about the future of environments also arise from children's, perhaps genetically endowed, interest in nature, life forms and the outdoors. Students of teaching frequently remark on the good behaviour of children engaged on well-planned fieldwork in a variety of open-air contexts. Schools with a clear environmental focus to their curriculum capitalize on this interest and use it to generate the feeling that individuals can do something to change the probable future of damaged or threatened environments. The Eco Schools project (Eco Schools, 2005, website), supported by the British Educational Communications Technology Agency (BECTA, 2006, website) is a good example of a well-supported initiative providing guidance and resources to feed these interests. Suggested and potentially engaging topics, such as litter, waste, energy, water, transport, healthy living and school grounds, however, require a range of very specific subject skills and knowledge to bring them alive for children. Other themes are discussed more fully in Chapter 7.

Recognizing the importance of relationships

Since the 1980s there has been a dramatic change in the casual magazine-reading habits of young people, particularly amongst girls. Comics with cartoons, moral stories, games and information are no longer as popular, but magazines and websites devoted to personal, beauty and relationship problems of young people have grown hugely in recent years (National Literacy Trust, 2005, website). Relationships are important to all of us but for the developing psyche of the child they may dominate everything. Each year the

Illustration 1.7   *Friends in a school in south India*

numbers of children who contact the charity *Childline* grows by more than 10 per cent. This UK charity gives support to children who are abused, fearful or worried, and in 2004 gave in-depth support to over 141,000 children. Eighty-three per cent of them were between 5 and 15 years old and about a third of cases concerned bullying and interpersonal relationship problems, by far the most common reasons for contacting Childline. Concerns about family, peers, friendships, who they can trust and who is caring towards them are central to children's lives. (Illustration 1.7)

The family into which a child is born provides the first and most powerful model of relationships. Most of us recognize that the interrelationships within that family go on influencing the trajectory of our lives well beyond childhood. Family support is often the key to a child's learning and development within school. A family member was given as the most important role model by 16 per cent of children in a recent European survey (Popenici, 2006). Yet there may be a mutual suspicion between schools and families, and few schools currently build family contacts into their curriculum. The establishment of multi-agency children's centres and the extension of the school day under the UK Children Act 2004 will, hopefully, have a positive effect on contact between school, family and community. There are several aspects of twenty-first century life, however, where mistrust seems to be growing.

Recent reports show a growing atmosphere of suspicion in some societies. One large-scale study involving 160,000 children shows, for example, that only 43 per cent of English children aged 11–15 (53 per cent in the USA) could agree with the statement, 'I find my peers kind and helpful'. By contrast, 70 per cent in Scotland, 80 per cent in Macedonia and 80 per cent in Switzerland agreed with the same statement (WHO, 2004, website). Growing distrust in children may be evidence of social polarization and increasing suspicion between sub-cultures and communities.

Polarization is likely to be increased by schools if they do not recognize and address the gulf between their aims and values and those of their children. Popenici found that in Romania most secondary aged children saw school as simply instrumental to getting a good job, but thought schools' interest in altruism, goodness, education and sincerity was somewhat irrelevant to their lives (Popenici, 2006). If schools feel these caring and community values are right then they may need to work hard to gain the agreement of children.

Intercultural and cross-community understanding is seen by many to be crucial to national and international peace and progress in the twenty-first century. Schools have their part to play in fostering this. Relationships between cultures and sub-cultures have been subject to a number of government-sponsored initiatives, especially since the Stephen Lawrence enquiry (1999) and the subsequent Race Relations Act 2000. The QCA site, 'Respect for All: Reflecting cultural diversity through the curriculum' (QCA, 2003, website), is a helpful attempt to show teachers how relationships of greater understanding between and across cultures can be developed through the curriculum. A number of websites, for example the DfES-sponsored Global gateway (DfES 2006c), promote international links between schools, where real contact across continents can be developed.

Wholesome relationships are, of course, an important part of the well-being of all individuals, and children need them to feel secure and ready to learn. We give little formal attention to building, maintaining and understanding relationships in our curricula and yet, as Daniel Goleman (1996, 1999) and Elizabeth Morris (2005) have reminded us – 'emotional intelligence' can be more important than other kinds of intelligence. By emotional intelligence Goleman means the ability to understand and handle one's own emotions (the subject of the next section) and understand relationships, others' emotions and how to deal with these. Emotional literacy programmes have been very successfully introduced into a number of schools partly as a result of the publicity Goleman has brought to the theme. Again the English PSHE and Citizenship curriculum maybe is relevant here, since the recommendations from the QCA for Key Stage 2 include:

- taking responsibility
- feeling positive about the self
- participating in decision-making
- making real choices
- understanding the different views of others
- developing relationships through work and play
- dealing with inappropriate pressure

- recognizing risks
- resolving differences (QCA, 2002).

But the danger is that these non-compulsory aspects of the English primary curriculum are left to chance and excessive pressure on timetables means that such issues are often only dealt with in a cursory and unplanned manner.

Helping develop a positive sense of self

As far as we know our sense of self is a defining human characteristic. It is argued to have massive survival and evolutionary advantages (Dawkins, 2003; Morris, 2004) and with it comes consciousness of everything good and bad about our world. The concept of 'self' is as neurologist Antonio Damasio puts it: 'the critical biological function that allows us to know sorrow or know joy, to know suffering or know pleasure, to sense embarrassment or pride, to grieve for lost love or lost life' (Damasio, 2000, p. 4).

The trend towards prizing and nurturing individuality has resulted in a great interest in selfhood. If you simply type the words 'self' and 'children' into Google Scholar, references to over a million recent academic studies on selfhood and children are called up. Damasio has devoted his career to research and thought in the area of self-consciousness and describes two identifiable selves in our minds: a *core self* and an *autobiographical self*. The core self is that sense of consciousness where objects, sounds and senses around us are not only perceived but understood within our mind to be being perceived at that moment by ourselves. Core consciousness is consciousness in the moment, here and now, 'ceaselessly recreated for each and every object with which the brain interacts' (ibid., p. 17). The autobiographical self consists of ongoing and systematized memories of situations which bear centrally and usually invariably upon an individual's life: 'who you were born to, where and when, your likes and dislikes, the way you usually react to a problem or conflict, your name ... your anticipated future' (ibid., p. 17). Significant to those involved in education, Damasio draws three key conclusions from his and others' work in the field of selfhood. His research suggests, first that both the core and autobiographical self are interrelated; secondly, that consciousness is inseparable from emotion; and finally, that the sense of self exists to maintain or promote the healthy equilibrium of the body.

The arguments about consciousness, reality and how we come to 'know' things are labyrinthine, but four questions of central educational importance emerge from this research:

1. If core consciousness is so totally dependent upon the senses, what do we do in our curriculum positively to introduce, develop and enhance experience across all the senses.
2. If the fully developed sense of self includes a clear sense of autobiographical self, what help are we giving children in school to identify

Illustration 1.8   *A 12-year-old introducing David Miliband (UK government minister) to his group presentation on identity.* Courtesy Gifted and Talented Summer Academy, Canterbury

their own *individualized* and special sense of identity confidence and belonging. How are we adding to their own *positive* memories, responses, talents and opinions? (Illustration 1.8)

3. If emotion is so closely linked with consciousness, are we spending enough time and effort in our teacher education on understanding emotion? In the education of children are we planning for the positive engagement and enhancement of their *feelings*?

4. If self-awareness has developed as nature's way of promoting, assessing and fine-tuning the health of our body, what are we doing in our curricula *holistically* and positively to involve both mind *and* body in the learning process?

It perhaps will not have escaped your attention that I have used the word 'positive' in each of the four key educational implications of Damasio's work. Damasio attempts to place his scientific conclusions outside any values framework; teachers and the curriculum can have no such luxury. Almost everything teachers do is interpreted in some way as support or denial of some value or another. Each facet of the child's world described so far has implied questions of value. Some kind of morality is always at the heart of what society has required of its teachers and this fact can be used to generate vital discussion and decisions in schools. If we agree, for example, on a desire to work to make the world 'a better place', common sense would suggest that we should start by establishing a culture in which a positive, sense of self, behaviour, feelings, relationships and environment is more likely than a negative one. The theme of promoting well-being through the educational choices we make runs through every chapter in this book.

Well-being is as important a factor in our learning as it is in our relationships. Based upon findings from a wide body of research (see Chapters 3, 4 and 5), the inner and underlying sense of what we often simply call 'happiness' seems the most common and useful foundation for the transferable and lifelong learning many of us aim for in our schools. Happiness is not always easy to come by, however; after basic needs are well catered for, increased wealth does not seem to increase happiness (Layard, 2005, 2006). The USA and the UK are amongst the richest countries of the world, but can only manage to be twenty-sixth and twenty-eighth, respectively, in a 35-nation survey of life satisfaction in 11-year-olds.

Not everyone thinks of happiness as an appropriate aim for education. Placing each child's and teacher's personal happiness as a necessary background to everything that happens within a school setting is sometimes characterized as an erroneous, over-idealistic and unrealistic aim. Detractors of this aim cite numerous examples of great but unhappy people, like Van Gogh, Schumann or Sylvia Plath or perhaps their own painful struggle to learn how to ride a bike, to suggest that good learning does not always come from 'being happy'. These examples do not necessarily negate the value of aiming at a default position of well-being. Neither does aiming at a generalized state of well-being deny the personal importance of accepting, empathising with, expecting, valuing and using periods of suffering, difficulty and pain.

The famous bipolar creators rarely created anything in their times of deep depression, but rather used their times of more positive emotion to process and make sense of their more negative experiences. Few would suggest that we deliberately make children depressed in order that they become better artists or thinkers. Neither is the depressed state typical of the mind at its most creative (see Csikszentmihalyi, 1997; Layard, 2005). I agree that lasting learning can be painful and stressful, but unless it is painful and stressful *against a background* of deeper personal security, learning is likely to be associated with negative feelings. A preponderance of negative life experiences seems more likely to result in a relative lack of resilience and self-efficacy (Bandura, 1994; Fredrickson and Tugade, 2004). The happiness I refer to is more profound than feeling smiley and light in our upper levels of consciousness, it's that deeper sense of security, contentment, rightness of being, health and inner peace which we refer to when we look into someone's eyes and ask, 'But are you *really* happy?' Even with no notice, most seem to be able to understand this kind of inner happiness enough to venture a sensible personal score on a scale of one to ten.

Personal happiness appears generally and deeply important to us. There is clearly something universally recognizable in the happy face (Ekman, 2004) positively interpreted even by children with neurological barriers to emotion such as severe autism (Howard-Jones and Pickering, 2005). Even very young babies respond positively to the smiling face from any cultural source. Several strands of current research now suggest that a feeling of positive emotion is a prerequisite for high-level efficient and creative learning on social, physical and intellectual levels. Placing emphasis on positive aspects of the child's self may not simply be a more efficient way of teaching them; it may beneficially affect their body and spirit too. Damasio's recent work (Damasio, 2003) puts forward a refinement to earlier thoughts about the links between consciousness and the body. He suggests that positive emotion, particularly the feeling of joy in an individual, signifies a biological state of: 'optimal physiological coordination and smooth running of the operations of life ... [Joy is] not only conducive to survival, but survival with well-being' (ibid., p. 137). In other words, when we are happy our body is in its optimal state for psychological and physical survival. Our body state indicates to our brain that we are in this optimal condition and our brain responds by 'feeling' happy in order to help us maintain this physical condition. Damasio describes an unbroken loop between body and mind according to this theory: the happy/healthy body promotes a more happy/efficiently working mind and vice versa. If this is the case then seeking curricular opportunities to create the sense of joy in as many children as possible must be considered a desirable way to for them to be and to learn. Teaching with *enjoyment* as a major aim seems to have the potential to serve mind and body, here and now, and also to create in children a positive sense of self which will benefit them well into the future.

These findings based on neurological research, mirror those by 'positive psychologists' like Mihaly Csikszentmihalyi (2002), Barbara Fredrickson (2003), Fredrickson and Branigan (2005) and Martin Seligman (2004), who also propose that positive emotional states are the optimum mental conditions for learning, social and intellectual connection making, discovery, creativity and invention. A particularly accessible hypothesis in this regard is Fredrickson's 'broaden and build' theory of positive emotions. This is examined in Chapter 4.

There seem to be strong links between happiness and creativity (Csikszentmihalyi, 1996). Recently the veteran 'people watcher', Desmond Morris, has suggested that our feeling of happiness relates to 'the degree to

Illustration 1.9 *Enjoyment is not always shown in the smile, but shows itself here in intricacy, concentration and application.* Courtesy Gifted and Talented Summer Academy, Canterbury

which we find ourselves able to exercise the particularly human skills of creativity, the use of symbols including symbolic language, and family relationships' (Morris, 2004). A recurring theme of this book is the relationship between the self involved in creative activity and the ensuring sense of contentment, achievement, fascination, engagement and joy we often call happiness.

The developing self of the child is also prey to a particularly powerful set of negative influences. Notions of rampant materialism, excessive wealth, risky behaviour, violence, fame and a particularly narrow concept of physical beauty are attractive and perhaps easily assimilated into the hoped-for self. These features of young life are constantly reinforced by toys, advertising, television, film, computer, Internet and video images. Human young are probably genetically predisposed to finding joy in these things, but it is also commonly held that such simple pleasures do not bring particularly long-lasting satisfaction. Indeed, studies of lottery winners throughout the world have demonstrated the short-lived nature of material wealth (see, for example, *Scotsman*, 2006, website). Left to their own devices without ICT to distract them, children quickly find enjoyment in physical and social activities. Physical play clearly engages the vast majority of young mammals. A casual observation of children during games sessions and at playtime always shows wide grins, sparkling eyes, relaxed faces and joyful conversation – the key signals of happiness. It seems particularly disastrous that school sport and

Illustrations 1.10, 1.11, 1.12   *Seek out the facial manifestations of happiness, the smile, the shining eyes, the raised cheekbones and the un-furrowed brow.* Photos: Cherry Tewfik

PE are so constrained by time, especially since negative body image and obesity are growing issues in developed societies like the UK and the USA (WHO, 2004, website).

Schools of the twenty-first century are right to be thinking hard about what implicit and explicit values they wish to teach their pupils. Perhaps the call for more complex and challenging activities in the curriculum results from a feeling that it is in creative, often symbolic, physical activity that lasting human satisfaction is to be found (Morris, 2004). Political demands on schools have sometimes resulted in significant conflicts of values in this regard. In the context of heightened 'back to basics' demands on US schools, Csikszentmihalyi castigated schools and parents for: 'making serious tasks dull and hard and frivolous ones exciting and easy. Schools generally fail to teach how exciting, how mesmerisingly beautiful science or mathematics can be; they teach the routine of literature or history rather than the adventure' (1997, p. 125). He goes on to give evidence from his own research which suggests that creative individuals in all walks of life go beyond the limitations of genetic or cultural programming to live 'exemplary lives … [which] show how joyful and interesting complex symbolic activity is'. Attitudes to the self – how I learn best, what I find fascinating, satisfying, pleasure-giving, helpful – can be developed through education, but it is probably important that we consider carefully what kind of 'selves' we are helping to create in our classrooms.

How can we know what it is like to be a child in the twenty-first century?

The current concerns of children remind us that it may not be easy being a child in the first quarter of the twenty-first century, anywhere in the world. At one extreme, children suffer disproportionately. In the developing world, five-sixths of the world's children have the least access to scarce resources and 16,000 of them die each day because of poverty (Bread for the world, 2005, website). Two hundred and fifty million children under 14 work for their survival (UN, 2006, schools website). On the evidence of researchers and current media headlines, many young people in the resource-rich and developed world live a pretty sad and lonely existence too. Poverty of all kinds singles children out for special problems. The United Nations Children's Fund (UNICEF) recently reminded us that 22 per cent of children in the USA and 15 per cent in the UK live in poverty which they describe as 'an environment that is damaging to their mental, physical, emotional and spiritual development' (UNICEF, 2005, website). The gap between rich and poor is as significant as poverty itself. Life expectancy correlates exactly with levels of inequality, and children born into low-status, low-income and high stress,

Illustrations 13, 14, 15 *Each child shows engagement in a different way, but it is recognisable across time and culture.* Photos: Cherry Tewfik

start life smaller and significantly more prone to psychological problems and illness (Layard, 2005, 2006; Wilkinson, 2005).

Beyond poverty, relative wealth may have brought its own problems. Young people in the developed world are reported to be increasingly involved in risky behaviour. Several studies demonstrate the rapid growth in behavioural and emotional difficulties amongst the young, and rising rates of 'teenage alcoholism, early smoking, depression, self-harm and suicide (Collishaw et al., 2004; Layard, 2006, website). Indeed, Collishaw's report records that in the UK behavioural and emotional problems among teenagers have risen by over 70 per cent in the past 25 years. The WHO report (WHO, 2004, website), already quoted, graphically presented a rise in many of the possible causes of such trends: family breakdown, bullying, loss of trust, lack of success or pleasure in school, stress, loneliness and subjective health problems. Within many categories of health-related behaviour, young people in England (not necessarily in the UK as a whole) and the USA were shown to be amongst the least happy in the western world. There may be a sensationalist element to some newspaper headlines and opinion polls about young people's health, but it is more difficult to argue with international organizations with a well-established research methodology and, hopefully, less culturally biased views.

The most important way of finding out about what concerns children is by asking children themselves. In *The School I'd Like*, Catherine Burke and Ian Grosvenor asked children their views on how schools should be (Burke and Grosvenor, 2003). The collected children's statements plead for a very different school environment to the one which many adults may *think* children would like. Here are a few provocative suggestions for the schools of the future:

- Children will learn more about the future than the past.
- Adults will listen to them and not dismiss their opinions.
- Children will be free to be children.
- Children will not be, 'treated as herds of identical animals wanting to be civilized before we are let loose upon the world. It will be recognized that it's our world too'.
- Playgrounds would have 'something to play with'.
- 'Power will be evenly spread throughout the school.'
- 'More time should be devoted to art, design and technology.'
- The curriculum will be 'concerned with fulfilment'.

Several case studies from this book will outline projects where children have taken the lead in successfully defining and achieving what they wanted to learn and make in environments where the 'locus of control' was passed to them. These may still seem radical more than 200 years after Rousseau's idealized and naturally good, 'noble savage' approach to the education of the child (see Introduction).

Less radical but very much in line with a 'reconstructionist' education ideology, the UK government and government agencies are now acting on the ground-breaking new Children Act, *Every Child Matters* (HM Government, 2004). This Act seen by some as far-reaching and bold, is constructed around *five outcomes* which arose from consultations with children about their hopes and needs from the adult-controlled worlds of the health, social and education services. These common outcomes, against which all government agencies working with children will in future be judged, are to:

- be healthy
- stay safe
- enjoy and achieve
- make a positive contribution
- achieve economic well-being.

Evident in this list is a newly articulated emphasis on feelings, security and well-being. A similar stress is also evident in a number of other government directives. The recent 'framework for inspection' (OFSTED, 2004, s. 4, p. 25) requires schools to self-evaluate efforts made towards enhancing the 'personal development and well-being' of all learners. Again the most recent Healthy Schools Status document (DH/DfES, 2005, and website) holds as one of its key areas of activity 'the emotional health and well-being' of children. It now seems clear that national education systems in the developed world and beyond are charged with not just the education and socialization of our young people, but also the active promotion of their personal emotional security, health and well-being. In many senses schools are the only agencies in a position fully to enact such policies and philosophies. Schools are designed to reach every child. In the next chapter we examine some schools' attempts to address the central issues for children of the twenty-first century.

Summary

The twenty-first century is to be a century full of challenges like every other century. Aside from the obvious implications of overpopulation, there are three major differences to the challenges of this century: the much more rapid *pace* of change (Figure 1.2), their perceived often *negative* character in the minds of modern children and their *global* characteristics.

The changes and challenges in our world, and consequently our minds, cannot be kept local; our global economy, instant communications and global pollution have meant that whatever happens in one place quickly affects every other. If they want, ordinary people, particularly teachers and

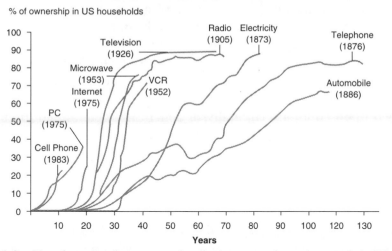

How long it takes new technologies to reach a mass market

% of ownership in US households

Figure 1.2 How long it takes new technologies to reach a mass market. Where cell phones, internet and personal computers penetrated 20% of the US market in less than 20 years, it took the car and the telephone 50 years to achieve the same take up

children, are now in a position to exert some influence over the interrelated future of this world, but to do so effectively we need to be very clear about what we value most. The answers to questions of value should underpin all our education decisions. So far we have selected and examined five key areas of special interest to children.

- the future (which is taken to include environmental as well as personal concerns)
- ICT
- global politics
- relationships
- the self.

Research and experience in these areas also suggests a number of related statements can be made which might impact upon a curriculum designed to liberate those children from the combined threats of materialism, fear, exclusion and lack of self-fulfilment. Each of the following statements rest on arguments for a more cross-curricular, creative, meaningful and child-centred approach:

1. *Security about the future is an essential prerequisite for the happy child.* A curriculum which addresses children's anxiety about the personal and global future (as well as insecurities about the self and relationships) is crucial if we agree that school activities should be relevant to their lives.

2. *A sense of personal control over aspects of their daily life is central to children's motivation for learning.* A concentration on developing emotional literacy, the constructive use of ICT and establishment of personally meaningful, curricular experiences to interpret and examine is more likely to generate personal engagement among children.

3. *It is possible for ordinary individuals to make a positive impact upon global and environmental issues.* It is suggested that cross-curricular themes that touch upon children's culturally or genetically determined interests in any area are more likely to generate interest.

4. *Opportunities to build and deepen positive relationships with others are embraced by children.* We should seek a curriculum, teaching methods, community links and classroom organization which offer a range of activities to promote and utilize such relationships.

5. *The child's positive self-image is fundamental to a healthy mind and body.* Education should therefore be physically active and individualized as far as possible and aimed to promote a personal sense of achievement, resilience and discover the strengths of each individual.

Education in the UK and USA is now in a position where *government policy* on health, education and social services could be seen to be broadly in line with *theoretical/professional* opinion on priorities for children. Key words which arise from both areas are all related to feelings:

- health
- security
- enjoyment
- positivity
- well-being.

Each of these concepts and each of the five key areas of special interest to children (pp. 18–20) are themes which require judgements of value where school and community based decisions will significantly impact on the character of twenty-first century life.

Key questions

+ Do you think that the 1990s were more optimistic times and that the 2000s are more pessimistic?
+ What do you think schools can do about integrating family learning into the curriculum and structures of the school?

✦ What can the playground tell us about children's learning? How could this be integrated into the curriculum?

✦ What are the pluses and minuses of ICT in the lives of children?

✦ How can we make relationships a more central part of our curriculum?

✦ How can we provide times of happiness and positivity for every child?

✦ What can the school do about the health of the child?

Further reading

Alexander, T. (2001) *Citizenship Schools: A Practical Guide to Education for Citienship and Personal Development*, London: Campaign for Learning/UNICEF.

Greenfield, S. (2003) *Tomorrow's People*, London: Penguin.

Robinson, K. (2001) *Out of Our Minds,* London: Continuum.

What Does Good Cross-Curricular Practice Look Like?

The wonder of human beings is our infinite variability. This variability does not apply simply to our DNA, irises or fingerprints, but to the almost infinite range of potential links within every human brain. There is an immeasurable variety of possible connections between neurons controlling our senses, memory, and physical and emotional responses, and those which process our conscious, rational and intellectual responses. Those variations suggest that we each experience the world around us in subtly (and not so subtly) different ways. Thus it would be foolish to give the impression that there could be a single or even a finite range of answers to the question, 'What does good cross-curricular practice look like?' The honest answer is that good practice in this area is as diverse as any cooperative group of human brains and bodies.

A second wonder of human kind is that we *can* communicate so effectively. Considering the potential for some of those of billions of connections to go wrong it seems little short of miraculous that we establish shared understandings so well. The teacher's job is to construct mutually acceptable perceptions in the interests of learning. Curricula are designed to provide intellectual and social settings for such learning and they can be good, bad or indifferent. To help you form an answer to the question, 'What does good cross-curricular practice look like?' I have chosen six case studies. These examples illustrate something of the diversity of successful cross-curricular learning. Each case study generated wide evidence of creative thinking on the part of children and adults involved. Each example uses carefully focused subject application, real and relevant activity, strong and detailed planning, and frequent and formative assessment to promote and challenge interdisciplinary thinking. The case studies cover:

- two examples of whole-school approaches to the entire curriculum
- a two-day teacher training module with a Year 7 group
- a primary school following the Royal Society of Arts (RSA) competences curriculum

- a whole-term project in mixed Years 5/6 class in a city centre primary school
- a week's cross-curricular work in a Year 4 class in central London
- an inner-city nursery school pioneering the idea of a children's centre.

In choosing these six I am aware that others appear disregarded, but when a school curriculum allows teachers and children to make links between subject disciplines which energise, motivate, provoke and sustain high-quality learning in a school, then good cross-curricular practice is happening. If the same curriculum helps the adults delivering it feel they are doing good work too, it is even better practice.

The arts form the focus for two, humanities for one, multiple intelligences another and science the main focus for two more. In each example, however, the required cross-curricular and creative thinking did not just 'happen' it was the result of long periods of thought and planning. Objectives were met because teachers and key workers were constantly aware of them during planning and whilst the children were working. Many of the case study schools brought in experts of one kind or another to take topics forward. Several teachers noted that their children were able cheerfully to accept pinpointed criticism and stretching targets from non-teacher experts in ways they would not have done from their regular teachers (see also Brice Heath and Wolf, 2005). The evidence of these case studies suggests that partnership with members of the local community is not simply good for citizenship education but has wider learning benefits. Whether the expert was a carer, the mayor, an imam, or a great grandmother remembering evacuation in the Second World War, his or her expertise helped raise standards of achievement, promoted the sense of belonging to a living, changing community and provided authoritative alternatives to standard assessments.

Very often cross-curricular approaches are associated with creative or, as Anna Craft calls it, 'possibility' thinking (Craft, 2000). Indeed in some schools, for example those using the International Primary Curriculum (2006), appear to have chosen a curriculum specifically intended to promote it. Arthur Koestler's (1964) insight that creativity is a result of 'bisociation' seems relevant here. Bisociation means the (usually unexpected) meeting of two distinctly different planes of thought. We may, for example, be analysing in some detail the decorative markings on a Victorian teapot while carrying out an investigation in history, and something makes us think of the markings as reminiscent of music. This unpredicted link between applied pattern and music may result in an imaginative, original and valued musical composition. The chances of making unusual juxtapositions of ideas, approaches and knowledge are high in a curriculum where the skills and thought processes of two or more different disciplines are applied to a single stimulus.

Illustration 2.1 *Children studying full sized paintings in their school hall.*

We will examine six quite contrasting settings where two or more curriculum subjects are brought together to help understand a particular stimulus, event or place.

Case study 1: A primary school with a whole-school arts focus supported by Creative Partnerships

This school works with Creative Partnerships (Creative Partnerships website), a government organization dedicated to promoting links between schools and local creative practitioners in disadvantaged communities. When the school introduces its curriculum to parents we read the words:

> The essence of creativity is in making new connections and this can be frustrated by rigid divisions in subject teaching. Hence the realisation for the need for a whole new approach.

> The Creative Learning Curriculum at School X was introduced as a result of dissatisfaction with the learning and teaching of the Foundation subjects together with the over emphasis of teaching of the core subjects. The creation of 'SATs robots' and bored, sterile teachers brought into question the nature of what we were trying to achieve with our children. (School Prospectus, pp. 4–5).

The same school has thought very clearly about its objectives which are to:

- achieve a radical change in children's learning styles in conjunction with teaching methodologies
- raise the profile of the foundation subjects
- develop learning and teaching through the arts
- foster creativity and inspiration in all children
- build confidence and self-esteem so that children are able to express their creativity and individuality.

Supported by Creative Partnerships, the school builds its curriculum around works of two- and three-dimensional art from a variety of different times and cultures. In every one of the six school terms, each year group uses a different work of art as the focus for their learning, so that during their time in primary school every child will have studied over 40 works of art in some depth. The work is carefully planned for progression with National Curriculum objectives embedded throughout, which ensures every child receives his or her full entitlement to the National Curriculum. Each subject is scrutinized by subject coordinators for appropriate skills' development, quality of content and resources. Teachers introduce each work of art in a variety of ways to the children, exploring themes raised by the children in early discussions. Work in ICT, Religious Education (RE), Citizenship, Dance, Music, Drama, Art, Design and Technology, Music, Geography, History and Modern Foreign Language (MFL) is recorded in loose-leaf folders divided by subject, but children are encouraged to document their understanding in personalized ways and present it according to their preferred learning and communication style. At the end of each term the children create their own bound 'proper' books with title and contents pages. Incredible pride is taken when they are able to present their work in this way.

Here is an example of the focus of learning activity in a single six-week half-term:

Spring Term 1 2005

Paintings

- Nursery, *The Postman Roulin*, Vincent van Gogh
- Year R Aboriginal painting of a Kangaroo
- Year 1 *Winter scene with Skaters*, by Breughel
- Year 2 *Storm over Southall shed*, by Terence Cuneo
- Year 3 Nebuman Hunting in the Marshes, Egyptian fresco.
- Year 4 *The Fighting Téméraire*, by JMW Turner
- Year 5 African Rock art from the Kalahari desert
- Year 6 *Michael triumphant over the devil*, by Bermejo.

Illustration 2.2   *Turning understanding of a painting into a dance*

Using the works of art as a starting point, many classes were able to link with a creative partner who helped facilitate learning in a number of curriculum areas. Some
works of art were used to generate 'creative visits'. For example in Year 2 the daugh-
ter of artist Terence Cuneo was asked to come into school to speak about her father's
life and work and join with the children in related activities. The children visited a
steam train centre, they watched a video of the painter painting, they learned about
life in the 1930s, 1940s and 1950s, and made their own paintings based upon their
own hobbies and interests in the world around them. In Year 5, pupils worked with
an African music group who performed and then taught the children dances, drama,
percussion techniques and rhythms. Their work on the African rock painting also
included sculptures of African wildlife and a concert for parents and friends of the
school.

Children and teachers are both clearly involved in evaluating and planning
this curriculum. Their comments are honoured in each section of the
school introduction to its curriculum and decisions on repeating each mini-
project are based on discussions and written responses from adult and child
participants.

Illustration 2.3 *Children and student teachers were placed together in the tiny carriages of a half-gauge railway to construct 'raps' about the journey*

Case study 2: The Canterbury HEARTS project (an Initial Teacher Education/Year 7 cross-arts project)

This cross-curricular project, which formed part of a teacher education pro-gramme, exemplifies many of the personal benefits for both teacher and pupil when they are involved in activities which seem to be mutually relevant.

The Canterbury HEARTS project, 'Strangely Familiar' (Barnes, 2005b, 2006a; Barnes and Shirley, 2005) started as a research study designed to investigate the power of the arts to enhance the learning of university tutors, trainee teachers and school children. It consisted of a series of practical encounters where cross-arts activities were used to answer profound questions and detailed investigations about environments. It aimed to challenge teachers, trainees and pupils to re-think their concept of education and by so doing bring about change in both teacher training and each participating individ-ual's mind. So successful was the initial externally funded module that it has become part of a standard BA (Ed) Teacher Education course.

The module consisted of four discrete but linked experiences.

Experience 1

30 Students began with a high-impact experience shared with 60 Year 7 pupils. Adult and child were thrown together unprepared as co-learners in an unfamiliar place, asked to make sense of it through the eyes of various arts. After instruction

on health and safety responsibilities, student teachers were given only two instructions for their day: avoid using the words 'you' or 'I', and allow the children to take control of activities as soon as possible. As they arrived at the site, each group of six students and pupils were simply left with a set of focusing tasks developed with conceptual artist Robert Jarvis, and asked to 'capture the essence' of their place for a short presentation to their peers when they returned to school.

Focusing exercises

- *A sense of touch:* each member to go into their own space and sit or stand alone. Feel walls, pebbles, plants, fence, etc. nearest you. Jot down FRAGMENTS of sentences which describe the fine detail of the physical sensations in the fingers as you feel the immediate environment

- *The micro scale:* find a place where two materials meet. Isolate a small area of this juxtaposition (perhaps with a viewfinder) and draw a sketch of the fine detail of this tiny place. (Avoid places which require perspective, shading, etc.; take a 'front-on' view.) Write single words around the drawing to indicate colour, feelings, associations, textures, etc.

- *The macro scale:* take a position where a wider view can be seen, perhaps the view over the whole place. Try to split the view into three different planes (foreground, middle ground and background). Draw or describe in words and phrases this general view and annotate any sketches with phrases which describe the place

- *Only words:* in groups list all the words or phrases which describe the place around a central symbol for your place.

- *Haiku:* each person in the group to write a three-line Haiku (five syllables, then seven, then five syllables only) that captures the essence of a tiny detail of the place they are in. A haiku often starts with a sensitive description in the first two lines and in the last five syllable line 'flips' the thoughts to a 'higher' or more profound association

- *Snapshot view:* divide into pairs. In each pair one of the partners closes their eyes and is led very carefully by their open-eyed partner. When the open-eyed partner sees an unusual or interesting image, they position their friend in the optimum viewing position and then squeeze the hand of their partner. The partner then opens their eyes for the length of the hand squeeze. Do this five times and then swap roles.

- *One shot only:* each member of the group is allowed one still photograph only (so it has to be a good one). Discuss shots with the whole group but each individual must take a photograph.

- *Spatialization:* with the group seated or standing and facing in the same direction get them to draw a circle on their page with a bump at 12 o'clock and two bumps at quarter to and quarter past. This will make an aerial view of a head. Everyone

Illustration 2.4   *Dungeness power station from the beach*

should write what they can hear and on which side of the head they can hear it. Moving sounds (for example, a plane) can be recorded as such.

- *A dramatic happening*: plan a dramatic modern (or future) event which could *only* have happened in your place. Act it out. Summarize the story in three freeze-frame montages. Discuss and draw/plan/note what you would absolutely *have* to construct on your school stage if you wanted to act the scene out back at school. For example, would the light need to be coming from a certain side? Would there have to be a step here, an arch there, would the arch have to be low/pointed/stone/crumbly? Etc.

- *Say it in one*: each group has to produce five 'one-shot movies' lasting one minute. Each person will have the opportunity to make a movie. It should be a planned and continuous shot taken by one member but the shot should be discussed by the whole group.

(With thanks to Robert Jarvis for many of these ideas.)

After a day together, students and children brought their collected data and impressions back to school, worked on creative ways of bringing several aspects together and presenting them, and finally performed them to the rest of the year cohort.

Experience 2

At a two-day conference, students began by handing control to the children and making themselves vulnerable by learning alongside them. A large

Illustration 2.5   *Initial Teacher Education students planning the Canterbury HEARTS*

majority of students reported they had gained more from the children than they had imparted as teachers. Typical comments were:

> 'I was surprised at how well they could take a small piece of information and come up with some really exciting imaginative ideas.' (Lily)

> 'I was inspired by the children's responses ... and their eagerness to explore, gather materials and discuss.' (Christine)

The student conference continued with workshops, tutorials or lectures on how individual arts skills, attitudes and knowledge and citizenship perspectives could be applied to a single place, and how they could use the high motivation of working outside school to raise standards of thinking within individual subjects.

Experience 3

Following this induction, students were to be sent to work in teams of three or four in one of nine rural primary schools. They were charged with planning and delivering a focused project which would address an identified citizenship issue through the arts. Citizenship issues identified by the schools included:

- making decisions together
- improving the local community
- cooperating

Illustration 2.6   Six year olds showing thoughts about the possible changes in the view from a classroom window in 5o years time. (Left hand side, present; right hand side future)

- making change happen
- understanding other points of view.

The stimulus and physical context for activities was to be a place outside the classroom: playground, school field, local streets or natural area. Activities in the place centred around what made it unique. The specialness of the place was to be communicated through a combined arts approach and eventually shared with other participating schools. The suggested pedagogy was significantly different to that used in 'normal' teaching practices; there were to be no detailed planned outcomes, just focusing tasks which were open-ended and control over the outcome was to be passed to the children as often as possible. Students were asked to act as coach-facilitators more than stereotypical teachers; the words 'we' and 'us' were to be common features of all interactions. Teaching *was* to take place but only when students or pupils recognized the need for a particular subject-based skill. Learning would be assessed in teams during performances at the end of the two days of activity.

Experience 4

Students were asked to make a detailed record of their impressions and observations, and write them up as an assignment which would include a rationale comparing the theory with their experience.

From these assignment several themes of general interest to those thinking of cross-arts work in schools emerged. Students noted many common outcomes from their work with children. In each case the taught and observed sessions were outside the classroom, answered personally significant questions, and in an atmosphere where control was placed in the children's hands for significant periods and where the arts were used as ways of interpreting and communicating the essence of a place. The following themes were commonly highlighted:

- Children's imagination was consistently recorded as being beyond that of the students' themselves.
- The activities generated a great deal of genuine questioning.
- Children seemed so highly engaged that behaviour never became an issue.
- The atmosphere seemed very relaxed.
- The children displayed facial expressions of happiness and contentedness.
- Cooperation and friendliness of the children involved in the project were frequently remarked upon.
- Children were handed control and it significantly enhanced engagement.
- Children responded well to the open-ended nature of the project.
- The normal barriers between teacher and pupil were significantly broken down.
- Both children and students reported that they had learned a great deal.
- A number of students commented that this activity had been the most enjoyable aspect of their whole course.

However in a setting where such positive outcomes are so evident, teachers need to be aware of the following pitfalls

- Having stepped out of the role of teacher, many students forgot to step back in. Students were happy to see well-motivated, well-behaved, active and link-making children during their engagement in the topic, but they did not use the opportunity to help the children 'raise their game'. They did not step in to offer new challenges, teach new and relevant skills at a higher level or question them about ways they could improve their products.
- Having attended a crash course on creative teaching and learning, some students left with the idea that it was going to be easy to generate creativity in their classrooms. They failed to understand that creativity does not 'just happen' when children are left to their own devices, but it needs serious preparation and discussion amongst teachers, and probably needs a clear framework to develop within.

Illustration 2.7   *These children are making independent choices about representing aspects of their 'weather' project for the term*

Case study 3: An urban primary school using the Royal Society of Arts (RSA) 'Opening Minds' competences curriculum

This school serves part of a garrison town and has a highly mobile population, with 60 per cent of its children likely to move into or away from the school in any year. Between 30 and 40 per cent of its non-armed forces children have free school meals. When the head teacher arrived at the school in 2001 it had a history of poor attendance, severe behaviour problems and low achievement. Within a term a new and rigorous curriculum had been established which for the first time satisfied all OFSTED Key Issues, the demands of the National Curriculum and the NNS and NLS. But, attention to teaching methods, a strong behaviour policy and 'more of the same' in standard curriculum terms did not seem to make any difference to standards or attendance or engagement. Standard Assessment Test results continued to fall. The head and her team decided only something dramatic would make a difference and so began a major and cross-curricular departure from the conventional approach to the curriculum. They adopted a primary school version of the RSA's competences-based curriculum called 'Opening Minds'.

Put succinctly, the RSA curriculum centres around five competencies:

- competences for learning
- competences for citizenship
- competences for relating to people

- competences for managing situations
- competences for managing information.

Each competence is chosen to cover an essential and generic aspect of modern life. Schools delivering the RSA curriculum decide upon curriculum themes which will generate development of the competences in a variety of experiential, learning and subject contexts. Working towards mastery of the RSA competences would result, they suggest, in internalizing essential and highly transferable life skills which will be meaningful to children whatever changes come about in twenty-first century society. In the context of children's' preoccupations and worries about the future, outlined in Chapter 1, such a curriculum appears deeply relevant and timely.

What the competences mean

Learning

Children will understand how to learn and manage their own lifelong learning, they will learn systematically to think, to have explored and extended their own talents and have opportunities to develop a love of learning for its on sake. They will achieve high personal standards in literacy, numeracy and spatial understanding and be able to handle ICT with confidence and understanding.

Citizenship

Children will have developed an understanding of ethics and values and have experience of contributing to society. They will understand how the institutions of society work and their relationship to it. They will understand and value the importance of diversity both nationally and globally and will consider the global and social implications of technology. They will also learn to manage aspects of their own lives.

Illustration 2.8   *Learning to cooperate. Children planning their presentation*

(Continued)

Relationships

Children will understand how to relate to people in a variety of contexts. They will have experience of operating in teams and understand how to help develop other people. They will develop a range of techniques for communicating in different ways and have an understanding of managing themselves and others emotionally. They will know techniques of managing stress and conflict.

Situations

Children will learn to manage time, change, success and disappointment. They will understand what it is to be entrepreneurial and how to take and use initiative. They will learn how to take and manage risks and uncertainties.

Information

Children will develop a range of techniques for assessing and differentiating information and will learn to be analytical. They will understand the importance of reflection and critical judgement and know how, when and where to apply it.

The school has made its own detailed levelled descriptors (levels 1–5) of each of these competences, but it is instantly obvious that this curriculum makes no, or little, reference to subject content. The school has made thoughtful and well-discussed decisions about curriculum. Their curriculum policy contains the following aims:

- For children to produce high-quality outcomes across all curriculum subjects – to bring out the best in everyone.
- To have a time effective, relevant curriculum with real-life and cross-curricular links.
- To educate children and staff in the broadest sense of the word's meaning – 'to lead out'.
- To focus on children and how they learn best as a priority.
- To ensure children have appropriate access to learning activities that promote physical, moral, social, spiritual, cultural, academic and creative development.
- To encourage children's understanding and tolerance of the world in which they live and its peoples.

To achieve these aims, the school divided the curriculum subjects into what they term 'knowledge subjects' (Geography, History, Science and Religious Education) each of which form the 'lead' subject for a term. The 'process subjects' (Maths, English, Design and Technology, Music, MFL, Art and PE)

Table 2.1   Key Stage 2 weekly curriculum

Key Stage 2 total	23.75 hrs	
Literacy	Hr/wk	%
Discrete teaching of writing	1	4.2
Cross-curricular writing	1	4.2
Guided reading	1.25	5.3
Handwriting	0.25	1.1
Word and sentence work	2.5	10.5
Reading by/with teacher	1	4.2
Total	7	29.5
Numeracy		
Oral mental work	1	4.2
Number	2.5	10.5
Cross-curricular	1.5	6.3
Total	5	21.0
Other subjects		
Science	1.75	7.4
History and/or Geography	2	8.4
Art and/or Design and Technology	2	8.4
Music	1	4.2
Physical Education	2	8.4
Religious Education	1	4.2
Information Communication Technology	0.5	2.1
Personal Education	0.75	3.2
Modern Foreign Language	0.75	3.2
Total	11.75	49.5
FINAL TOTAL	**23.75**	**100.0**

feature throughout the learning programme. Next they made sure that each subject was represented fairly throughout the year. Then they made a whole-school decision, based on consultation with the children, that a literacy and numeracy 'hour' was too long and that the daily sessions should be cut to half an hour. Other English and mathematics and all science was to be subsumed in topic-based work and other times throughout the week. Science is a term's focus three times a year, and English and mathematics have extra weighting to reflect their 'core' status. Look, for example in Table 2.1 at the way the subjects are shared throughout the week during Key Stage 2.

As well as linking all curriculum subjects to developing skills within each of the competences, the ongoing theme of 'weather' was used to unite work throughout the school. The school also requires a religious education theme for each year group so that children from many cultures represented in the school can respond to different religious festivals throughout the year. Within

Illustration 2.9   *A weather painting generated from infants' direct experience of weather*

this framework, each year group team chooses a strong and emotionally engaging shared 'event' as the end of term focus for each of six terms. For every year group, the event and lead subject for the term define teaching decisions for every six-week block. Every term ends with the special event which has formed the focus and motivation for cross-curricular work for the preceding six weeks. So a Year 1 or 2 group may be working towards the following end-of-term happenings:

- 'a day trip to India'
- Easter fun day
- the opening of a wildlife garden
- trip to the seaside
- art exhibition
- Christmas nativity.

Between 65 per cent and 70 per cent of all work in the subjects comes within the cross-curricular theme. Teachers are encouraged to use texts and examples in the remaining 35 per cent or 30 per cent , which also relate to the main theme, the RE theme or weather. Throughout the school all of the learning done by children is interrelated and contextualized – the learning makes sense to the learners.

Planning is done on a general and whole-school framework across both Key Stages 1 and 2, and brings together, religious and weather focus, National Curriculum (NC) subjects, the special event theme and focus subjects so that progression and coverage can be mapped. The planning table (Table 2.2) used throughout the school can be seen partially filled in.

Table 2.2 Format for medium-term curriculum plan

National Curriculum Year : 2		Term: 5			
Subject and theme: *Wildlife in our garden*		**Event and visits:** *Opening ceremony for the wildlife garden*		**Role play:** *Vet and environmental scientist*	
Weather topic: *'From spring to summer'*					
Year topic:					
Religious Education topic:					
Displays: *Posters for wildlife garden*					
Parental involvement: *Parent helpers for visits, bird-watcher parent, insect collection*					
Literacy tasks and NC references time:	NC levels and key vocabulary	Numeracy tasks and NC references time:	NC levels and key vocabulary	Science tasks and NC references time:	NC levels and key vocabulary
					E.g. Level 2: Arrange in an orderly way e.g. say in your own words. Observe and compare, then describe similarities, differences and changes in the objects and events observed.
Art and design tasks and NC references time:	NC levels and key vocabulary	Geography tasks and NC references time:	NC levels and key vocabulary	History tasks and NC references time:	NC levels and key vocabulary
			E.g. Level 2: Independently organize and classify. Select and use equipment from a given range. Work together		*E.g. Level 2: Record and respond through talk, writing (lists, matrices, labels, simple sentences), drawing,*

Table 2.2 *(Continued)*

			to carry out a task. Adapt and amend to improve.		*models. Say in your own words what has happened.*
Music tasks and NC references time:	NC levels and key vocabulary	RE tasks and NC references time:	NC levels and key vocabulary	ICT tasks and NC references time:	NC levels and key vocabulary
Design technology tasks and NC references time:	NC levels and key vocabulary	PSHE/ Citizenship tasks and NC references time:	NC levels and key vocabulary	RSA Competences **No time allocations required. The competences are to be planned into lessons across the curriculum.**	
Gymnastics tasks and NC references time:	NC levels and key vocabulary	Games tasks and NC references time:	NC levels and key vocabulary	Dance tasks and NC references time:	NC levels and key vocabulary
	Level 2: Explore whole body actions independently varying speed, level, direction e.g. forwards and backwards and turning, on floor and apparatus. Remember and repeat simple sequences of up to 3 actions independently and share these with a partner using meeting and parting; focus; unison and leading and following.		*Athletics: E.g. Level 2: Children explore, copy, repeat and remember simple skills of running, jumping and throwing, with a range of simple equipment. They show increasing control and co-ordination.*		*E.g. Dance Level 2: Explore whole body actions independently varying speed, level, direction, and strength. Remember and repeat simple sequences of up to 3 actions independently and share these with a partner using meeting and parting; focus; unison and leading and following.*

Teachers from England will notice that generic National Curriculum language is used to define the levels and types of activities in each selected subject. Detailed planning for each subject is taken from the 'Progression in … ' guidance published for each curriculum subject.

Case study 4: A combined Year 5/6 in a city centre school – a two-term project in the local environment.

Behind this school for 210 children lies a derelict tannery site which in former years pumped out noxious smells which must have affected the house prices. The site was large, scattered with functional and undecorated Victorian industrial buildings, dangerous pits and stores, and had a sluggish river running through it. Photographs taken from the air showed the children that large areas were now covered in brambles, long grass and dumped rubbish. The school decided to make this site the focus of a 12-week project for its Years 5 and 6 children. Their challenge was to make a serious proposal to the local council for the development of this site. The council planning committee was contacted and it offered to send its senior planning officer to outline the kind of brief such proposals would require and the 'Tannery Project' was started.

Through funding from English Heritage, the school was promised an architect and town planner to help children throughout their project but, first, teachers and town planning experts had to come up with a thorough programme of activities. Two staff development days and a week of after-school planning went into the curriculum proposal which looked like this:

Focus subjects	History (PoS 7), geography (PoS 2, 3, a and b, 5 a and b, 6a) , Design and Technology (PoS. 1, a, b, c and d, 2 d and e) and Citizenship (1, a, c, and e, 2a, g, h, j); Learning objectives for each to be taken from National Curriculum level three, four or five and programmes of study.
Time allocation	Two full days and one afternoon per week for 12 weeks.
Other subjects	Maths, English, Science, Art, RE, PSHE. Some already programmed work with relevant objectives to be addressed within the Tannery theme.
Staffing	Two class teachers, three TAs and head teacher, architect, four days, town planner four days, builder (a parent) half a day, architect (governor) three days, planning officer half a day, council planning committee, one meeting, and mayor meeting and exhibition.

Week one	Introduction to the project and partners. A series of surveys; asking local residents about their views of the site, their hopes for the site, mapping and recording specific aspects of the character of the area, natural life in the area, street furniture, materials and a photo record of every building surrounding the site.
Week two	Continuation of surveys. (*These were conducted in supported groups of six or seven children with an adult.*)
Week three	Presentation of the results of the surveys using ICT, posters and dramatization. Assessed and appraised by the two year groups themselves, the architect and the head teacher.
Week five	Decisions on how the site should be redeveloped based on the survey results. (*Children decided the site had to be used for new housing, some recreation facilities such as a running track, undercover tennis courts and a swimming pool. There also needed to be a supermarket for those who could not travel to the out-of-town industrial estates, and some small food shops which they said people preferred. They were also worried that the river was an underused resource and could be a really beautiful thing to design the development around.*)
Week six	General historical survey led by the local archaeological trust. Archaeological information, historical records going back to 1200 AD, illustrations and photos from 17th century to later 20th century. This was assessed and appraised by the archaeology team.
Week seven	In-depth survey of the school site with members of the archaeological trust and their technical equipment including a loaned Surface Proton Magnetic Resonance Machine. Some art and design work using small details of the environment to apply to products such as china crockery, handkerchiefs and wall paper. Again assessment was continuous, formative and led by the archaeologists.
Week eight	Divide into teams of six (architect, planner, non-working citizen, worker, child and tourist) to decide on what the project should look like/include. Town planner to assess work and advise during its progress.
Week nine	Learn from architect how to start planning a redevelopment scheme, using Ordnance Survey maps, aerial photography, Internet information. Learn from town planner how to make proper models of the scheme and how to present information in most attractive way.
Week ten	Construct detailed and accurate scale models from sketch plans, using appropriate model-making techniques and materials taught by architecture student. Supported by governor/architect.

Week eleven	Small group of Year 6 to observe town council planning meeting to see what happens to proposals for redevelopments. Report back to rest of the year groups and lead discussion on plans for exhibition.
Week twelve	Mount Tannery exhibition and invite the mayor and planning committee to judge the most acceptable proposal. Invite parents and tannery owners to the exhibition.

Teachers reported after the project that attainment targets in each of the focus subjects had been met at level 5 by the majority of pupils engaged. The rest of the curriculum went on undisturbed, though teachers reported a significant improvement in behaviour and general motivation. A child requiring *School Action Plus* to support him in his complex behavioural and learning needs, was unanimously elected by the class to take the mayor around the exhibition. He confidently answered a host of detailed and complex questions and knew the fine points of each of the 10 different proposals. The mayor reported that she had never seen such a comprehensive, relevant and well-presented school exhibition and that it would significantly influence decisions taken by the planning committee in the coming years. The tannery site is currently being redeveloped – using a professional company – as a mixed housing, shopping and recreation area of the town using the river more imaginatively – the same mix the children had recommended.

Teachers observed that the children's attitudes to their local community and environment had been significantly changed for the better. They also noted that skills in surveying, model making, imagining the future and understanding the complexity of planning were transferred readily to subsequent projects.

Case study 5: A nursery Education centre with a 'thinking curriculum'

This nursery is located in a large city centre and serves an ethnically rich and economically mixed population. It takes 106 children from 6 months old to 5 years and its policy ensures the continuation of a philanthropic approach by reserving 20 per cent of its places for children with special educational needs and by providing free places for the children of homeless and refugee families. Its doors are open to children from 8.30 a.m. to 5.30 p.m. and the nursery forms part of a *family campus* which supports parents and carers, providing various therapeutic, health and social support as well as education.

The nursery school has a system of 'key workers' and co-workers for each class. Each child is assigned to a key worker who plans, observes, records and assesses learning in her or his own group of children. Co-workers support the learning and help discuss developments and needs in children. The school feels that the peer group is the best seedbed for the development of friendships and the growth of confidence, tolerance, compassion and caring. It also aims at developing in each individual a creative and curious mind which is both appreciative and appreciated.

Against this strong and values-based background the nursery is organized around several key principles:

1. *The importance of parents as primary educators of the child.* Parents are consulted and interviewed throughout the school year about their child's achievements and targets. They have daily opportunities to share news with the school and collect information about their child's day. Specific 'social time' is timetabled for this use. Through a parent's room, the parents' centre next door, regular newsletters and notices, and the provision of a comprehensive language service, parents are helped to feel an important part of the school.

2. *The importance of the inside and outside space for learning.* Rain or shine, children are encouraged to play and learn through play outside as well as in. A *key group* may have an activity planned which involves using water pipes, large pedal cars, earth and seedlings, hunting for natural materials to construct a house or a collage. These and similar activities will take place outside under large and colourful umbrellas if necessary. 'Garden play' is timetabled each day for most of the day and meetings with parents are as likely in the school garden as in the head's office. Tidying and arranging the toys and resources and natural life of the garden is as important as tidying the classroom.

3. *Scaffolded and social learning is highly valued.* Children and parents are made well aware of Vygotsky's concept of the *Zone of proximal development*, 'the gap between the child's actual and potential level of understanding' (school website) and the importance of peers and adults in supporting or *scaffolding* each individual's understanding. The school's stated objective is 'developing practice which is based upon a philosophy of responsibility towards each other'. And helping children become 'respectful of themselves and others' is very evident in the ways that children play and the relationships the adults model in front of the children.

4. *The significance of real experience.* Key workers plan the experiences of the keygroup according to emerging themes and needs recognized within the group. They use the *Curriculum Guidance for the Foundation Stage* (CGFS) (QFES/QCA, 1999a) to plan *stepping stones* through these experiences and the children's processing of them and long-term planning ensures that there is full curriculum coverage at appropriate depth and breadth. Curriculum coordinators monitor and evaluate regularly to ensure that planning and output continue to challenge and engage the children.

5. *The centrality of play.* The website list of examples of current science activities implies a playful attitude to learning. Science includes caring for class pets and indoor plants, gardening, exploring materials, cooking, making circuits with batteries and bulbs, using 'treasure baskets' for heuristic or 'trial and error' play, investigating, exploring and devising experiments. The nursery website states:

> We understand from the work of Claxton in the UK and Csikszentmihalyi in the US, that those who succeed economically and financially in adult life tend to have perceived their own learning as

'more play-like than work-like,' and nursery classes like this are not simply ensuring the sense of security, enjoyment and meaning we examined earlier, but also laying essential foundations for successful adulthood.

6. *A responsive approach to the curriculum.* Because key workers are constantly observing and assessing children, they can confidently say what each child's strengths, needs and interests are. Key workers' review and planning sheets, and the forms they share with the parents, have significant space devoted to children's interests so the curriculum can be quickly responsive to newly developing or discovered interests. Thus there are no set themes or projects in the school's curriculum plans, only an expectation that the key worker will identify them with her or his group of eight or nine children. Once identified, it is the key worker's responsibility to ensure coverage of the early learning goals and the keeping of a portfolio for each child to represent milestones in their learning.

A look at the generalized time allocations for a typical kindergarten day will give a flavour of the flexibility of this kind of timetable, one which with minor adaptations could easily form the core curriculum organisation for much older children.

Time	Activity
8.00	Nursery staff arrive and prepare for breakfast
8.30	Children having breakfast arrive and eat
9.30	Social time: parents' teachers, and children mingle in garden or class to exchange news, etc.
9.45	Key group time starts in special key group locations around classroom and garden.
10.30	Drinks and fruit and play
11.15	Tidy garden and or classroom
11.30	Maths and language groups
12.00	Lunch and 'garden play'
13.00	Focus activities with key group and child initiated experiences inside and out
14.40	Tidy up
15.00	Key group time to reflect on the day
15.15	First group ready to go, key worker discusses day with parent/carer. Room set up for activities for children staying on later

Cross-curricular activities arise naturally from simple resources and generative play structured by teaching staff. For example, free access to a set of pipes, a wide variety of different containers, some sticky tape, a raised water container and a paddling pool are used to help children develop their social, communication and emotional skills, and provoke creative thinking as they work out how best to transfer water from the raised water container to the dry paddling pool in their school garden. On another side of the garden a group of children develop their understanding of number and direction as well as social communication through playing bus journeys on the various four- and three-wheeled vehicles available to them. Inside the school a group of children may be drawing their plans for a new piece of play equipment and discussing their ideas with an adult or using the role-play area to listen to sitar music, dress in Indian saris, sample fruits or help cook some rice with a parent helping them to develop their knowledge and understanding of the world.

Case study 6: A cross-curricular week for Year 4 children, set around the felling of a tree in Kenwood House gardens

A 200 -year-old beech tree in the grounds of Kenwood House, London, which had withstood the ravages of war, disease and development but had begun to suc-cumb to rot, was becoming dangerous and likely to fall. English Heritage decided the only option was to fell it. A number of local schools were invited to witness the felling of the giant tree and base some of their curriculum on this rare event. One school decided to approach other similar trees in the garden through a range of personally significant starting points. They were to become for the day:

- movement experts
- artists
- naturalists
- musicians
- mathematicians
- wordsmiths
- lone philosophers
- geographers.

Children were asked to choose which activity group they wished to belong to, knowing that they would all act as researchers into the history of the place and the tree when they returned to school. The spread of the choices was remarkably even but their teacher felt it was important to give children a choice of reflecting upon the tree alone.

Each group was given a different data collection sheet to use with an alter-native, safe tree.

Artists had to make a rubbing of the bark describing it in precise words, and then had to make a detailed drawing of the tree to show its actual shape and the way it had grown to catch most sunlight. They also had to draw a single branch of the tree and how it joined to others. Finally, they had to draw every facet of a single leaf and make detailed colour notes around it. Together the children decided to make a group pattern which was suggested by these elements of the tree. When they returned to school they decided they would mount an exhibition of their drawings and some paintings inspired by their experience.

Movement experts were asked to watch how the leaves and small branches were moving and imitate these movements with hands, arms and fingers. They were also urged to notice how the whole tree moved slightly all the time, even in a gentle breeze, and to mimic that slower, subtler movement with their whole body. Sitting down at a distance from the tree the children were then asked mentally to divide the tree into several flat shapes: a long rectangle, two large circles divided by a small square, several contorted lines and a triangle at the top. The challenge was to 'do' something with this information. Children responded by drawing each shape separately on the ground in found twigs. They then made up a dance where the two-dimensional shapes of the tree were combined with the several movements they had observed. One child made a side show dance showing the growth of the tree from 1780 to the present day.

Mathematicians found the approximate age of the tree using a rough formula whereby they measured the distance between two metre sticks, placed either side of the trunk, and then multiplied the answer (in centimetres) by 2. They also measured circumference and the area of an average leaf on graph paper. They were asked to measure its height with a clinometer and then checked it with the rule-of thumb method below.

Finding the height of a tree using a pencil

Hold the pencil **vertically** at arm's length and walk backwards until the tree looks the same height as the pencil. Then turn the pencil **horizontally** and ask a friend to walk outwards from the base of the tree until she has walked the 'length' of the pencil. Then measure the length of her walk with a metre stick or tape measure.

They finished their day by planning an illustrated poster 'report' on the dimensions of the tree.

Naturalists started by placing a small branch with leaves inside a plastic bag and sealing it with tape. They noted what happened in the bag as the day progressed. They lay down under the tree to see how each leaf was arranged to get maximum light and, with some sample leaves, made a mock-up of the arrangement of a small area of the canopy above them. They were then asked carefully to wipe a low leaf on the tree with a clean white muslin cloth and note exactly what they could see on the cloth. They also placed a sheet of white paper under a low-lying branch and gave the tree a gentle shake and observed what fell from the tree onto their paper. They sketched and noted the location of lichen, and also sketched leaves, labelling veins, stalk, galls, marks and holes. They sought small animal life in the soil, under and in the tree, and catalogued and classified what they found. Again their findings were presented in poster form back in class.

Geographers used their spatial skills and their interest in the similarities and differences between places to understand the tree. They marked out the shape of the shadow of the tree canopy with lolly-stick stakes, joined the sticks and then observed whether the canopy was regular or irregular and why this might be. They plotted the shape onto graph paper and then set about mapping several other nearby trees and placing them on their own map of planning around the garden. They compared temperatures and winds under the tree with those in the open part of the garden and near the house, and marked their 'micro climate' findings on a base map.

Wordsmiths were asked to focus on the tree and its surroundings with a quick drawing but to concentrate upon collecting a rich list of words all around their drawing to describe emotions, materials, sounds, smells, physical feelings, colours or condition. Taking their list they were asked in pairs to add as many adjectives to nouns so as to make up colourful phrases to describe aspects of the tree. They were asked very minutely to observe and make fragmentary notes on the appearance of one of their friends as they moved dramatically around the tree. These observations were later to become the setting for a piece of creative writing back at school. One child wrote:

Peeking behind the rough trunk

Creeping

His white shirt glossing

Cars in the background

Into the sunlight slowly walking

Rustling of leaves

Snapping of twigs

Less than half of him seen behind the stone and leaves

His hair blending in with the red-brown bark behind. (Dori, 5 June 2000)

Two *lone philosophers* chose the thinking route towards understanding the tree. Their collecting sheet asked them to list the best words they could think of to describe the place and also asked them to write a haiku about a very tiny detail of the place. One child wrote:

Twigs and snapped branches

Surrounded by wild shadows

The bird's cheep still sounds. (Jonathan 5 June 2000)

To provoke focused thinking the two philosophers were asked to complete four sentences:

- When I look at the old beech tree I am reminded of ...
- When I look into the shadows near the lake I think of ...
- When I hear the breeze blowing in the leaves ...
- When I see the grasses and flowers growing in the gardens I think ...

Musicians concentrated on sounds in and near the tree. They made lists of the sounds describing as far as they could the distinctive timbre. They talked with each other about how the sound could be translated into instrumental sound and experimented with a range of instruments they had brought with them. They looked for patterns in the tree, natural patterns, patterns of movement, or sound patterns and began to piece these aspects together to produce the beginnings of their tree music. They also used the tree itself, the trunk, the boughs, branches, twigs and leaves as a kind of 'graphic notation' and interpreted the tree in musical sound. In the garden itself, with their box of school instruments, the children evoked roots and trunk in dark rounded drumming sounds on the bass tambour. They used a range of hard wooden musical instruments to produce the boughs and twigs in sound and then metallic tinkles to represent the myriad leaves.

Each of the described activities focused and engaged children and their adult 'assistants' for over 90 minutes. After a short period of sharing insights they returned to school and during the following week the mass of data and really creative ideas were brought together in an extraordinary class exhibition based upon a single tree, which by that time had disappeared for ever.

The case studies above used focused subjects, real and relevant activity, strong and detailed planning, and frequent and formative assessment to promote and challenge interdisciplinary thinking and learning. Clearly the core business of education is children's learning. Education-based solutions must start with teachers thinking seriously about how we humans think and how we learn. The following three chapters will outline current understandings of human learning.

Key principles arising from the case studies

- Each study illustrates different forms of local and child-centred relevance.
- There is no optimum timescale for good cross-curricular practice; a day a week, a term, two terms and a whole-school curriculum are each represented.

- The fewer the curriculum subjects represented within a single theme, the more teachers are able to help raise subject standards and ensure curriculum progression and coverage.
- Each case study relied upon and promoted maximum physical and emotional involvement in a authentic setting.
- Each generated creative links across the curriculum.
- Each integrated working adults as experts from the wider community.
- Activities and themes held equal fascination both for adults and children involved.
- Each activity required and was founded upon detailed and lengthy planning in order to ensure progression and curriculum coverage.
- Every case study was reported by teachers to have generated a high degree of focus, motivation and exemplary behaviour on the part of children (and adults).

Further reading

Brice Heath, S. and Wolf, S. (2004) *Visual Learning in the Primary School*, London: Creative Partnerships.
Csikszentmihalyi, M. (2003) *Good Business*, New York: Hodder and Stoughton.
Wilson, A. (ed.) (2005) *Creativity in the Primary Classroom*, Exeter: Learning Matters.

CHAPTER 3

What Is the Contribution of Neuroscience to Ideas about Cross-Curricular Learning?

One response to the kind of practice outlined in the case studies is to suggest that this approach is a result of changing and ephemeral fashion. Recent developments in neurology, psychology and teaching imply, however, that such cross-curricular, meaningful and emotionally engaging approaches should become a new norm, if education is to keep pace with the accelerating rates of change outlined in Chapter 1.

We are beginning to understand in more detail what interests, worries and motivates twenty-first century children. Improved technologies and scientific method over the past 30 years have also helped us to become much more aware of the ways in which they think and learn. Chief amongst the new insights from science is the contribution of neurology. Neurology applied to education can raise fears of chemical interference in learning reminiscent of Orwell's *1984* (see, for example, *Guardian*, 2006). Some teachers suspect that in the hands of neurologists, ordinary human differences in learning could rapidly be perceived as problems and learning itself become pathologized. These and similar worries underline the importance of establishing dialogue and a shared vocabulary between educationalists and neuroscientists. Happily in both Europe and the USA such dialogue has begun (for example, Bransford, 1999; Howard-Jones and Pickering, 2005).

Dialogue has rapidly shown that each side of the debate may see a different truth. Neurologists and experimental psychologists rightly look for a 'scientific' truth represented by the evidence of numbers trials, controlled experiments repeatable in the laboratory. Teachers, however, tend to hold to an 'experiential' truth based on qualitative interpretation of their everyday experience in the classroom. Teachers may, for example, observe beneficial learning changes in children which appear to stem from the adoption of new 'brain-based' approaches to learning but which are dismissed as scientifically baseless by the neurologists.

A second line of debate concerns starting points for neuroscience. Psychologists and neurologists are most commonly involved in thinking about children with various learning difficulties but teachers may be more interested in the implications of neuroscience for the learning of all children. Conversations between scientists and educators are rich and fruitful, but teachers and other educators need to be aware of the detail of relevant neurological research before they engage in the debate and apply any findings. Equally, teachers are the professionals working with children on their learning and need to feel confident in their own observations and experience. The most effective and transferable professional skills of the teacher perhaps more closely resemble an art than a science.

The neurological view on learning

Current neurological thinking suggests that specifically human ways of learning conferred survival advantages on our species as it evolved. We continue to exploit these unique ways of making sense of the world. It is unlikely we would have survived as a species if we were not self-conscious, good at using language, making lasting relationships, understanding and making signs or symbols, synthesizing input via the senses, remembering and creating. Our species has been successful to the degree that it has been able to share and build upon these abilities. Neurologists argue that the plasticity and complexity of our brains and our prodigious capacity to learn has made this success possible. Teachers need to make full use of the advantages evolution has conferred upon humans when they make choices relating to the style, means and context of learning they offer their children.

Education in the twenty-first century will increasingly be influenced by the findings made possible by brain scanning and imaging techniques which were impossible only a generation ago. Through brain scanning, neuroscience offers independent corroboration of what teachers already 'know' about emotional and sensory engagement in learning, but it has also revealed a great deal of new knowledge about our learning. Teachers should know a little about how information on the brain is gathered and seek to be fully informed about the insights neurology brings. (Blakemore and Frith, 2006)

Brain scans

Brain-imaging technologies such as functional Magnetic Resonance Imaging (fMRI), Positron Emission Tomography (PET) and Near Infra-Red Spectroscopy (NIRS) have added new dimensions to our understanding of the ways in which we think and learn. Before extending the discussion to some significant implications for education, it needs to be remembered that fMRI scanners, the machines most often used to measure brain activity in children, are noisy, large, cumbersome and very expensive. (Positron Emission Tomography scans are not frequently used because their images use a radioactive dye to indicate diseased or damaged areas of the brain.) These costly scanners are confined to universities,

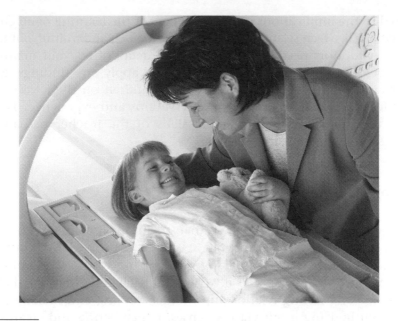

Illustration 3.1   *Child entering an fMRI scanner.* Courtesy of Siemens

hospitals and neurology departments and, until very recently, their main use has been to research or diagnose abnormalities. This may have resulted in the patho- logical tendency in neuro- educational research to look for neural evidence of dyslexia, attention deficit hyperactivity disorder (ADHD), dyscalculia and autism and their treatment, rather than trying to understand learning in general. It is still impossible to measure activity in children's brains while they are engaged in 'nor- mal' everyday learning activities. (A neurologist at a recent conference remarked that it was difficult enough to find a scanning machine where the child could even remain sitting up for an experiment.) Neurological research into learning is therefore still very much in its infancy.

Neurologists have, however, been able to observe several significant aspects of normal brain development in children. These observations have impacted on our understanding of thinking, learning, the influence of the emotions, the influence of environment and the concept of self. Through findings in these areas, neuroscientific research is poised to make observations which could influ- ence the curriculum our children follow. This is why teachers should be cen- trally involved in the debate. Since one of our assumptions is that learning is a consequence of thinking, we begin by considering the neurology of thought.

Thinking

Thinking is not a simple activity. Our brains and bodies, work as a whole organ- ism with individual parts taking on a variety of functions depending upon which other parts are working with them. Connections within the 100,000,000,000

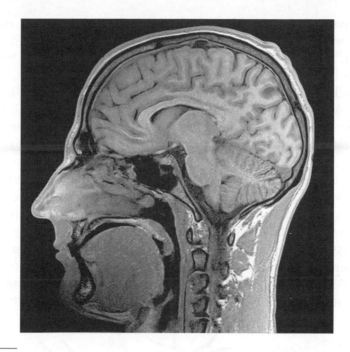

Illustration 3.2   *An fMRI scan of the head, showing skull, brain and other soft tissue.*
Courtesy of Siemens

neurones (or brain cells) which make up the normal brain, control everything that happens in and through our body. We are not conscious of the activation of clusters of neural connections responsible for survival and simple physical operations. Such neural activity cannot be called thinking. Even complex and conscious movement, such as playing a piano sonata, may for some become almost as automatic as breathing. When consciousness (or sometimes semi-consciousness) is involved in our mental or physical processes we mark the qualitative difference with the word 'thinking.' The thinking elements of our brain – aspects of memory, planning, monitoring, learning, language, feelings, emotions, spiritual and self-consciousness itself – we call our mind. These faculties depend on even more complex linkages between networks within the brain and beyond.

Close your eyes and place the tip of the index finger of your right hand on the base of the underside of the index finger of your left hand. Gently stroke your right index finger up to the tip of your left index finger. Even with your eyes closed you can probably sense exactly where on your finger the sensation is. Each located sensation you register involves the connection of separate pairs and groups of neurones governing the feeling in that finger. When we think of the implications of this simple exercise we are involving thousands of other connections: between aspects of memory and feeling, between neurones governing sight and sound, and between the networks which establish the present understanding of self and this book. Almost half the brain is involved in this activity (Blakemore and Frith, 2006)

Unlike living skin or bone cells, neurones generally do not replace themselves when they die, and they die when they are not used (see Giedd et al., 1999). Neurologists argue that exercising, or simply using these neural connections is vital to the survival of individual neurones and our continued learning. Each working cell in our brain carries a minute part of the inherited or learned self. Every cell is able to connect with another through some 1000 tiny root-like filaments called *dendrites*. Cells 'connect' via the transmission of a tiny electrical impulse along an *axon* towards receptors on the dendrites of another cell. This pulse results in the emission of chemical neurotransmitters which move across the miniscule gap between an axon and a dendrite and are either accepted or rejected by the receiving dendrite. The meeting point between an axon and a dendrite is called a *synapse*. Neurones fail to connect when an electrical or chemical inhibitor is released at the synapse. In making consciousness itself and allowing the conscious act of thinking, these microscopically small synapses become the very stuff of intelligent behaviour (LeDoux, 1999, 2002). Each concept we develop – pain, mother, comfort, god – consists of networks of thousands of such connections. Individual linkages

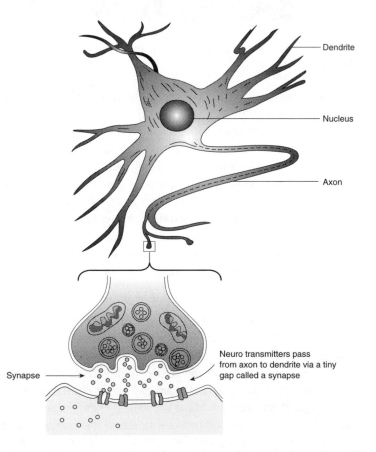

Figure 3.1a　A diagrammatic representation of a neurone, showing; dendrite, cell, body, axon and nucleus

Structure of a Typical Neuron

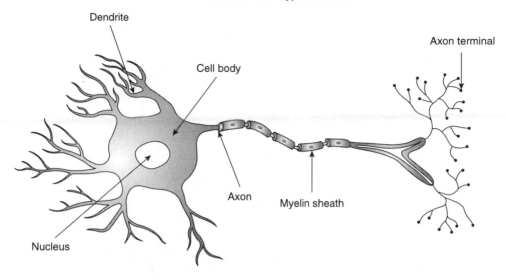

Figure 3.1b A myelin sheath develops to insulate the connection between an axon from one neurone and a dendrite from the next

and wider networks which prove useful, become physically conjoined as a *myelin* sheath grows to protect and make the connection more efficient. Frequent use thus establishes networks of cells which fire almost simultaneously when required. Each human brain is wired up uniquely and, as Susan Greenfield observes, 'reflects, in its physical form and function, personal experiences with supreme fidelity' (Greenfield, 2003, p. 148).

An old brain trick illustrates the way these connections work in our mind.

Point to a piece of white paper and ask your audience what colour it is. Point then to a whiteboard, or white teacup and ask again what colour it is. Repeat the question for two or three other white things in the room. Then simply ask, 'What does a cow drink?'

The immediate response to this quick-fire question is usually the (wrong) answer ... 'milk', after which people usually correct themselves and say, ' no, water'.

What has happened in our brain?

When the concept, 'white' is visually brought to mind, all previously experienced mental associations with white – summer clouds, milk, snow, drawing paper, the colour of a childhood bedroom or a hated school blouse – will also be brought into or near consciousness. So will the respective associations of each of those concepts. The areas of the brain involved with the concepts milk, paint, blouse and snow, 'glow' and are ready for action if needed. When the aurally introduced stimulus 'cow' is added, our brain circuitry races to fire up all the concepts related to cow. Since the concept milk is already primed by association with white, our reflex answer will be that a cow drinks milk, though we 'know' that only calves drink it.

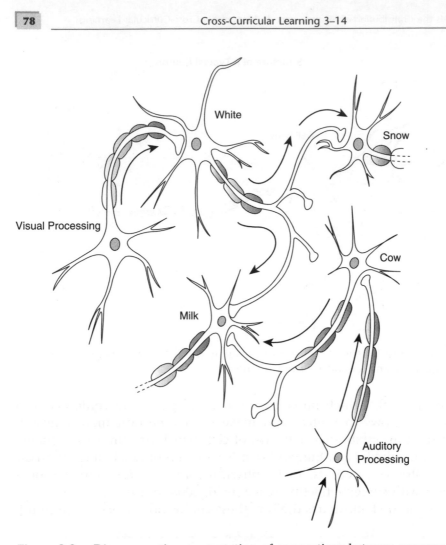

Figure 3.2   Diagrammatic representation of connections between neurons on processing sensory inputs relating to the concept 'white'

The linkages between certain clusters of neurones via their axons and dendrites and across the synapses in the brain are the beginning of thinking. But thinking is not a purely cerebral activity. Neither is it as simple as involving activity in just one discrete region of the brain. A highly intricate system of two-way links between various parts of the brain and body is activated when we think. The advanced and developmentally recent frontal lobes or *neo- cortex* in the human brain have connections which link with much more primitive areas of the brain controlling the metabolism, senses, muscles, stomach, the immune system, and emotions and memory. Neurologists now have evidence that these unconscious, largely automatic, but primitive systems, which we share evolutionarily with many other vertebrates, are involved in the conscious act of thinking. Thus scientists are increasingly clear that what affects the body impacts upon thinking and that thinking deeply influences what happens within the body (Damasio, 2003; Goleman, 1997; LeDoux, 2002).

Since thinking appears to have given us evolutionary advantage, and since it is so closely linked with senses, memory and emotions, neuroscience might be used to suggest to teachers that they should consider their use of;

- the sense of personal security
- the multi sensory
- the emotionally significant
- the memory using and enhancing faculties
- the intellectually challenging.

Using such approaches may take advantage of the unique thinking ability of the human. Exercising the distinctive mix of mind/body skills in each individual is likely to enhance the sense of achievement in every child.

The maturing brain

More than a quarter of a century ago, scientists noted periods of especially rapid cell production in the growing brains of very young children. Confirming observations from developmental psychology, neurologists established that between 0 and 3 years the neurones in the brain multiply at unusually rapid speeds. The volume of the brain does not increase significantly after about 3 years of age (Thompson et al., 2000) but scans show that the *matter* of the brain does undergo very significant reorganization as the density of the brain increases through childhood and early adulthood (see Illustration 3.3).

Between the ages of 8 and 14 there seems to be a second major 'growth spurt' of neurones with copious connection-making dendrites. Neurologist Jay Giedd and Colleagues (1999) has demonstrated that despite this extra capacity the volume of the brain does not increase. Unused connections are rapidly 'pruned away' if they are not used. This finding suggests that the second period of neurone growth may be as vital to optimum mental development as that of the early years. Giedd himself has commented, 'If a teen is doing music or sports or academics, those are the cells and connections that will be hardwired. If they're lying on the couch or playing video games or [watching] MTV, those are the cells and connections that are going to survive' (Frontline, 2002, website). If the 'use it or lose it' principle applies to the immediately preadolescent brain, as other neurologists have suggested (Baird and Fugelsang, 2004), then it is surely incumbent upon schools and teachers to ensure the experience of children is particularly rich, positive and stimulating between these ages. This is especially true for those parts of the young person's brain most susceptible to environmental influence.

Over the period of our education, as more connections within our brain become 'hard wired', a physical change in brain density occurs. The fatty

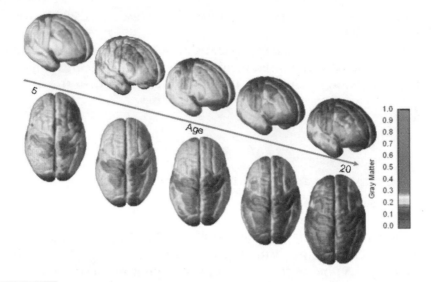

_____
Illustration 3.3   *Thompson and Giedd's illustration of the maturing brain 0 – 21years. Increasing white matter (myelin-sheathed neural connections within the brain) is shown by the darkening colours as the brain matures.* Courtesy Paul Thompson

myelin sheath which develops over frequently used connections causes the observable change in colour from grey to white as we gain increasing control over physical and mental faculties. This colour change denotes maturity. But not every part of our brain becomes mature at the same time. Quite recent research (Gogtay et al., 2004; Thompson et al., 2000) has suggested that the pre-frontal areas of the brain are not *fully* matured or 'wired up' until we reach our early twenties. (Illustration 3.3) Physical and sensory areas of the brain mature first, but the much more complex abstract thinking, decision-making, impulse controlling networks seem to be among the last to mature. A research example (Luna and Sweeney, 2004). may illustrate this.

> Adults and 14-year-olds were asked to perform a similar experiment which tested their ability to control a 'natural' impulse to look at a light. Whilst they were exerting this control their brains were being scanned using fMRI. It was found that whilst many 14-year-olds showed the same degree of success in avoiding looking at the light, adults and teenagers used different parts of their brains to assert that control. Adults used a range of areas distributed throughout the brain whereas those used by young teenagers were very localized and easily susceptible to emotional 'hijack'.

Maturation involves the reorganization of the brain into more complex networks consisting of numbers of checks and balances. Significantly these include the ability to envision, or ask, 'what if?' what are the risks? and mentally to model alternative outcomes. These abilities generally show themselves in the late teens and early twenties and the extensively dispersed neural networks which make such weighing-up possible are now known to be amongst the last to mature. Again these findings may have implications for education. Neurologists tell us the mature brain is one where connections and inhibitors are widely distributed and collaborative, and less susceptible to impulse or purely emotional responses. To help 8–14-year-olds' brains reorganize and refine in this direction, perhaps social collaboration and distributing intelligence between various members of a group should be more frequently modelled within an educational setting. This social activity in learning would be an external metaphor for what is invisibly happening within the developing brain. Future neurologists may well be interested in researching the impact of curricular and class organization attempts at such 'help'.

If the thinking, predicting, reflecting parts of our brain come slowly to maturity and if through education we can make an impact upon which parts of the brain mature more quickly, then this would tend to affect the curricula we plan. Findings from neurology might be used to suggest that the school experience of children aged 8–14 should:

- be social
- continue to be physical
- use all the senses fully
- not expect too great a degree of abstraction
- be fully aware of the strong impact of emotions.

It is worth noting, however, that currently in England many children between 7 and 14 years old are heavily tested. They have national tests at 7, 11 and 14, and school-based tests at 8, 9, 10, 12, 13 and 15. For significant periods when the brain is growing at its fastest and the higher functions of the cerebral cortex are maturing, children are either under stress or cramming for tests. Large periods of time which should be devoted to new learning, are lost in what has been called the 'never ending cycle of demoralising, childhood-destroying examinations' (Dawkins, 2003, p. 70) which summarize educational experience for many between these ages.

Excess stress may cause difficulties for younger children too, perhaps establishing negative attitudes to learning and the self as a learner. The neurological research above may suggest there are optimal periods for introducing material in the school curriculum. Both listening to and playing music, for example, has been shown to have a strong impact on young children's developing brain. Several studies for example, have shown close relationships between musical activity and high scores and improvements, particularly in maths (Jensen, 2000). If we know that the progress of brain maturation makes musical, linguistic and physical activities more readily learned in the early years, should we delay the teaching of subjects more likely to be abstract? If

Illustration 3.4   *Involvement in practical musical activity, such as rhythm and tune, is primarily fun, but also helps develop skills of coordination, confidence, and an understanding of pattern and structure.* Photo: Cherry Tewfik

we find that good health, positive emotions and feelings of security disproportionately affect the thinking of the young, should we angle the curriculum more towards activities which promote these things? Focused discussions between neurologists and educators are clearly overdue.

Implications for school:

- Introduce physical, practical, sensory, emotional and language learning early.
- Maintain physical, practical, sensory, emotional and language learning throughout Years 3–14.
- Do not expect abstract thought too early.
- Do not expect judicial behaviour too early.

Thinking can be good or bad, efficient or inefficient, complex or simple. One condition which apparently *prevents* some otherwise useful thinking connections being made is when we feel under some kind of physical or emotional threat.

Stress

Stress is a vital survival mechanism. We could not learn some things without a considerable degree of stress. The stress of being run over by a car has taught

Illustration 3.5   An upset and angry pupil. Note the position of her shoulders, the configuration of mouth, eyes and cheekbones and the closed body language. This information was provided by Clinical Tools, Inc., and is copyrighted by Clinical Tools

me to be very careful when crossing roads! We know from experience that in stressful situations the parts of the brain which control our secretions of hormones such as adrenalin cut in. Through them our 'fight or flight' reflexes are activated, we think less consciously and react in a more reflexive way (Jensen, 1995; Smith and Call, 2000). This can be a very useful in everyday life. Today I was washing up and was, not very sensibly, piling up the wet crockery too high on the draining board. When a cup slipped off the pile and headed for the floor, before I had time fully to register what was happening my right knee had jerked up to block its fall. The cup then rebounded (unharmed) from knee to cupboard and my left hand was ready to catch it. I could never have achieved this feat of juggling if I had been asked to do it. This balletic response was a simple reflex action triggered at the lowest levels of my nervous system. It did not involve thinking or learning in the terms already discussed, though I have learned that I can trust my reflexes to get me out of trouble … sometimes.

The remembered stress of accidents and unpleasant situations is present in much useful learning. Some aspects of stress may be vital for learning, though I would want to make a distinction between stress which I feel when I do not have control and challenge, which pushes me towards achieving a goal which currently may be just outside my reach. A *lack* of response to stress hormones, particularly the catechoramines, has been implicated in attention deficit hyperactivity disorder (Arnsten and Li, 2005). Many of us are very aware of the benefits of stress in meeting deadlines, winning races or provoking creative solutions to problems. But too much stress over too long a period, or stress which threatens our psychological or physical being, may be damaging. The hormone *cortisol* (a hormone produced through stress) has been shown to provoke cell death in the hippocampus (p. 89) area of the brain (Lee, Ogle and Sapolsky, 2002).

There is a close relationship between our immune system, nervous system and our state of mind. Neurologist Francisco Varela goes as far as calling the immune system our 'second brain' (in Goleman, 1997, p. 50) in that it responds to emotions and external influences in a parallel way to our 'neurological' brain. The feeling of stress, for example, seems to affect the connections between neurones within the brain by restricting blood supply. It also causes the secretion of hormones that weaken the immune system, which of course affects our physical well-being. Physical disease in its turn directly affects the behaviour of the limbic system of the brain which, to complete the vicious circle, makes us feel bad (ibid., p. 58).

Our brain has evolved a tendency to restrict blood supply to parts of the brain inessential to basic physical or psychological survival when under stress. The feeling of being 'unable to think straight' in times of stress can be very inconvenient – think of particularly nerve-racking examinations, angry teachers, unreasonable deadlines or stage fright when you were a child. Stress can restrict activity in the evolutionarily 'younger' parts of the brain which are involved in appraising situations, making fine judgements, analysing consequences, remembering, applying experience and planning.

Recent neuro-scientific study therefore may suggest that:

- the stress of *unthreatening* challenge may be seen as helpful in some learning
- too much stress may actually reduce brain functioning
- our brains are likely to be less rational under stress
- if a child is feeling worried, embarrassed, sick or scared, they are less likely to be able to think or learn (Greenhalgh, 1994)
- a curriculum which is designed to produce challenge without stress is likely to maximize learning.

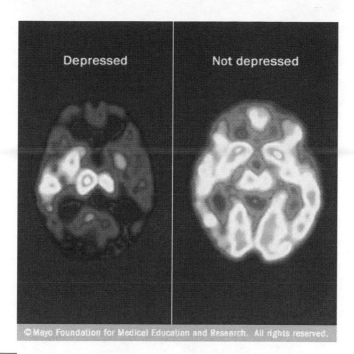

Illustration 3.6   *PET scans of a brain before (left) and after (right) treatment for depression. Notice increased blood supply (shown by paler areas) to the recovered brain*

The pair of PET scan images in Illustration 3.6 show a depressed patient's brain compared with their brain after treatment. The lighter parts have the greater supply of blood which activates the connection making essential to thinking. The frontal parts of the brain where thinking is most clearly registered appear relatively dark and therefore poorly supplied with blood. In the image on the right, taken after three months of treatment for depression, a much more general supply of blood is shown; this is especially evident in the frontal areas associated with high-level thinking.

Emotions and feelings

The external manifestation of feelings – the smile, the frown or the grimace – we call emotion. These superficial features impact upon our minds and provoke further changes in our bodies. Psychologist Paul Ekman and neurologist Richard Davidson, working at the boundary between neurology and psychology, found that even pulling the face of happiness had a positive impact upon inner feelings (Ekman, 2004; Goleman, 1997). 'Whistling a happy tune' when we feel worried or upset really *does* seem to make a positive difference to our minds and bodies.

Illustration 3.7   *A happy face. Note crinkles around the eyes, raised forehead, cheeks and eyebrows and the broad smile.* This information was provided by Clinical Tools, Inc., and is copyrighted by Clinical Tools

Both our externally shown emotions and our more secret inner feelings appear to be involved centrally in learning. The neurological connections through which body and mind are linked are well illustrated by examining what we call 'feelings'. A feeling is the word we give to our sensing of that exquisite network connecting memory, nervous and immune systems, muscular, visceral and intellectual systems as we respond to a particular event. Feelings, including intuition, serve to help us weigh up the pros and cons of a situation, decide on a course of action and plan our future actions (Claxton,1998; Damasio, 1994, 2000; Goleman, 1996; LeDoux, 1999; Salovey and Sluyter, 1997). We are beginning to understand more about the complexity of these interrelated systems. British neurologist, Hugo Critchley, has shown how EEG, PET and fMRI scans can now be used to measure the impact of events on the living brain so that we are able to say with some confidence, for example, that *negative* non-speech intonations, and sounds like groans, sighs, squeals, shouts and cries, provoke increased activity in the parts of the brain which process threat, just as pictures and words associated with danger do. Numerous other imaging studies have confirmed the link between what is

Illustration 3.8 *This student, linked to a computer which painlessly reveals electrical activity in parts of her brain, is learning, through neuro-feedback, to control aspects of her own thinking*

emotionally significant, current attention and long-term memory (Critchley, 2003) it appears we can also learn to control electrical frequencies within our brain through neuro-feedback (Gruzelier, 2003).

Neurologist Damasio argues that the sense of joy or happiness is the optimum condition of the human organism. He examines biological evidence which supports seventeenth-century philosopher Spinoza's view, that the brain/body is constantly seeking ways of promoting its physical and emotional survival. The goal of the human mind he says, is to 'provide a better than neutral life state … well-ness and well-being' (Damasio, 2003, p. 35). Translating this into a school context, we could take this to mean that children are likely to be attempting to find aspects of their classroom life which generate those secure, relaxed, fully engaged and exciting feelings we interpret as happiness. Such feelings, whether provided by a stimulating curriculum or peer popularity gained in other ways, will affect body, mind and immune system positively – a condition we generally want to prolong. It is obvious that there is no guarantee that feelings of happiness are always generated by culturally or morally 'good' things. It does seem likely, however, that teachers and all those who work in schools would share the desire to provide in their classes:

- a comfortable and warm place where basic physical needs are supplied
- a place where positive experience for each individual is more likely than negative experience
- a curricular concentration on promoting the conditions of well-being
- a close knowledge of the lives of the children beyond the classroom.

Growing numbers of local authorities are convinced that 'emotional literacy' programmes, where pupils are helped to 'recognise, understand, handle and appropriately express emotions' (Sharp, 2001, p. 1.) have a direct impact not only upon well-being, but on learning and achievement also. Recent thinking supporting a curriculum based around 'well-being' has only recently gained the attention of many teachers and head teachers (Antidote, 2003; Hanko, 1999; Morris, 2005; Warnock, 1996; Weare and Gray, 2003, pp. 33–6).

Memory

Three different kinds of memory affect learning. The *working* memory involves present-time operations such as adding numbers in the head, remembering what you just said and following directions. These aspects of memory are controlled in various parts of the pre-frontal cortex. The *declarative* memory, storage of facts, figures, faces and names, all experiences and conscious memories, is largely controlled by the limbic system including the *hippocampus*. We also have what is sometimes known as 'muscle memory' the memory of *procedures*, actions, habits, or skills that are learned simply by repetition. These procedural memories are probably controlled in the *cerebellum* at the back of the brain. Learning is the result of consciously connecting sensory inputs, all three types of memory, language and the emotional charge connected with most aspects of the declarative memory.

We seem to store negative memories in different areas of the brain to positive ones. Equally, different organs within the brain have predominance in negative and positive situations. One of the principal brain organs considered to be centrally involved in even mildly threatening situations is known as the *amygdala*. The amygdala and other areas are activated in fearful situations and seem to facilitate rapid but minimally processed responses which evoke alertness and escape behaviour (Garrett et al., 2002; LeDoux, 2002). Even when we 'know' situations are not really threatening, such as those measured during a boxing scene in a DVD or a violent video, studies have shown that the areas of the brain linked to threat, escape and those which store long-term memory of (real) traumatic events are significantly engaged (Murray, 2001,

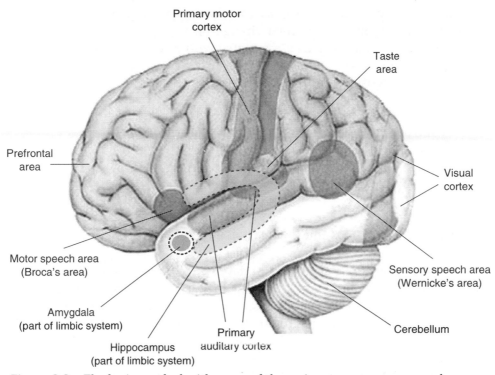

Primary motor cortex

Taste area

Prefrontal area

Visual cortex

Motor speech area (Broca's area)

Sensory speech area (Wernicke's area)

Amygdala (part of limbic system)

Primary auditary cortex

Cerebellum

Hippocampus (part of limbic system)

Figure 3.3 The brain marked with some of the major sensory, memory and thinking areas referred to in the text. The amygdala and hippocampus are deep within the brain

website). The concentration of such events in the memory has been argued to affect the degree of aggression, desensitization and generalized fear experienced by individuals. Some argue that our brain makes very little distinction between what is 'real' and what is imagined to be real. Corroboration of such research would have serious implications for assessing the impact of what children experience in television, video, and video games.

Positive emotional stimuli tend to arouse quite different and equally complex areas of the brain. Brain areas associated with relaxed, content, secure, 'approach' behaviour are generally distinct from those which provoke withdrawal behaviour typical of feelings of fear, pain and disgust. Even in young babies the reflex response to their mother's approach activates the areas of the brain which in adulthood process positive emotion. Positive feelings appear to involve larger and more dispersed areas of the brain usually concentrated on the *left* side than the right. In emotionally significant situations, the engagement of these areas facilitates more detailed, measured responses and enables analysis, correction or reinforcement. Recent research has suggested that children with a tendency to use the pre-frontal lobes on the *right* side of the brain in response to emotionally engaging stimuli are correlated most frequently with anxious and withdrawn personalities. However, neurologists now note that since areas, such as the amygdala, appear to respond to environmental stimuli by molecular changes, it may be possible to provoke the physical growth of other areas associated with positive memories through education (Davidson, Dane and Kalin, 2000).

Neurological research into memory would suggest that schools and teachers:

- provide many situations likely to provide positive memories
- avoid realistic negative scenarios
- cultivate 'approach' atmospheres and relationships in the classroom
- avoid situations where withdrawal is the natural response.

School learning, memory and brain science

Teachers and other adults are understandably interested in how thinking and learning are affirmed, provoked and reorganized. The links between learning and memory are vital and, again, neurology has helped us understand them. Learning happens when brain and body combine to make experience part of the conscious memory to be recalled to solve future problems. We have seen how the brain does not mature in a linear fashion, and this is true of the memory in particular. As the connections between senses and amygdala and hippocampus become hardwired, we can memorize more easily. Between ages 3 and 14 we can memorize things more easily if our already matured senses are involved. Repetition also significantly helps us memorise. Through establishing repeated neural connections, we create changes in the brain which become permanent or semi permanent. In general, this is the type of higher learning teachers aim at and could be called 'quality learning,' Quality learning is the kind of learning which is accepted by the culture as benefiting individual and society. Quality learning may also include the ability to inhibit inappropriate behaviours and thoughts, focus attention and monitor our own actions – each of these abilities, Gogtay and colleagues' (2004) research reminds us, are subject to gradual maturation.

Memory is also enhanced by frequently talking about the things we think are important. National or state curricula have helped us by establishing what *politicians* think is most important to remember, but each institution may arrive at other aspects of knowledge the community feels is worthwhile (see Chapter 6). By establishing and revisiting conversations, by making links between present and past class activity and by connecting school learning with learning in the rest of life, teachers can help build useful memory banks in each child's mind. Key, usually subject-based, vocabulary is important here also and forms part of proposed lesson plans discussed in Chapter 8.

Adults construct much of the physical and emotional environment within which the child learns. Teachers plan progressive sensory and intellectual experience to support the child in building new concepts and reassessing earlier

Illustration 3.9   *Children engaged with an interactive museum exhibit.*
Photo: DorotheeThyssen

misconceptions. It is therefore of great importance that teachers and other adults involved in education are aware of new research on the workings and development of the brain.

Many schools are currently using 'mind mapping', 'brain gym', visual, auditory and kinaesthetic (VAK) divisions or 'brain-based learning' methods. This interest in ideas traceable to neurology suggests that neurological perspectives have already made significant inroads into education. In the view of most laboratory neurologists, however, these 'brained-based' ideas are poorly understood, based on faulty science and likely to be ineffective in the longer term. Such well-intentioned initiatives have been dismissed by neurologists and other academics as 'psycho-babble' (Howard-Jones and Pickering, 2005, p. 7) and consequently insights of potential worth may be undermined, undervalued or thought of as 'fads'. A teacher's understanding of neurological research is unlikely ever to be as detailed and deep as a neurologist's and, in any case, experience, agendas and audiences are very dissimilar. The popularity of brain-based approaches with teachers, however, says much about the contemporary need for 'quick fixes' and external verification from science to justify what might in the past have been called good and intuitive teaching. An important challenge for twenty-first century education is to ensure dialogue between educationalists and neurologists so that the insights and specialized experience of both sets of professions can work together to the benefit of children.

Implications for schools:

- Agree on what 'quality' learning and 'worthwhile' knowledge should be.
- Continue to use multi-sensory approaches shown to be effective in helping children learn and remember.
- Talk a lot about important principles, bits of knowledge and skills which have already been introduced.
- Assess the effectiveness of new approaches by small-scale research projects within school.

Multiple intelligences

The widespread interest in the theory of multiple intelligences (Gardner, 1993, 1999b) is a case in point. Gardner's theory is popular with teachers because it closely matches their experience of children and it gives them academic support in their genuine attempts to be more inclusive and positive. Gardner suggests a biological basis for eight and a half specialized 'intelligences' (one has not yet [2006] passed the full list of eight tests he applies to each proposed intelligence). To Gardner, an intelligence is 'A neural mechanism or computational system … genetically programmed to be activated or triggered by certain kinds of internally or externally presented information' (Gardner, 1993, p. 63).

Gardner suggests that the following are each discrete ways of making sense of the world, highly valued in at least one culture and capable of isolation through brain damage (see Gardner, 1999b):

- linguistic
- logical mathematical
- spatial
- bodily kinaesthetic
- musical,
- naturalist
- intra-personal
- interpersonal
- existential.

Each of us has a mix of all intelligences but every individual has a unique profile of strengths and weaknesses. A related cluster of brain areas distributed

Illustration 3.10   *These fully involved children are using musical intelligence to compose music based around the skin patterns of African animals*

around the brain is involved in processing one particular mode of mental processing. For example, the way we understand the world *spatially* uses observably a different set of brain connections than those used to understand it *linguistically*. The same brain area, however, may fulfil a number of different functions and be shared by several different 'intelligences'.

Whilst it seems that in normal situations our brains work as a complex whole, each of Gardner's intelligences has been shown to be capable of relatively independent existence. Each proposed intelligence also matches a range of psychological and social-scientific criteria. Usually, we use several intelligences to process what is going on around us, but nonetheless we may display positive dispositions towards one or more. So one of us may be more prone to understanding practically through the use of our body and gross and fine motor movements (Gardner's *bodily kinaesthetic* intelligence), whilst another may prefer to understand through reflection and quiet analysis (using his *intra-personal* intelligence).

Since this neurologically based theory is seen as, 'uncontroversial (in scientific terms), unthreatening and simple.' (Howard-Jones and Pickering, 2005, p. 13) it is argued to be, 'easily accepted and owned' by education. Whilst it might be owned, it may still not be very deeply understood. My observations in schools which purport to put this theory into practice would suggest that many fail to grasp some of its founding principles (Barnes, 2005a). Multiple intelligence theory was proposed to help *teachers* and other adults understand that children may learn and show their intelligence in various and contrasting ways. The fact that some primary school children are currently tested for their particular intelligence or encouraged to pigeonhole themselves by deciding between eight or nine categories of being 'smart' runs counter to Gardner's intentions. An understanding of the different ways a child could show intelligence was meant to suggest to teachers different ways of mobilizing the brain so that important content could be learned. Gardner is clear that he does not support the categorizing of individuals, the creation of a 'new set of losers' or ignoring the possibility that the profile of intelligences may change with the situation, maturity or experience (Gardner, 1999a, p. 98).

Interest in Gardner's multiple intelligence theory might suggest the following changes in school:

- Avoid labelling children as having one intelligence or another – this will limit their development.
- Provide as many entry points to learning as possible – this will maximize the chances of engagement.
- Be more inclusive in the use of the term intelligence – look for *how* each child is intelligent not *if*.
- Value equally all ways of being intelligent.
- Choose a curriculum which provides many powerful and multifaceted experiences to interpret in a wide variety of ways.

Environment

The social, economic, physical, cultural and mental environment in which we live seems to have a powerful effect on how we develop intellectually and physically. The nature–nurture debate has raged for centuries, but neurology is helping us see the two sides of the argument in more dynamic balance. Professor Ian Robertson, an expert on stroke and traumatic brain injury, has argued that environment has as big an effect on intelligence and our neural circuitry as our genetic inheritance, and therefore our minds are susceptible to 'sculpture'. He quotes a number of studies which demonstrate a marked improvement in children's mental processing achieved simply by changing the home environment of children (Robertson, 1999). Experiments on domesticated rats placed in enriched and stimulating environments have consistently shown that environmental factors influence the growth of neural connections and production of neurones themselves. As a result visual spatial learning and simple problem-solving improve markedly (Faverjon et al., 2002). The fact that environment so clearly affects the brain development of other mammals might lead us to examine closely the relationship between

Illustration 3.11   *Working in less familiar environments beyond the classroom can quickly involve children in memorable learning experiences.* Canterbury HEARTS project

the environments our children work in and their mental, physical and spiritual development.

Neurologists have been able to demonstrate that our brains, particularly the complex pre-frontal cortex (PFC) which distinguishes us from other similar animals, are especially shapeable by experience, (see Greenfield, 2003; Robertson, 1999). The PFC is involved in cognitive, social and emotional processes such as the regulation of attention, planning, self-control, flexibility and self-awareness, and seems very sensitive to environment. Studies of children with neurological damage due to accidents have already shown that family and physical environment are key factors in the degree and rate of recovery from such injury (Yates et al., 1997), but the environment consists of much more than family. Neuroscientists have noted that the PFC is also connected with working memory, mental imagery, audio and visual associations, mental representation of the body in space and the integration of memory with present circumstances. Each of these facilities are shaped and organized according to environmental considerations which will include the individual's experience of sub-culture, socio economic class, peer group and geographical location.

The plasticity of the brain may be illustrated by a study on the brain areas concerned with topographical memory of London taxi drivers (Maguire et al., 2000). Taxi drivers' memory for streets, landmarks, routes and shortcuts is

Illustration 3.12   *Recording fine detail and personal impressions in a unique and authentic environment*

unsurprisingly increased by repetition practice. This progressive experience results in observable growth in the relevant brain areas, chiefly the *hippocampus*, which was observed to become more complex, denser and physically bigger over time. We have already seen that the hippocampus is also involved in our affective response to situations, and research in the past 10 years has shown that the hormone *cortisol*, produced as a result of stress, can provoke cell death in the hippocampus. Other studies have shown *neurogenesis* (the growth of new neurones) occurring as a result of more positive experience. Experienced musicians, for example, have an auditory cortex some 25 per cent larger than control groups of non-musicians (Pantev et al., 1998). Brain scientists guess that other areas of the brain, particularly those involved in our feelings and emotions, are similarly susceptible to the environment (Davidson, Daren and Kalin, 2000).

Some educationalists have taken the concept of the plasticity of the brain to imply that it ought to be possible to teach other aspects of thinking and being. Gruzelier (2003) has shown how it is easily possible for students to learn (through neuro-feedback via a monitor screen, see Illustration 3.8) to control the *theta* brainwaves associated by neurologists and experimental psychologists with creativity, improved memory, anxiety reduction, self-confidence and a sense of well-being. Experience tells us that simple practice in something like playing an instrument, learning a script or finding our way around, makes a great deal of difference to our performance, but research has also shown more complex outcomes. Given extra music lessons, for example, children made unexpected and considerable developments in mathematics, emotional literacy and language (Overy, 1998) Such findings coupled with other neurological insights would suggest that schools need to see intellect and attitude as:

- teachable and able to be changed through experience
- subject to non-maturational influence in particular supportive, stimulating environments
- responsive to learning situations throughout life.

Summary

The implications for education of modern neurological study are only lately being discussed by educationalists (Howard-Jones and Pickering, 2005). The techniques of brain scanning are still in their infancy and we should therefore be tentative about conclusions from neurology and beware of unthinkingly adopting what scientists are already calling 'neuromyths'. However, when neurology reports publish findings which match the experienced observations of teachers it seems inevitable that teachers will take this scientific evidence as corroboration and support for their own professional judgements. When rapidly developing modern imaging technology makes it possible to see images at the detailed level of connections being made between neurones in response to particular stimuli, and if we were able to observe the neural effects of well-being in non-laboratory contexts, then the implications for schools and curricula would be huge. Schools must be prepared for this likelihood. The meeting points between neurology and education are still being forged, but this area is one of the most significant and potentially paradigm-changing developments of the past few years.

Neurology can support many of the principles of cross-curricular learning. A curricular approach which maximizes the use of the widest range of mental and physical faculties is likely to be more effective than one which only uses some. The faculties which evolved to ensure human survival and flourishing are those which continue to ensure the most productive learning. The common ground between cross-curricular learning and our current understanding of neurology of learning is in the following areas:

- the crucial role of the senses
- the unique human skill of making finely judged discriminations
- the centrality of emotional engagement

- the long-lasting effects of positive experience
- the positive impact of challenge
- the negative impact of threat
- the positive effect of stimulating and supportive environments
- the importance of rich, authentic and multilayered experiences
- the existence of multiple modes of interpretation.

Illustration 3.13 *Using emotions, senses, intellect and body in a holistic learning experience*

+ Does neurology tell us anything new?
+ Why do we need evidence from neurology?
+ What is the difference between stress and challenge?
+ What can education tell neurology?

Further reading

Damasio, A. (2003) *Looking for Spinoza; Joy, Sorrow and the Feeling Brain*, Orlando, FL: Harcourt.
Gardner, H. (1999) *Intelligence Reframed: Multiple Intelligence for the 21st Century*, New York: Basic Books.
LeDoux, J. (2001) *The Synaptic Self*, New York: Viking.
Robertson, I. (1999) *Mind Sculpture,* London: Bantam.

CHAPTER 4

What Are the Contributions of Modern Psychology?

Psychology and the cross-curriculum

Neurologists may see thinking and learning as evolved survival techniques, but educational psychologists are interested in how we make *meaning* out of sensory and mental experience. They observe children's behaviour and focus on what children *say* and do about their thoughts and actions. Children themselves often point to the fact that learning seems to be easier if it makes sense to them. Amongst many other questions, educational psychologists ask how schools and teachers can make use of experimental findings that we all tend to learn what is useful and meaningful to us.

Old concepts of intelligence have been systematically challenged over the last few decades. To take a few examples: the concept of the 'plastic' brain (Robertson, 1999) and learnable intelligence (Jensen, 1995; Shayer and Adey, 2002) are now mainstream. David Perkins, Harvard Professor of Education, has pioneered the concept of *distributed intelligence* which sees other people's minds, tools and technologies as playing a significant part in our own individual problem-solving and 'intelligent' behaviour. Vera John-Steiner has demonstrated what she calls *creative collaboration* amongst many of the key shapers of the twentieth century (John-Steiner, 2000). 'Traditional' and individualistic methods of instruction have also been challenged by many psychologists during the past 70 or 80 years. Teaching heavily reliant on whole-class tuition, drilling facts, rote learning lists, texts, formulas and patterns is not primarily intended to teach understanding. Such pedagogies are seen by many as engendering only short-term learning. (see Gardner, 1999a, p. 82; Shepard, 1992, p. 319).

Educational psychologists have offered models of learning aimed at fostering 'deeper', more transferable, longer-lasting mind change. Ference Marton and Noel Entwistle have most recently pioneered work in this field in Europe (see Chapter 7 for more details of their work). They argue persuasively for an active approach to learning which concentrates on understanding; transforming 'surface' knowledge by relating ideas to each other, looking for patterns and principles and extracting meaning. They suggest the most effective methods to generate 'deep learning' are within groups and in solving problems which are, or have been made, significant to pupils. The same group of educational psychologists also champion the concept of 'teaching for understanding'. Their argument is that teachers should help students to learn *how* to learn (Entwistle, 2000; Rhen, 1995). It is the central argument of this book that the cross-curriculum is the most powerful educational context for such learning.

One key idea put forward by cognitive psychologists (psychologists particularly interested in thinking and learning) is that we can learn *how* to learn. Some education psychology writers have popularized aids to thinking. Ideas like 'Mind Mapping'® (Buzan, 2002) '6 Thinking Hats'® (De Bono, 1999) and the 'new 4 Rs' of resilience, resourcefulness, reflection and reciprocity (Claxton, 2003) have, like 'brain-based learning', been embraced by many teachers because they appear to work to help children and adults order and deepen their thoughts. Perkins has termed such tools designed to assist thinking, 'Mindware'.

There are, however, many other enlightening possible answers to the question, 'How do children learn?' locked away in erudite journals and rarely visited websites. This is a huge field and for the purposes of this book I have singled out a few educational approaches which suggest developing an attitude to learning, founded on: experience, understanding, cooperation, relevance and transforming knowledge. Teachers wishing to make education more relevant to today's children may be helped by suggestions brought together from current psychological research, under the following headings:

- Children thinking
- The 'thinking classroom'
- Children playing
- Children and their feelings
- Children and 'Flow'
- Children and language.

Children Thinking

A lifetime of working on children's learning resulted in Perkins famously stating 'learning is a consequence of thinking' (Perkins, 1992, p. 34). He argues that rich, stimulating and multi layered environments, real world investigations, and active participation in discovery and challenging questioning, all promote thinking. But experience and stimulation alone are not enough make learning deep and transferable. Most cognitive psychologists now argue that *metacognition,* thinking about our thinking, is essential to 'deep learning' (see Chapter 7). By calling to mind the *way* in which we think, we rehearse and externalise that thinking. Even at the age of five and probably younger, children can be led towards thinking about their own thought processes. Being asked to think about our own thinking appears to result in measurably positive benefits for young learners in mathematics, science and design technology. Grades dramatically improved in national and school tests in a number of London schools in which an emphasis on thinking, explaining and hypothesizing about subject-based activities was adopted (Shayer and Adey, 2002). Shayer and Adey's research also suggested that the change of teaching and learning style provoked marked improvements in attitude, autonomy and motivation.

Thinking needs preparation time and teachers themselves need to be very aware of what works best. In 1994 Adey and Shayer provided five simple pointers to generating better thinking:

1. Prepare the child's mind with experience of concrete and practical examples and relevant vocabulary.
2. Arrange some kind of 'cognitive conflict', an apparent contradiction of common sense, a genuine challenge or a problem.
3. Work with others to construct an answer to the problem through speculation and collaboration.
4. Think about your methods of finding an answer to the problem.
5. Transfer the newly formed theory to a new situation. (Adey and Shayer, 1994).

When children are asked to explain their thinking, teachers and the children themselves quickly become aware that we do all not think in the same way. A simple musical listening exercise shared by Robert Fisher, will help demonstrate this;

Find a section of video where a single slowly changing scene is depicted for about three or four minutes. Several sequences from the documentary film Powwaqqatsi (1988) directed by Godfrey Reggio are highly suitable, but this will work with the opening sequences from many modern films. Play the same video clip through three times, but each time play it against a different musical soundtrack (perhaps one with rock music, one reflective and quiet church music and one silence). Ask children independently to write down, or discuss with a neighbour what they saw in the video clip or what it made them think. A discussion after each clip will reveal dozens of different connections have been made between the sounds of the music and the details of the image you have chosen. This will remind children of two important messages: that they are (a) all thinkers and (b) all different thinkers.

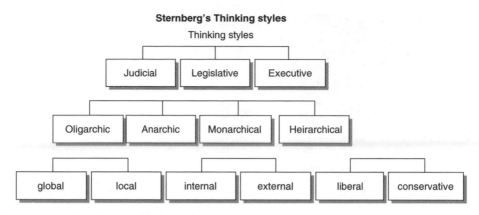

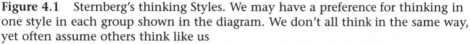

Figure 4.1   Sternberg's thinking Styles. We may have a preference for thinking in one style in each group shown in the diagram. We don't all think in the same way, yet often assume others think like us

The suggestion that there may be many different ways of thinking has been developed by psychologist Robert Sternberg. Sternberg, a past president of the US Psychological Association, postulates some 13 distinctly different 'thinking styles' (or styles of 'mental self-government') and uses the metaphor of contrasting styles of political government to illustrate them. Within Sternberg's theory, some of us are, for example, *monarchic thinkers* who like single goals to think about and work towards. Others may be *judicial* thinkers who weigh up the alternatives for some time before deciding on the goal. *Oligarchic thinkers* are motivated by several, sometimes competing, goals of equal importance. Other possible thinking styles are listed in Figure 4.1.

Understanding one's own preferred thinking style and the bias it will bring to judgements and preferences is clearly essential for all teachers. There is a danger that without this understanding we may expect children to think in exactly the same way as we do. Sternberg argues that it is vital for teachers to expect children to think in many different ways and that none of them are intrinsically wrong – if they work. Most thinking styles may be effectively pooled in group discussions and collective activities to produce much more satisfying and rounded outcomes than would be possible through one style alone.

Sternberg has also made major contributions to our understanding of intelligence itself. His *triarchic theory* of human intelligence, suggests that alongside requiring a good memory, intelligence consists of analytical, creative and practical profiles which differ in each of us (Sternberg, 1997b). He describes research which shows that pupils taught by teachers who share their intelligence strength are much more likely to succeed, but those with a teacher with a different intelligence strength are more likely to fail. A child with a strongly analytical approach, for example, who finds him or herself taught by a highly (but exclusively) 'creative' teacher will more often receive bad grades and in all likelihood a negative attitude to learning itself. The obvious advice is for teachers to be aware of their own preferred style but also to plan for many

Illustration 4.1   *Making sense of a view through the window - teacher and pupils thinking and learning together as equals*

different thinking styles and teach to all types of intelligence during each lesson so as to maximize the number of pupils that can be reached.

Recent work in cognitive psychology has significantly widened the concept of intelligence. We have already seen how Gardner, Goleman, Sternberg, Salovey and Fisher amongst others have challenged the simple IQ test. Such work has quite literally changed teachers' minds. Many teachers and educational psychologists today seek to discover *where* the intelligence strength lies in each individual before deciding upon 'treatment'. The key suggestions for teachers to consider are that:

- we all think differently
- we should be aware of the range of thinking styles/preferences
- we should seek the specific ways in which each child shows intelligence
- we need to help the child to learn to think better.

The thinking classroom

The classroom itself can promote thinking. It is a place where displays, stimulus resources, learning aids, the arrangement of furniture, use of the window

Illustration 4.2　*A group discussing a proposed drama. Each brings a different perspective to the discussion*

view, corridor space, ICT and easy access to outside may all be used to help generate thinking. A classroom is not simply a physical space; it has social and personal dimensions too. Expensive and excellent physical characteristics will be worthless unless the social, personal and spiritual classroom is equally well resourced and cared for. Teaching experience shows that thinking is generated by an atmosphere where questioning is part of the classroom culture. Piaget and hundreds of psychologists since him remind us that learning growth happens when children are not embarrassed to make mistakes, where relationships are warm and supportive, where goals, instructions and expectations are clear. Well planned and arranged physical resources and secure interpersonal relationships come together in the provision, by teachers and other adults, of multiple opportunities for each child to find the entry points appropriate to his or her own learning.

Psychologists argued that environment had a profound impact on our thinking and learning well before such thoughts were confirmed by neurology. The nature–nurture balance debate reappears throughout this book because understanding the relationship between environment and heredity is so fundamental to understanding how we learn and how we should teach. If we believed the environment had no impact on learning, we would all still be teaching in the high-windowed, crowded, stuffy and unstimulating classrooms of the nineteenth century. Psychologists have, however, consistently put the case for enriched and multifaceted class-room environments, and children's learning has flourished in the institutions which have embraced such advice.

The social, cultural, spiritual, intellectual and physical environment a child is born into has a powerful impact upon him or her for better or worse. If recent research into intelligence is taken into account, then this broad definition of environment may well be a crucial factor in the development of intelligence. Psychologist Robert Fisher, for example, identifies three dimensions of the child's intelligence; two of them, *developed intelligence* and *self-developed intelligence*, are clearly prey to the particular set of environmental circumstances the child is born into. Only Fisher's concept of born-*with* intelligence seems beyond environmental influence (Fisher, 1999).

The social, emotional and physical environment we live in is in many ways exclusive to us. Psychologist of language, Steven Pinker suggests a roughly 50/50 split in environmental and genetic influences on our learning (Pinker, 2002). He thinks that up to 50 per cent of what we *are* (character, abilities, intelligence, even habits) is the result of our genetic inheritance The other 40–50 per cent he postulates, is the result *not* of our generalized, home, family, school or cultural background (or nurture), but what he calls our *unique environment*. The unique environment is what uniquely surrounds us as individuals; exactly what happened to us, where, with whom, what we heard, smelt, touched, saw, felt and thought in the billions of separate incidents which make up our unique lives. Thus identical twins, physically clones of each other, are likely to be nearer to 50 per cent alike in character and intelligence than the 100 per cent we would expect, because each of them inhabited a different unique environment from shortly after conception. Pinker's concept of the unique environment, could have major implications for schools and teachers. Teachers, as influential adults, consciously and unconsciously control much of the physical and emotional environments that surround the child. Whilst the unique environment experienced by the child could never be directly under a teacher's control, teachers are still likely to influence its general character. Teachers can strive to build the kind of environment most likely to generate meaningful, positive, affirmative, constructive connections within the mind.

Many cognitive psychologists of the past 20 years have also agreed on the importance of meaning-making in education, (Bruner, 1996; Csikszentmihalyi, 1997; Gardner 1999a; Marton and Booth, 1997; Shepherd, 1991). Such writers argue that personal meaning may only be found if an appropriate and personalized language of learning is discovered. Gardner likens the ideal learning, thinking classroom to a painter's palette, with many different

Illustration 4.3 *Meaningful engagement found in a museum. How was each child's 'unique environment' manipulated by the teacher?* Photo: DorotheeThyssen

colours tints and hues on offer. In the thinking classroom it is the teacher's responsibility to provide many opportunities for the child to discover the right 'colour' to support their learning. Discrete areas of the classroom for practical, literature-based, group-based, sound-based, thinking-based, movement-based, ICT or observation-based learning are a good start, but practical considerations and cramped conditions may make the construction of such spaces difficult.

The provision of multiple aids to understanding does not obviate direct teaching of facts and skills. The human child, and the human adult for that matter, seems to learn best through interpersonal and intra-personal relationships. Most psychologists involved in education argue for balance between structure and freedom, the didactic and the discovery approach (for example, Hallam and Ireson, in Mortimore, 1999). Space in a classroom must be provided for instruction too. Many teachers have therefore taken to choosing furniture for its flexibility. They redesign their classroom term by term, or even weekly, to offer a changing palette of opportunities depending upon the term's theme and most appropriate teaching and learning styles.

Case study

Creative Partnerships UK (a government-led initiative encouraging long-term links between schools and creative practitioners in the community) set up a project about the deliberate marooning of a conceptual artist on a mid-English Channel fort for a month. Local high school children with a wide range of barriers to learning were provided with well-resourced spaces for construction, music and drama activities. Using these spaces they worked in mixed age groups to provide comfort, entertainment and food for the mind of the marooned artist. These were delivered to him on the dangerous and isolated fort. In the following term the same groups of 11–14-year-olds worked in art rooms, comfortable common rooms and ICT suites to produce high-quality brochures and visual presentations on the project. Children reported very positively about their experience. The provision of multiple entry points changed the teacher's view as well. As a result of engagement in the project their teacher said, 'I think at the start it was subject knowledge I was passionate about … but now I think I'm more passionate about the children's learning and learning something new from each other' (Grainger, Barnes and Scoffham, 2006).

Educational and cognitive psychologists suggest that learning which takes place in a relevant context is learning that sticks and is transferable (for example, Perkins, 1992; Shepherd, 1991). 'Situated learning' in school starts within a classroom made relevant for the activities the children will follow, but quickly moves to the even richer settings beyond the classroom. In such contexts meaningful learning is easier to construct. Each context is real world, complex and stimulating. Each needs cross-curricular approaches to provide fuller understanding.

The work of cognitive psychologists suggests that classrooms should be arranged, resourced and 'ethos-ed' to generate intrinsic motivation and help the child become aware of their own thought processes. The concept of the unique environment suggests that we construct a classroom in which the chances of positive experience are greater than the chances of negative. In summary, recent research suggests that teachers need to:

- make classrooms visually exciting and change the stimuli often
- resource classrooms so that children find it easy to construct mental images of new concepts
- arrange furniture and resources so that stimulus displays, artefacts, other people, tools, machines and technologies are all used to generate, sustain and deepen thinking

Illustration 4.4 *Positive relationships between teacher, child and resources generate thinking and deeper learning.* Photo: DorotheeThyssen

- use space flexibly to allow for teachers to move between being instructors, facilitators, observers and coaches
- capture learning in the classroom environment through celebratory and informative displays, exhibitions, gallery walks and collections
- widen the definition of the classroom to include views, corridor, school building, grounds and locality
- ensure that they spend as much time constructing a positive atmosphere as providing a stimulating room.

Children playing

After a gap of 30 years, greater emphasis has once again been placed upon play. Psychologists and psychology researchers since Jean Piaget have seen exploration, intuition and imagination as key sources of all, and especially early, learning (Claxton, 1998; David, 1999; DfES/QCA, 1999a). Guy Claxton argues that, to generate more creative attitudes in children, teachers should make less distinction between work and play. Music educator Keith Swanwick (1994, 1999) sees unstructured play with sound as an essential foundation for musical development at any age. Research on the 'Forest Schools' recently set up in Wales and some counties of England has added weight to the suggestion that simply having the opportunity to play in safe, stimulating environments adds significantly to social skills, self-esteem and positive attitude to learning (Maynard, 2004). Playing with language, the voice, body sounds, patterns, objects and social situations is part of the controlled risk-taking and invention which characterizes childhood (David, 1999).

The associated humour, abandon and risk of playfulness has serious purposes for learning. Children may play with power relations and the meaning of things, and this activity may help them establish social and conceptual boundaries. Laughing which often accompanies play helps them overcome anxieties in the neurological sense already discussed, but its positive effects are frequently observable in the external world of children too. Tricia David (1999) has also discussed the importance of the irreverent, challenging and subversive behaviour of young children who are discovering personal meaning, creativity and the possibilities of their personality. In play, children learn and practise the rules of their particular culture or sub-culture. The curricular implications of such observations are many. There are times when simply to observe and record young children at play is all a good teacher needs to do to: 'Teachers need without intruding into their "tribal culture" or hijacking children's play, to capitalise on children's highly motivated and playful use of language [roles, objects and places] and learn to celebrate it and use it as a tool for learning' (David, 1999, p. 28).

At other times the teacher's role may be to make learning take on the character of play. Opportunities to play with movement in dance, with sound to compose new music, with words to write an original poem or with the concept of roles, symbols or boundaries in history or geography abound in the National Curriculum. Equally, opportunities to play with the links between subjects are overtly encouraged by government advice (DfES/QCA, 1999; Ofsted, 2002; QCA, 2005 website). Permission to play with ideas on a cross-curricular level is already given, for example, in the case of drawing:

> Drawing, in a variety of media, is associated with play and playfulness in much early years teaching. Children often tell stories through their drawings, talking about what is happening as they draw. In secondary schools

Illustration 4.5   *Play in the sand, making an imagined world real by involving all the senses*

the potential of drawing for releasing and articulating ideas, while an integral part of art and design and design and technology (D&T), was also evident in other subjects such as religious education and geography. In one geography lesson, for example, Year 8 pupils produced annotated drawings of the potential effects of particular planning decisions on a local landscape. (OFSTED, 2003 website, para. 21).

Such advice is built upon recognition that children may enter an understanding of a particular subject from many contrasting starting points but it also points to the importance of play. Even at the Year 8 level, children are playing with ideas about the future through drawing. The recent work of psychologists has simply reminded us of the importance a fundamental human activity.

Playing across the curriculum

Teach children using an example from the classroom to take a tiny aspect of their world and weave it into a haiku poem (5+7+5 syllables). Suggest the ideal haiku might have two lines of description and one (usually final) line which flips the reader onto a higher plane of thought level. One 12-year-old looking at a single candle in a cathedral wrote for example:

A lone white candle

Hopeful against dark vastness

Folly or symbol?

After this teaching, take children into the school playground and ask them to identify a tiny object, plant or corner that for a few minutes can be theirs. (They might choose a dandelion clock, a spider's web, a discarded crisp packet, see Illustration 4.6.) Allow them time to reflect and then write and correct their own haikus. On return to class ask them to gather into groups of five or six and decide on one which might be a good candidate for putting to music. When children have chosen give them time and resources to construct a piece of music to either accompany or even replace the haiku. It should have the same 'feel' as the poem. They may use the words imaginatively, recite, chant, sing or mumble the words as part of the music, or abandon words entirely and let the sounds speak for themselves.

Illustration 4.6   *Here a teacher joins in the haiku writing exercise with the*
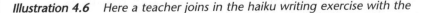

Research on the significance of play from Piaget, through Bowlby to Claxton or David, suggests that teachers should:

- consider plentiful opportunities for children of all ages to play with ideas, materials, and senses
- shift the balance of their teaching towards the playful aspects of their subject
- not fear failure and encourage adventurousness
- observe children's play to get ideas for teaching
- play with the application of the skills in òne subject to the understanding of another.

Children and their feelings

Psychological as well as neurological insights point to the importance of what we feel about ourselves or what we feel to be true, important or relevant. Daniel Goleman, a scientific journalist from the USA, has brought together a considerable weight of research by neurologists and psychologists such as Bandura (1994), Damasio (1994), Ekman (2004), Gardner (1993) LeDoux (1999), Davidson and Saron (1997) and Salovey and Sluyter (1997) to support his notion of emotional intelligence (Goleman, 1996, 1999).

The identification of personal engagement in and ownership of the curriculum has been a favourite theme of UK educational writers too. They maintain that positive views of the self as a learner, a belief that mistakes are part of learning and a feeling of personal emotional security are fundamental to transferable learning. These views on learning have arisen partly in response to the stubborn and sizeable 'tail of underachievement', disaffection and feelings of social exclusion which still remain after decades of government education initiatives intended to address them (Abbs, 2003; Black and Wiliam, 1998; Gipps and MacGilchrist in Mortimore, 1999; Halpin, 2003; Seltzer and Bentley, 1999). We have already seen evidence of how the sense of well-being may be compromised for many young people in our post-industrial societies. For the last 50 years US and UK societies have become increasingly richer and yet there seems no appreciable increase in recorded happiness indicators (Layard, 2005). A recent report has noted that depression and chronic anxiety are the biggest causes of misery and incapacity in Britain amongst 16–60-year-olds (Layard, 2006).

Schools, their staff and their children are all affected by the alarming statistics on depression. Encouraging debate on children's and teachers' feelings about themselves must be central in this new social context, and psychology has important contributions to make. Educational psychologists offer some practical answers chiefly through cognitive behavioural therapies, but they

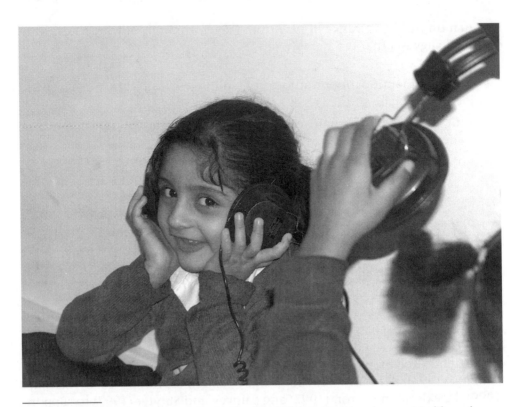

Illustration 4.7   *Look for the smiles and other facial signs of involvement in life and learning in classrooms*

also frequently offer teachers some corroboration of their intuitive and experiential professional knowledge of children's learning. Good teachers quickly develop a knowledge and understanding of what works to promote children's learning but, if they are unsupported, often lack confidence to fully and adventurously apply it. The work of experimental and educational psychologists may help give the extra encouragement for teachers to act on their 'gut feeling' regarding the curriculum.

The debate regarding children's and teachers' feelings about themselves and their learning, hinges on values. How highly do we value individual happiness? What is the importance of individuality? Where do we place children in our hierarchy of value? What is the value of a school, a community a society? Educational psychologists are not above such questions, indeed they are subject to the same pressures and worries as the rest of the population, but they do offer some corroboration for the intuitive and experiential knowledge that teachers and others who work closely with children develop.

The sense of inclusion or exclusion deeply involves feelings. If a child or family feels excluded in school, it is unlikely they will enter into any meaningful learning contract with school. At its fundamental level, inclusion concerns each individual's emotional response to the people in institutions with which they come into contact. The internationally acclaimed research of Mel Ainscow and Tony Booth (Booth and Ainscow, 2002) has contributed centrally to the debate on inclusion in our schools. Their work, initially written against the background of the institutional failures exposed in the Macpherson Report on the murder of Stephen Lawrence (Stephen Lawrence Inquiry, 1999, website), suggests a forensic examination of the social and structural character of our schools is essential before many adults and children begin to feel included.

At a personal level, finding an emotionally significant entry point to any subject is a powerful route to deep learning. Writer Peter Abbs (2003) suggests that not only is education a cultural and cooperative occupation but that it also has to be seen by the learner as an *existential* activity to be effective. Psychologists from Freud and Jung to Frankl, Seligman and Davidson remind us that the search for meaning is a typical human attribute. Sadly the age-old pupil question, 'Why do we have to do this?' continues to be seen as a threat rather than a plea for personal relevance.

We have already seen neurological corroboration of the assumption that we learn better when we are happy. Psychologists confirm this intuition too. Recently schools of 'positive psychology' have been estab lished by psychologists who have argued strongly for a renewed focus on aspects of psychology which seek to study enrichment of the human mind rather than just its repair. Physio-psychologist Barbara Fredrickson and colleagues (Fredrickson and Branigan, 2005; Fredrickson and Tugade, 2004) suggest for example that remembered states of 'positive emotion' provide a bank of positive scenarios which support us in developing resilience in times of difficulty. In her 'Broaden and Build' theory of positive emotions (Fredrickson, 2004) she argues that states of positive emotion such as calm, interest, security, fascination, joy, elation and love provoke the ability of the mind to broaden its 'thought-action repertoire'. By this she means that when we feel good, we are more able to make new links, explore new ideas, places or materials and make new and deeper relationships. She also suggests from a wide research base that adults in states of positive emotion show significantly enhanced ability to build new ideas, to be creative and to integrate past knowledge and present circumstances. In states of prevailing negative emotion she notes that experimental subjects were less able to think of new ideas, build relationships or explore possibilities.

A positive mindset results in a strong sense of 'self-efficacy', the ability to persuade oneself that one is able to reach a particular goal or set of goals (Bandura, 1994; Baron and Byrne, 2004). Numerous psychological studies have suggested a strong link between positive engagement with others and an expressed sense of well-being. Even more have shown that negative emotional experiences have a detrimental effect upon health, relationships and longevity (for example Fraser-Smith, Kawachi et al., 1994; Lesperance and

Illustration 4.8   *A positive experience shows itself in the detail and concentration shown by this 5 year old redesigning his playground*

Talajic, 1995). Scientific study now provides evidence that constructive relationships, affirmative experiences and an optimistic mindset can positively affect learning, intellectual activity, physical functioning and enduring personal resources (for example Fredrickson, 2004; Isen, 2002)

Teachers do not have the time to read these serious and often tentative scientific studies, and it is left to others to summarize and apply their conclusions to schools and teachers. Inevitably the work of these scientists is oversimplified and conclusions are overgeneralized. Popular books and courses of guidance on 'accelerated learning' (for example, Smith and Call, 2000), whilst sometimes accused of being based only tenuously on psychological evidence, have successfully challenged and changed the character of teaching towards a more inclusive, engaging and effective curriculum. It is perhaps unhelpful to demean such developments, considering the implications of doing nothing to make the curriculum more engaging.

Research in psychology on the importance of emotions in learning suggests that teachers:

- make inclusion a priority
- create a classroom life which seeks to generate the secure, relaxed, fully engaged or exciting feelings we call happiness

- promote positive relationships in the classroom and school as a priority
- seek emotionally relevant starting points – 'speak to the heart'.

Children and Language

From our first moments, language forms an key part of our environment. The 6-month-old baby is able to recognize the specific nuances of her mother's language probably by its dominant tunes and the musical tones. Until the child is 2 or 3 they may learn the *exact* tones and tunes of any world language they are exposed to – as Patricia Khul says they are true citizens of the world. After our infancy, however, it becomes increasingly difficult to speak a foreign language exactly as it is spoken (Khul, 2002). There are possibly windows of opportunity for language development, opened at different times during a child's development that make language acquisition a programmed affair. Understanding seems to develop before spoken language, fluent and grammatical speech, using the home tongue or tongues come next and the detail of 'foreign' languages may come after. If we are deprived of opportunities to develop language until the age of 12, the case of *Genie* suggests, it may be difficult to learn any language (Wikipedia, 2006, website).

The language we use and the ways in which we use it are powerful means of constructing the emotional and social setting within which learning might occur. Many parents and teachers recognize truth in Chomsky's arguments that the growing mind is dependent upon a brain apparently already wired up for language learning. Chomsky also argues for the existence of a universal grammar. Regardless of theory, style and philosophy, language is clearly the chief means of most school learning. An understanding of what Pinker (1995) has called the 'language instinct' is considered by many teacher educators to be a prerequisite to good teaching. Our brains seem prepared for ever more complex, symbolic and abstract uses of language, but clearly these need exercising. The challenge for the teacher is continually to find ways of enhancing the talk of children. Language can be significantly improved by attention to the learning context, and a recent study by anthropologist, Shirley Brice Heath illustrates this well:

Language is so much part of what we as humans are, it is hardly surprising to find researchers identifying a pivotal role for language in a project linking art with science. Shirley Brice Heath watched and recorded the interactions between Early Years children and an artist provided by 'Creative Partnerships' over a year. She observed that whilst using drawing to help them understand aspects of the natural world, children's language developed as strongly as their understanding of science and art. She points out that in concentrating on drawing detail, careful observation of skulls, eyes, the face and fruit, children were subconsciously naming the minutiae of what they were observing, and refining their language accordingly. Their language skills – fluency, use of vocabulary, expression – were all significantly enhanced simply by the act of focusing so strongly on single objects during the act of drawing or painting. Their use of complex language not only improved dramatically through working with a 'real' artist, but Brice Heath notes that the types of language they used in art was remarkably similar to the language needed for science because both disciplines 'testified to the power of curiosity, fascination and mobility of thought (Book 2, p. 13). She noted also that in talking about their art and the art of adult artists, ordinary children of just 4, 5 and 6 used complex, multi-syllabic words, expressed complex and sometimes profound and emotional thoughts (Brice Heath and Wolf, 2005).

Language is inherently creative. We create new sentences moment by moment, and with great ease, to provide commentary on the unique situations which we encounter. We cannot assume that this commentary goes on in all households, however, and one of the roles of the school could be described as establishing a minimum base of language experience in a population. Helping children play with language is seen by many as a vital component in developing their creativity. Creativity requires more than simple consciousness of the moment, it requires as Damasio puts it, 'abundant fact and skill memory, abundant working memory, fine reasoning ability and language' (Damasio, 2000, p. 315). The more words they can play with the bigger their world can become. Language progressively gives children the ability to translate feeling and thoughts into words, and words back into feelings and thoughts. It gives them the ability to classify and to express the imaginary, and to be still more creative.

There is a language of learning too. When teachers and children build a shared vocabulary regarding learning itself, learning is enhanced. The language of metacognition has been vital to children finding success with Guy Claxton's *building learning power* programme, for example (Claxton, 2006, website). In metacognitive contexts, the innate ability of all humans to be conscious of themselves means that children learn quickly to identify and improve the fine detail of their own learning. By using evaluative conversations, reflections, talking about their learning strengths and difficulties, they become conscious of themselves as 'independent learners'. How did I learn that? What difficulties did I find? How could I do it better next time? How did I deal with that distraction? How did I memorize that? Do I need to practise? Whatever the shared language of learning, it can be reinforced by being made visible in wall displays and social with 'talk partners' or a sustained learning dialogue with adult learners. In various commercial or 'home-grown' ways, cognitive psychology suggests that specific language should be used by children to track their own development as learners, thus externalizing and extending their learning.

Illustration 4.9 *Children arguing in role play. The class notes down the changes in language they use.* Photo: DorotheeThyssen

Role play, 'hot-seating', discussion, 'exploratory talk', problem-solving and making sense of authentic situations are time-honoured ways of extending language and the deepened thinking which emanates from a broadened language world. The NLS and other strategies of the past six years may, however, may have had the effect of diminishing the use of classroom dialogue, through an unintended narrowing of the curriculum (Smith et al., 2004). Guidance from the DfES/QCA (2003) used research findings from linguists, anthropologists and psychologists to reaffirm the importance of genuine dialogue, drama, debate and discourse in improving speaking and listening of children aged 3–14 (see Illustration 4.9).

Recent work on language suggests that teachers should be aware that:

- the language world of children should be extended daily (Khul, 2002)
- art, music and science can very effectively stimulate language development (Brice Heath and Wolf, 2005)
- children should have multiple and contrasting opportunities to play with and extend their language world (David, 1999)
- using words to explain feelings, problem-solving techniques, new understandings, differences and similarities is an important part of extending learning (Shayer and Adey, 2002)
- teachers should strive use the language of thinking: *hypothesis, hypothesize, believe, predict, guess, think, suggest, understand, compare, contrast, metaphor, analogy, analyse,* and so on (see Costa, 1991)
- teachers should provide a clear sense of progression in the complexity of language within a real context (Perkins, 1992).

Children and Flow

The environment is, of course, not simply physical. We have already seen how classroom atmosphere can become the all-pervasive influence on what and how much is learned. There is general consensus that the most productive of learning atmospheres is one in which all participants are fully involved in learning. Ferre Laevers is well known in Europe for the *Leuven involvement scale* (Laevers, 1994), which attempts to measure such engagement. Differences occur when psychologists, pedagogs and others argue about the way to construct such an atmosphere. One answer has come from Hungarian psychologist Mihalyi Csikszentmihalyi, who coined the term *flow* to describe that sense of deep engagement (see Illustration 4.10). We are said to be in a state of 'flow' when we experience: 'that almost automatic, effortless, yet highly focused state of consciousness,' which is so enjoyable that we will seek it at considerable risk and expense to ourselves' (Csikszentmihalyi, 2000, website).

These moments of flow remain treasured parts of our memory and seem familiar to all audiences in all cultures. From asking 100,000 people from a wide cross-section of cultures, socio-economic backgrounds and ages, what this state of total involvement feels like, Csikszentmihalyi constructed the following list. In these periods of deep and satisfying engagement:

- time seems altered
- skills match the challenge presented
- present worries fade
- self-consciousness diminishes

Illustration 4.10   *Lost in the music. This 5-year-old shows signs of flow as she listens to her favourite music*

- confidence is strong
- the activity is engaged in for its own sake
- there is a sense of fusion between self and activity
- there is rapid feedback (usually from the self).

In further questioning, researchers discovered that apart from sex, the most common conditions to provoke the state of flow was during creative or physically challenging activity. Flow was not common when watching television or resting, neither was it recorded as being particularly prevalent in school, although frequently particular teachers were credited with stimulating it. These findings suggest that a curriculum which gives plentiful opportunity for physical and creative activity is one which would be most likely to generate flow amongst its pupils. This conclusion is of much more than academic interest, because Csikszentmihalyi goes on to argue that the condition of flow is the optimum condition for learning.

Many teachers will have experienced situations where children are in flow, for example when children are so involved in an activity in class that they do not want to go out to play (or come in *from* play!). Laevers describes such total involvement as follows:

The child is clearly absorbed in his/her activities. His/her eyes are more or less uninterruptedly focussed on the actions and on the material.

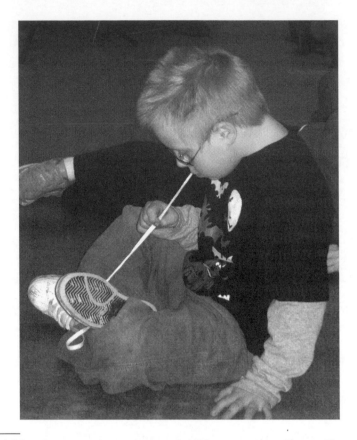

Illustration 4.11   Concentration may show itself in many ways. Photo: Cherry Tewfik

Surrounding stimuli do not or barely reach him/her. Actions are readily performed and require mental effort. This effort is brought up in a natural way, not so much by will power. There is a certain tension about the action (an intrinsic not an emotional tension … the signals concentration, persistence, energy and complexity abound. (Laevers, 1994b, p. 39)

In the specific context of children and schools, Csikszentmihalyi has controversially recorded the greatest concentration of flow activities are found in school club activities and practical sessions, in homes with plenty of books, in poorer communities, in children with *fewer* technological aids at home, in families where discussion is common and in families where group activities are common (Csikszentmihalyi, 2000, website).

Work on involvement or flow suggests, therefore, that teachers consider:

- providing more opportunities for creative activity in all subjects
- finding more time to involve children in physical/practical activities
- making more field trips and visits

- encouraging discussion both at home and in school
- encouraging the availability of a wide range of club activities.

Summary

We have made a rapid tour through some of the most exciting work in modern psychology. The conclusions are necessarily oversimplified and perhaps reductionist, but the work of these leaders of the field demands a thoughtful response from teachers. Much of the work discussed was not designed for direct application to the classroom, however, many teachers will recognize the congruence between these findings and their own professional judgements. Gardner himself in the introduction to the second edition of his book introducing the theory of multiple intelligences writes:

> Whilst working on 'Frames of Mind' I viewed it principally as a contribution to my own discipline of developmental psychology and more broadly to the behavioural and cognitive sciences. I wanted to broaden conceptions of intelligence to include not only the results of paper-and-pencil tests but also knowledge of the human brain and sensitivity to the diversity of human cultures ... my eyes were not beamed toward the classroom ... In fact however the book has exerted considerable influence in educational; quarters ... Psychology does not directly dictate education, it merely helps one to understand the conditions within which education takes place ... (Gardner, 1993, pp. xii–xxvii)

Such thoughts remind us that what psychologists say is tentative, not focused on the realities of the classroom, and is always provisional (see White, 2005). Teachers must make daily decisions which affect children's lives and do not have the luxury to investigate ideas enjoyed by the experimental psychologist. Nonetheless, each research finding cited in this chapter has possible implications for schools and their curricula. Each has cross-curricular ramifications too. In summary, current psychological research suggests to teachers that:

- we should not blindly accept IQ, background, current ability, socio-economic status or apparent learning difficulty as a limit on children's aspirations or our aspirations for their learning
- we should see intelligence as learnable and the mind as malleable
- we should make the generation of thinking one of our prime concerns
- we should be concerned about the whole physical, social, spiritual and emotional environment for learning
- we should consider seriously whether a positive, affirmative and happy environment produces better teachers and learners

- we should reflect on and research the effects of multifaceted, contextualized and relevant learning settings
- we should carefully plan the learning experience of children to include a balance of instruction, coaching, facilitating and challenge
- we should seek to maximize on those learning experiences which promote flow or involvement
- we should take care to enrich understanding and perception by a particular concentration on new language acquisition.

Key questions

✦ How can we construct within our schools shared, social, intellectual and physical environments which optimize the chances of positive experiences for each individual?

✦ Do we need to change the curriculum to do this? And if so,

✦ How must we change the curriculum to make the positive and secure learning experience more likely?

✦ Do we agree that we want children to be steered by a set of positive experiences in school?

✦ What sorts of positive experiences do we feel would be most valuable?

Further reading

Claxton, G. (2003) *Building Learning Power*, London: TLO.
Csikszentmihalyi, M. (2002) *Flow: The Classic Work on How To Achieve Happiness*, New York: Ebury Press.
Fisher, R. (1999) *Head Start: How to Develop Your Child's Mind*, London: Souvenir Press.
Sternberg, R. (1997) *Thinking Styles*, Cambridge: Cambridge University Press.

CHAPTER 5

The View of the Pedagog: 'We Learn According to How We Are Taught.'

'Start from where the children are.' This exhortation has been given to teacher trainees for generations. It can sound glib, simplistic, even idealistic, and yet as pedagogical advice it has profound implications for teaching philosophy, style and the curriculum itself. Paulo Freire, Brazilian activist, educator and thinker clarifies the meaning of this big idea;

> The educator needs to know that his or her 'here' and 'now' are nearly always the educands' 'there' and 'then' … The educator must begin with the educands' 'here' and not with his or her own. At the very least the educator must keep account of the existence of the educands' here and respect it. You never get *there* by starting from *there*, you get *there* by starting from *here*. This means ultimately that the educator must not be ignorant or underestimate or reject any of the 'knowledge of living experience' with which the educands come to school. (Freire, 1994, p. 47)

The lives of children should be central to the curriculum they are offered. The 'here and now' of today's children is clearly not a homogenized whole. Children growing up in certain areas of some towns and cities, such as, Bradford, London, Manchester, New York, Nottingham or Washington, may have to add the fear of gangs and gun crime to the 'regular' fears of childhood. In more traditional, often rural environments, some may still experience aspects of the idealized childhood of the 1950s. Few urban or rural areas today, however, escape the additional challenges of drug culture. Few UK or US homes are beyond the negative and positive influences of the Internet, television or the so-called 'cult of celebrity'. As discussed briefly in Chapter 1, such aspects of today's world are not a noticeable feature of national or state curricula, though they may be addressed in individual schools. If one of the purposes of education is to transform society, or in Freire's words 'to change a wicked world, recreating it in terms of making it less perverse' (Freire, 1994, p. 55), opportunities to address issues from the daily and weekend life of children must feature in their weekly curriculum. A curriculum for hope must start with the child and the child's world. If the world is the subject of the curriculum, then the curriculum must surely be an integrated one.

We may not subscribe to Freire's analysis, however. Modern approaches to teaching incorporate liberal ideologies in the context of a pragmatic acceptance of the present language of targets, objectives and accountability (see, for example, Arthur Grainger and Wray, 2006). Beyond liberal westernized education systems, and in the minds of many western parents, the *delivery model* of teaching and learning is remarkably resilient. The delivery model suggests simply that learning is a result of the teacher transmitting packages of 'relevant' knowledge to children – not necessarily what the child sees as relevant, but what the adult deems relevant. The view that in school we learn what teachers teach, seems to most lay people the obvious and proper way things should be. Throughout the developed and developing world most educational institutions are organized on the basis of a knowledgeable teacher standing in front of a class and using some kind of syllabus and their own education to impart what the culture, or more accurately the government, proposes as relevant knowledge to children. Modern information and communications technologies, the success of the scientific method, secularism, multiracial and diverse societies, the findings of modern psychology and neurology, and the continuing philosophical legacy of the eighteenth-century enlightenment and the politics of liberation have all challenged this paradigm.

Teachers themselves are potentially powerful agents of change and challenge to the status quo. They work with, and think about, children's experience for much of their lives and build up a considerable body of expertise and evidence. Teachers and their unions are consulted with regard to public policy on education, but their intimate knowledge of children's learning has not been taken into account until recently (DfES, 2006a, website). The word *pedagogy*, though not often used in Britain or the USA, is used here to denote the art and craft of teaching. Pedagogy is the fusion of theoretical knowledge, practical experience and intuitive response displayed minute by minute in the practice of the 'good teacher'. Experienced teachers are well equipped to make judgements, almost always better in teams, on a wide variety of areas related to the curriculum. They become the experts on:

- motivation
- social learning
- pedagogy – the art and craft of teaching
- creative teaching
- barriers to thinking and learning
- values and teaching.

Illustration 5.1   *Teacher physically coming down to the child's level will help equalize the relationship*

Motivating children

Motivating children is a highly complex part of the professional role of the teacher. Children may be motivated from a range of sources. They may be engaged by their beliefs about the relevance of a subject so a teacher may need to appeal to, or attempt to change, beliefs in order to involve a particular child. They may be motivated by fear or a desire to be accepted; motivation does not always arise from positive impulses. In a positive values context, however, children may be motivated by desire to reach a goal, to be involved in a specific and much loved activity or to please someone else. The expert teacher will orchestrate such diverse motivations in an attempt to involve all in the task ahead. If we accept that children's participation is important, then the teacher's professional skill in knowing how to involve children in a conversation which results in them feeling heard, and included, is crucial from the very first session.

In a school in south-east England (Barnes, 2005c) children are told the theme of the term's work in their first lesson. The teacher then elicits and collects the questions children want to ask or have answered and the remaining sessions are devoted to considering answers provided by the lead and other relevant subjects. In a cross-arts project in another school, children were asked to take the lead in deciding how to bring collected data together in a performance (Barnes, 2005a). The teacher's role in this context was to raise the standard of presentations by teaching the skills necessary to enhance children's initial decisions. In a third school (Barnes, 1994) pupils decided on the direction of a 12-week project, (to redevelop derelict land behind their school) only after they had analysed the results of a number of local surveys they generated themselves. In each case the degree of positive motivation and meaning was evident in the faces and body language of the children involved in the activities. Faces were relaxed, focused, alert, often smiling (particularly the *Duchenne* smile with crinkles around the eyes), conversations were easy and animated, eyes were sparkling and bodies were focused upon the activity or partner in learning, non-verbal sounds were ones of pleasure, amusement and calm (Barnes, 1994, 2004c, 2005c).

Social learning with the teacher

Few today would venture that we learn very much in isolation, and Lev Vygotsky's suggestion that knowledge is socially constructed within our various cultures is now a well-established concept (Vygotsky, 1962, 1978). His and related theories were accepted by many educators of the 1970s and there was general encouragement to arrange primary classrooms and curricula for group work. However an influential government report (Alexander, Rose and Woodhead, 1992) resulted in group work being viewed with suspicion and 'whole-class' teaching methods were again argued to be more effective in passing on knowledge. The UK literacy and numeracy strategies (DfEE, 1998, 1999) recommended a teaching approach which addressed these concerns. Both strategies prescribed a detailed curriculum, with significant periods of whole-class instruction and highly controlled group work and what, in the case of literacy, were taken as strict timing guidelines. The fact that organizational difficulties meant that children were often discouraged from social learning during the first run of these strategies may have been detrimental to their deep learning.

In the world of work beyond schools, most people still work in teams and these teams tend to contain people with different skills and strengths. The 'economic' justification for group work and shared projects in schools is that they prepare children to contribute more fully to an economy where people work in teams. But perhaps a more profound justification lies in the suggestion that working together, sharing experiences and solving problems in groups is beneficial to the physical and mental health of the child now. 'Social and emotional factors are key to effective learning,' says the DfES National Strategy site on developing children's social, emotional and behavioural (SEB) skills (DfES, 2005b, website). Self-awareness, empathy, motivation, managing feelings and social skills are obviously best developed in some kind of social setting. As current Department for Education and Skills (DfES)

Illustration 5.2   *This student teacher in dancing with children demonstrates a playful aspect of social learning*

and Department of Health (DoH) advice (DoH, 2005, website; DoH/DfES, 2005, website) makes clear such skills are not simply caught; they need to be taught within a whole-school framework.

Teaching SEB skills should not be a separate activity. Opportunities arise naturally from a curriculum designed around children's participation in meaningful, shared experiences and shared responses. Research quoted by the Department of Health/DfES suggests that academic achievement, self-esteem, personal responsibility, mental health, tolerance of difference, workplace effectiveness, behaviour and sense of inclusion are all positively affected by a curriculum and ethos which takes SEB seriously.

Since the UK government's *Excellence and Enjoyment* primary strategy (DfES, 2004, website), schools have begun to abandon the perceived straitjacket of a rigid interpretation of the NLS and NNS. A more flexible approach, never specifically outlawed, is now evolving in many schools. Teaching approaches which use 'thinking partners', group investigations, problem-solving, role play, links with other subjects and practical situations are now common. This change of style takes account of different school and cultural contexts, various styles of thinking and learning, multiple emotional needs and a variety of ways of showing intelligence. In the best practice the teacher becomes part of these groups and shares learning with the children.

Illustration 5.3   *Emotional and interpersonal aspects of learning dominate the day for both teacher and child*

Recently an experiment in alternative modes of teacher education, The HEARTS project (Barnes and Shirley, 2005; see Chapter 2 for more detail on this project) took the idea of 'teacher as learner' still further. Third-year student teachers were given the opportunity to work in small groups of six Year 7 children on an open-ended project to 'capture the essence' of an unfamiliar place. They were instructed to avoid the words 'you' or 'I' and to take the role of deputy to any budding child-leader who arose in their group.

Neither students nor the children knew the place. They only knew they had to prepare a presentation on the essence of the place for the whole school the following day. For this two-day session there were no lesson plans, no clear objectives, no differentiation and no assessment criteria. The challenge strongly focused both students and children. The results of the two-day challenge were 15 powerful, inventive and highly creative presentations which were very well received by the school. But a key finding for researchers monitoring this approach was that a large number remarked upon feeling they understood children for the first time, though facing the same challenge together.

Pedagogs may come to a variety of conclusions from examples like the case study above, but a number of issues are worth discussion:

Illustration 5.4   *Head teachers rediscovering their own creativity on a Creative Partnerships staff development day*

- Are children genuinely working collaboratively in their groups?
- Are we as teachers genuinely planning and constructing opportunities to learn alongside children?
- Are our groups promoting social, emotional and behavioural skills?
- Have we got the balance right between direct teaching and social learning?

Pedagogy – the art and craft of teaching

Formulaic, *one-size-fits-all* approaches to teaching are still very evident. To a degree Initial Teacher Education (ITE) has fallen behind some of the more innovative and adventurous primary schools. The 'Standards' for Qualified Teacher Status (QTS) (TTA, 2003) have spawned a pragmatic approach to the preparation of teachers in which *training* has become the operative word. Initial Teacher Education courses and various series of teacher education publications encourage a 'training manual' approach to the art of teaching. Many books on how to achieve QTS are dominated by grids and instructions which advise how to demonstrate the standards but give less help as to *how* to make curriculum choices that promote learning and thinking. There is a tendency to fall back on bland exhortations such as, 'aim for effectiveness through efficiency' and the admission that successful teaching requires a considerable degree of confidence and practice (Hayes, 2003). Perhaps such confidence can only come after many years in the job, but since so many leave teaching in the first five years, maybe our ITE and in-service courses need to consider how their own students can themselves become deeper, more creative learners and enjoy the job satisfaction of more creative teaching and learning.

Teachers and teach*ing* have a vital role in promoting and shaping children's learning, but learning and teaching are not the same. The idea that armed with a basket 'tips for teachers', teachers will effectively teach and children learn, denies the utter complexity of children's (and adults') minds. Ivan Illich reminded us in the early 1970s that most learning happens outside schools, casually and as a by-product of some other activity (Illich, 1971). The skilful and open-minded teacher recognizes that children come to school with a rich understanding of their world, which is already entrenched and largely sensible, but knows he or she can help the child develop and shape that know ledge. Understanding and respecting the child's world, his or her popular culture and 'knowledge of living experience' is very important for the student teacher, but the successful teacher needs more. Illich and that other arch progressive, Freire, also recognized the importance of discipline, the teaching of skills and subject knowledge. The good teacher should look for the deeper meaning of the content being taught, but not shy away from occasional decontextualization and simple direct teaching. The strongly motivated pupil says Illich, 'may benefit greatly from the discipline now associated with the old fashioned schoolmaster' (Illich, 1971, p. 20). The disciplined approach to learning was as important as respect for the lives of the learners. Freire puts it clearly:

> Teachers who fail to take their teaching practice seriously, who therefore do not study, so that they teach poorly, or who teach something they know poorly, who do not fight to have the material conditions absolutely necessary for their teaching practice, deprive themselves of the wherewithal to cooperate in the formation of the indispensable intellectual discipline of the students. Thus, they disqualify themselves as teachers. (Freire, 1994, p. 69)

The teacher, in other words, should balance respect for the child's world with a craftsperson's skill at their subject, pedagogy.

Current advice on teaching effectively should take serious account of the child's world. Today their world is one in which children learn from their peer group, television and other media, but also still very much from adults. Gardner (1993, pp. 34–8) has suggested three ways in which children learn from adults: direct or *unmediated* learning, where the child observes an adult engaged in activity, *imitation*, where the child reproduces the actions of an adult who deliberately models them, and *outside the context* learning in which a skill is introduced and practised under adult supervision but in a situation unrelated to the need for the skill. He notes that most formal learning within 'modern technological societies' occurs in specialized institutions far removed

Illustration 5.5   *Roles are reversed as a child leads a 'blind' teacher in investigating an environment*

from the context in which the knowledge will be applied. By implication this would suggest that the de-contextualized learning which has become dominant in western schools, leaves out major opportunities for unmediated and imitation learning.

Significantly more children would reach their potential in school settings which valued the practical, creative, physical, spiritual and interpersonal as much as the symbolic and logical. Perhaps we should re-examine metaphors for teaching and learning, such as David Feldman's 'The child as craftsman' (Feldman, 1976), a generation after it was written. In his analysis Feldman suggested that teachers looking to an uncertain world future should start by seeing the child as a person who *wants* to be good at something, take a pride in his or her work and feel an increasing sense of mastery over an area or areas of experience. Feldman argues that:

- the sense of engagement and purpose involved in doing what one feels good at is not possible without developing the related subject knowledge
- mastery cannot be aspired to without a belief that knowledge and understanding within the field can be continually enhanced
- a child's capabilities can only truly be assessed once we have identified an activity which truly engages them
- what might personally engage child craftspeople will be found within, 'the full range of activities that enrich and sustain social life ... and diverse occupations'. (Feldman, 1976, p. 144)

To work within this idealistic framework, teachers, Feldman suggests, we need to combine four different teaching roles:

- To teach the core skills and knowledge of writing, reading, number, citizenship required by society for all, but to ensure they are taught in meaningful contexts.
- To teach bodies of knowledge in a range of other subject areas chosen by community or school and considered necessary for all children.
- To discover the 'propensities and proclivities' of each child and then to organize resources progressively to 'further the child's mastery'.
- To promote each child's engagement through introduction to and progressive guidance in the principles, key skills and attitudes of discrete areas of knowledge they have chosen.

As children develop from early years to maturity, they should have increasing opportunity to refine and deepen the subject areas which teacher and child have jointly identified as personally engaging. Working in a school community which 'fosters commitment, satisfaction and joy in accomplishment', (Feldman, 1976, p. 146) will, Feldman proposes, require each child to go beyond the limits of their current understanding of their chosen craft. This I would suggest is especially likely when a teacher sets up a group with a range of personal entry-points to solve a joint problem or examine a shared experience. Recent work by a sometime colleague of Feldman's, David Perkins, has corroborated this analysis. Perkins (2006) suggests that children need experience of 'playing the whole game', 'undertaking holistic endeavours that make learning meaningful and engaging'. Playing *any* whole game involves receiving coaching, learning the rules, having opportunities to play 'junior versions' of the game, identifying with the experts, having chances to play and be affirmed publicly and, of course, finishing it. In the social settings which involve playing the whole game or being an apprentice craftsperson, children are likely to learn creatively. They will inevitably make unexpected links and connections between areas of knowledge, experience and relationships.

Such observers of teachers teaching suggest that we consider the following advice for our practice:

- Show respect for the child's background.
- Give attention to subject knowledge.
- Learn the arts of pedagogy.
- Identify the areas of strength in each child.
- Work at engaging each child.
- Give plentiful opportunities for holistic, contextualized and meaningful learning.

Illustration 5.6 *Head teachers rediscovering the child in themselves*

Creativity for teacher and child

Creativity is one of a small group of features which distinguishes humans from other animal species. We know that birds, primates and dolphins may show a degree of creativity in their responses, but in terms of capacity breadth, and expression it is surely a quality which marks out our species. The ability to be creative currently makes us different from machines too. Arthur Koestler's (1964) definition of creativity which involves *bisociation*, the, often unexpected, coming together of two contrasting planes of thought, is central to understanding the purpose of cross-curricular learning. Creativity according to Csikszentmihalyi, is a central source of meaning in our lives (Csikszentmihalyi, 1997, p. 1). Its apparent rediscovery by governments, advertisers, economists, planners and many teachers may be a belated realization of the importance of maximizing those abilities which make humans distinctive. The current push towards *creative teaching, creative thinking* and *teaching for creativity* in schools is a reflection of this preoccupation, but treating it as a temporary fashion would risk losing for many children all that is humanizing and sensitizing in the impulse to be creative. A number of costly new government initiatives have creativity at their heart and in their title (Creative Partnerships Kent, 2005; DfES/QCA, 1999a and b, website; QCA, 2003, website) and provide further evidence that government advisers have accepted the advice of teachers, neurologists and psychologists that relevance is central to learning.

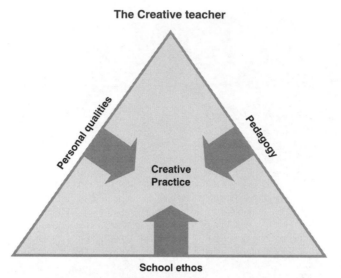

Figure 5.1 Creative practice depends on the interplay between a teacher's personal qualities of creativity (such as curiosity, humour, adventurousness, flexibility and enthusiasm), a creative pedagogy based upon multiple opportunities to make links and a child-centred supportive ethos established in the class and school

There are other important factors influencing creative learning too. The teacher's personal qualities, the ethos of the school and the particular pedagogical style all impact on the learning of the child. For learning to be creative, a particular set of characteristics needs to apply to each category.

The creative teacher (Figure 5.1) will be a personality who typically is playful, enthusiastic, flexible, committed and involved. His or her teaching style will commonly be personalized to the child, respectful, trusting, diverse and with a clear learning focus. The ethos in which the child is most likely to learn how to respond creatively is safe, secure and supportive of adventurous thinking (Grainger, Barnes and Scoffham, 2006).

No kinds of learning can be 'conferred' on the child. Throughout time good teachers have discovered myriad ways of *creating* relevance and engagement so that children will want to learn. Through force of character, story, anecdote, humour, display, drama, movement, music, games, debate, surprise, visits and visitors (but also by pressure, stress, threats and tests), teachers capture their audience. Ask a cross-section of teachers when their class seemed most engaged, most happy to work through playtime, and it is likely to have been during some kind of creative or physical activity, perhaps a combination of both, such as a football match, play, concert or dance. Research (for example, Brice Heath and Wolf, 2005; Harland et al., 2000) confirms the massive motivational and positive affective impact of the arts and artists in education, but potential for creative thinking and action spreads far beyond the arts into every subject of the curriculum. Creative approaches to teaching

Figure 5.2 The creative state of mind recognizes an inherent creativity in itself. Recognizing its own creativity may help it generate more connections, originality, questioning and autonomy

and encouraging the whole range of creative activity can do far more than motivate, however; it can also engender the new connection-making we earlier described as thinking (Arthur, Grainger and Wray, 2006; Grainger, Barnes and Scoffham, 2004).

Teaching is itself a creative act and relies continually on chance meetings of ideas and materials, curiosity, flexibility and adventurous thinking. Although each teaching and learning situation is unique, there are a number of characteristics which seem common to most creative teachers. Creative teachers are simply those who adopt and apply a creative state of mind. This mindset on the part of the teacher seems particularly effective in promoting creativity in children. The core characteristics which appear consistently to recur in creative teachers and which result in creative practice are:

- curiosity and questioning
- connection making
- originality
- autonomy and ownership.

Illustration 5.7   *Collaborative creativity: a group of 14 year olds planning their visual response to a haiku*

Thinking and barriers to thinking

Much of what we learn, whether creative or not, involves thought. Wherever we live and whatever we are doing a stream of thoughts accompanies most actions. Through devoting focused attention to an aspect of our world, we bring together past thoughts and present thoughts and if we do this with other people we also incorporate some of their thoughts as well. In thinking, groups of neurones make connections. We know that these connections become insulated and 'hard wired' if they are subsequently, recalled or reused a number of times. We generally recall such connections when they are relevant and meaningful to us. Thus if we think and rethink and think *about* our thinking, we learn. If we agree that *learning* is one of the consequences of thinking, the obvious question the teacher must ask is, 'Am I promoting thinking in what I plan to do with these children?'

Children can be helped to think more productively and satisfyingly. A whole range of books on thinking for primary and secondary school children have become popular with teachers who recognize this important aspect of their role (see, for example, Higgins, Baumfield and Leat, 2003). We know, however, that there are myriad barriers to children's thinking too. Good pedagogs are always aware that they may be a barrier themselves. Through reflection and evaluation an effective teacher can consider the impact of his or her own differing thinking or learning styles, school or class ethos or interpersonal difficulties before blaming the child for not learning.

The good school will constantly ask itself the question, 'Have we erected barriers to children's thinking which are therefore stopping them learning?' Is the 'hidden curriculum' that Illich referred to in the 1970s, stifling personal growth in individuals? One way of answering such questions is to use the comprehensive, whole-school approach recommended by the *Index for Inclusion* (Booth et al., 2002). The Index starts with questions for school self-evaluation. Staff are asked to examine fundamental values and the way they influence school policies, practices and cultures. Going through such a procedure quickly reveals the hidden and often unarticulated barriers to inclusive practice in a school.

Children already know many of the barriers which surround them. One Year 5 teacher in London recently took her children into an empty playground and gave them just such a theme to examine themselves. This is what she observed on her 'Barriers and boundaries' mini topic:

It did not take long for the children to realize that the list would consist of more than walls and fences – and they began to become engrossed as they came to realize that nearly everything can be a barrier or boundary – including flower beds, stinging nettles and other people. They began by asking 'Can I put down ... ?' and when I asked them what they thought, and explained that there were no right and wrong answers so long as they could explain their reasons, they were unstoppable. We walked the rest of the school the next day, and if anything the children were even more motivated than the day before – there was no bad behaviour and their lists grew. One child working at level 1 in writing (and who had not produced more than a line or two of writing for me to date) produced a list of 30 items, nearly all correctly spelt and legible.

In class we divided the lists into three columns: physical barriers and boundaries, signs (from the children's lists) and invisible barriers. We started the last column with language, which they had already identified, and the further suggestions (attitude, silence, culture, racism, hate, loss of senses, words) were very thought-provoking and

Illustration 5.8   *The open face of learning in an atmosphere of trust.* Photo: Cherry Tewfik

although received mainly from children of high ability, were not exclusively so. Had there been time, there was a wealth of opportunities for the children to have more freedom to explore themes in Citizenship, PSHE, Literacy and Drama, Geography, RE, ICT, History and PE/Dance.

Given control of the agenda, the children in the above example made multiple and unexpected connections. They were learning and, as the teacher noted, learning was happening in all sorts of apparently unrelated areas (like spelling and concentration). Affording children this kind of respect, establishing dialogue between teachers and children, building on the 'social capital' already present in children's lives and their community, and making their 'lived experience' a focus of education are approaches powerfully argued by Freire. He was also one of the first modern pedagogs to stress the importance of learning to learn.

Teachers and all learners gain considerably by thinking about their own learning. Modern developments in psychology and neurology have helped us to learn more about the conditions in which we are likely to learn best, but few teacher education or in-service courses offer advice on *who* to learn from. Of course, the children we teach are rich sources of learning. Recent experiments where trainee teachers were instructed to pass the locus of control to children for an arts and the environment project (HEARTS project, 1995; see Chapter 2) provoked significant and positive changes in students' respect for children as well as promoting major learning progress in the children involved (Barnes and Shirley, 2005).

As teachers, we should constantly and consistently examine what we are doing to the ethos of our institution and our classroom. The advice of key pedagogs suggests we consider:

- how we help children think
- where the barriers to learning are
- what are the unseen influences on the wider curriculum and atmosphere of the school
- the range of sources of learning we employ
- how to engage all children in satisfying learning.

Revisiting old absolutes

In a postmodern world, conscious of few anchor points, it is interesting to see an academic and educationally focused re-evaluation of 'old-fashioned' concepts such as 'hope' (Freire, 1994 Halpin, 2003; Wrigley, 2005), 'good' (Csikszentmihalyi, 2003; Gardner, 2004; Gardner, Csikszentmihalyi and Damon 2000), 'wisdom' (Sternberg, 2002), 'happiness' (Layard, 2005; Morris, 2005; Seligman, 2004) and 'love' (Bowlby, 1988; Darder, 2002; Goldstein, 1997, 2000). Pedagogs such as Comenius, Freire, Pestalozzi, Rudolf Steiner, Montessori, Dewey, Isaacs and Malaguzzi were unabashed at using terms like these. The progressive education philosophies of the past were anchored in clear understandings of such concepts, which were for them the ultimate purposes of education. These words, holding concepts that most of feel we understand, remain personally powerful regardless of our religious or political beliefs. Perhaps they should to be near the top of our consciousness as we think about the curricula our children follow. Old absolutes still form the basis of the 'here' and 'now' for most of us. Improving the emotional atmosphere of a school may involve using community discussions on hope, wisdom, love and good to help change many entrenched attitudes and practices.

We may need to examine our own institution critically and ask difficult questions. David Halpin for example, feels that schools often fail to provide a learning environment which leads to a broad sense of security. He reminds us of proto-psychologist, Sigmund Freud's use of the German word *sicherheit* (translated as 'security'). Freud regarded *sicherheit* as the chief gift of civilization and by inference, the prerequisite for education:

> This word manages to squeeze into a single term, complex phenomena for which the English language needs at least three terms to convey – security being one, and certainty and safety being the other two. According to Freud, all three ingredients of 'sicherheit' are conditions of self-confidence and self- reliance, on which the ability to think and act creatively depend. The absence or near absence, of any of the three ingredients has much the same effect – the dissipation of self-assurance and the loss of trust in one's own ability, followed in quick succession by anxiety and growing incapacitation. (Halpin, 2003, pp. 110–11)

For Halpin, no child should leave school feeling a loser. Equally, no teacher should end a school day feeling depressed. The cross-curriculum is well placed to turn the dream of a *liberating curriculum* into reality. Through it children can be freed to be children. Teachers are in a persuasive position to work with communities towards achieving this utopia. They need only to agree on the meaning of the four exhortations at the end of Terry Wrigley's (2005) book, *Schools of Hope*:

- We need commitment to a better future.
- We have to be visionary.
- We must dare to dream.
- We will have to rethink education and not simply improve schools.

Summary

Even in today's largely secular, increasingly diverse and global culture we cannot escape the fact that education will be value laden and attitude rich. The values we display either consciously or in the equally powerful 'hidden curriculum' will not always be the same as those which sustained very different societies of the past. If we do not address them, then the learning experience

Illustration 5.9   *Fourteen-year-old pupils performing their own musical composition about a garden in the garden which generated it*

of the child has no coherent context and perhaps the majority will find little meaning in it. We should therefore not dodge questions such as:

- Who decides on what 'worthwhile knowledge' is?
- What is *good* behaviour?
- Who chooses the topic under discussion?
- How can we agree?

A suggested way forward is to focus on children's well-being and, equally, the well-being of teachers and all those working with children. This means discussing the questions above in the light of staff and children's well-being and designing a curriculum based around enjoyment, experience and personalized ways of making sense of the world. I would suggest this is most possible in a cross-curricular context.

But we should keep the debate open and free from extremes, and be aware of the provisional nature of any of our decisions on what worthwhile knowledge is. In the light of previous chapters, key questions a school might ask before rethinking its curriculum might be as follows:

Key questions

+ Do we (adults in school) feel fulfilled and secure as people *ourselves*?
+ Are we modelling lifelong learning?
+ Is the teaching and learning in our classrooms promoting each child's well-being?
+ Is the social, spiritual and physical environment we control helping to develop positive attitudes to learning and the self?
+ What is the role of popular knowledge?
+ Does each child have an opportunity to find and develop an area of expertise?
+ Is the physical, emotional and intellectual environment we control keeping them safe?
+ What content *should* we teach and learn? Who selects it and how do we decide how it is to be taught?
+ What is the role of the teacher?
+ Are schools able to change the world?
+ Is our curriculum giving hope?
+ Are we teaching wisdom?
+ Is this school preparing all to make a positive contribution to future society?

Such questions are not very far from those posed by Plato, Comenius, Rousseau, Pestalozzi, Froebel, Dewey or Plowden. As professionals we are now in a good position to use the daily experience of today's successful primary teachers to help us judge which are *for this time*, the most appropriate attitudes, what is the most useful knowledge, the most helpful skills for children's lives now. Because we also serve society we also need seriously to consider what kind of people we want to shape this increasingly fragile world in the coming years.

Further reading

Craft, A. (2005) *Creativity in Schools: Tensions and Dilemmas*, London: Routledge.
Freire, P. (1994) *The Pedagogy of Hope: Reliving the Pedagogy of the Oppressed*, New York: Continuum.
Richhart, R. (2002) *Intellectual Character: What It Is, Why It Matters and How to Get It*, New York: Jossey-Bass.
Wrigley, T. (2005) *Schools of Hope: A New Agenda for School Improvement*, Stoke-on-Trent: Trentham Books.

CHAPTER 6

What Principles Should We Apply?

Principles for effective cross-curricular teaching and learning

If they want to be effective, teachers should be clear about why they want to teach and what they hope for children to learn in their classes. Teachers and children both need opportunities to develop their own values and to have a chance to discuss them. A thriving school is a place where debate about principle and big questions is alive and well. David Perkins once remarked, 'the quality of your organisations can be measured by the quality of its conversations' (Perkins, 2002). The conversations he was referring to were the ordinary daily chats in staff rooms, by the water cooler, in the playground and on the way to or from school. Overheard snatches of dialogue in successful schools are so often rich, caring and concerning the deepest purposes of education. Such conversations feed and inspire the novice teacher as he or she is forming his or her values (see Gardner, Csikszentmihalyi and Damon, 2000) and also sustain the seasoned teacher in times of pressure and doubt (see Barnes, 2006b).

Schools need to subscribe to values just as much as individuals and societies. Without a clear and well understood set of values, no organization can move very far forward. For some time now schools have published in their compulsory prospectuses 'mission statements', 'key aims' or 'overarching goals' outlining the values which underpin pupils' spiritual, moral, cultural and social development through curriculum and other activities (DfES, 2002, website). For some schools these statements are the vital and often revisited core of everything they do; for others the creation of a mission statement is little more than another bit of paperwork to be done before the next inspection. As the thinking behind the UK's *Every Child Matters* (HM Government, 2004) and the US Department of Education's *No child left behind* (USDE, 2002, website) begin to influence schools, local councils, health authorities and social services across our lands, clarity about underlying principles will become even more important and a principled approach to school curriculum decisions particularly relevant.

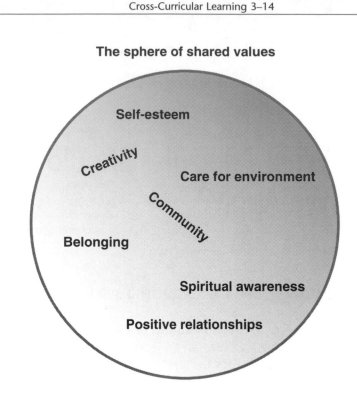

Figure 6.1 The sphere of shared values: discussing core values should be the school's first, most frequent and most important conversation

The all-encompassing sphere of shared values will be different in every school, but must arise from genuine and sustained conversations. A recent study of a single infant school has shown how it keeps ideas alive by talking about them (Jeffrey and Woods, 2003). Perhaps before they embark on any *other* discussion, a school community – teachers, children, leaders, support staff, parents and governors – together should decide on their individual and, eventually, collective answers to some of the following questions.

- What is education for?
- What is our attitude to children?
- How should adults behave towards children?
- What kind of children do we want our children to be?
- What kind of adults do we want our children to become?
- What kinds of education do we want our children to have?
- What kind of education do *children* want to have?
- What are the most important issues for this community?
- What assumptions do we make about the wider context of which education is a part?

(Continued)

- What sustains, motivates and give the adults in the school community optimism for the future?
- How can we build hope into children's lives through the curriculum?
- What things do we treasure most?

Taking the last two points first, it is arguably the teacher's prime professional responsibility to be optimistic (Halpin, 2003). This optimism might stem from religious, political or philosophical beliefs, from a shared but non-religious spiritual understanding or from a deeply felt, personal attitude towards humanity, children and the environment. There will inevitably be a variety of answers, but even embarking on conversations which try to arrive at a shared understanding is valuable. A rational discussion on the meaning of education goes straight to the roots of our thinking. How does education here help us all make sense of our lives and our world? In a postmodern, western, educational context, Peter Abbs argues that without engagement there is no deep learning;

> education cannot take place against the intentions of the student or without his or her active participation … Learning may be released by the

Illustration 6.1   *A typical primary school classroom in action*

teacher but it can never be conferred – for it is not an object so much as a particular cast of mind, a creative and critical orientation towards experience. The student has to learn to be the protagonist of his or her own learning. (Abbs, 2003, pp. 14–15)

One of the ideas that underlies Abbs's contribution to educational thought is that 'existential engagement' is vital. Put simply this means that we most deeply learn what is truly and personally relevant to us. The concept of education itself lies outside any single morality or world view. Education takes place in *any* and every cultural setting but only becomes really effective when it is meaningful. Meaning may be generated by fear, economic, cultural, political or religious obligation, duty, ambition, pleasure, self-fulfilment, self-actualization or a desire for the loss of self. In secular societies the challenge is to find a commonly acceptable formula which can bring shared meaning to all. The outcome of such discussions, seriously held, should profoundly affect the content and organization of the curriculum. The UK government has provided a lead in publishing the statement of values from the National Forum for Values in Education and the Community (DfES/QCA, 1999b, pp. 147–9), and in the Standards for Qualified Teacher Status (TTA, 2003) where teachers are charged with teaching and showing positive values and treating children with respect and consideration. The British government has also lent support to the *Index for Inclusion* (Booth et al., 2002) which, through its sections on creating inclusive cultures, establishes a firm link between values and the curriculum.

Appropriately, half of the discussion questions above (p. 146–7) contain the word *children* and a number of writers, have recently drawn our attention to the importance of the child's voice in making curriculum decisions (see Burke and Grosvenor, 2003; Catling, 2005). Valuing the views of children alongside the experience and (hoped for) wisdom of adults involved in education, now seems crucial to its success. From an adult perspective we might want education to promote creativity, make the world a better place, address the key issues of the day. Teenagers, however, can take a much more instrumental view of education, at best seeing it as the route to a better job and at worst totally irrelevant to their aspirations (Popenici, 2006). On the other hand, adults may feel that education should make our children more obedient, less challenging or more aware of 'high culture'. Either way the curriculum will be the route through which we attempt to achieve those aims. The school curriculum would be very different if an understanding of the world of 3–14-year-olds were taken seriously and represented in the programmes of study they follow.

As an example let us take several commonly cited but general aims of education, gleaned from school websites:

1. To promote a feeling of well-being for all children.
2. To ensure that the beliefs and values of the Christian/Jewish/Muslim/ Sikh/Hindu/Buddhist faith underlie all we do.

Illustration 6.2   _Peace Art: school children in Uganda have worked with schools in British Columbia to turn their war toys into a whitened peace sculpture._ Anthropological Museum, British Columbia, Canada

3. To support the development of self-esteem and personal responsibility.
4. To promote lifelong learning.
5. To develop high standards across the school, striving to reach and go beyond national standards in all subjects and key stages.

These aims clearly imply a specific ethos which, in turn, should require particular approaches to the curriculum. Perhaps a progressive, creative and child-centred curriculum may be suggested by the first aim. If we want to ensure that a particular religious belief system 'underlies all we do', our playground expectations, lunchtime rituals and our science, geography and English curricula will be affected as much as the RE curriculum. If we are aiming to support the development of self-esteem, this should show itself in the behaviour policy, but also has implications for the ways in which we teach all subjects. The fourth aim has similar implications but the focus may be more on the pleasure of learning. The last aim reflects the realities of a pluralist society. None of these aims is likely to have come from children, though all can be readily understood and acted upon by them. They will most likely have been decided upon in good faith, by adults who feel they know what is best for children. It is surprising how few school aims directly mention the environment, sustainability, relationships, new technologies or the global dimension.

Detailed aims such as the following examples may have more precise implications for their schools' curricula.

Illustration 6.3 *Walking the talk; children from the Scottish Children's Parliament leading adults on their 'health and happiness' march.* Courtesy Scottish Children's

- To appreciate all forms of human achievement: scientific, literary, mathematical, artistic, physical, humanitarian and spiritual. (Wingrave C of E Primary School, Buckinghamshire, prospectus accessed 21 July 2005)

- To enable children to become innovative and creative learners who achieve the highest possible academic, artistic and technical standards throughout all areas of the curriculum. (Priory School, Slough, accessed 21 July 2005)

- Our school community is multi-cultural and we promote equality of opportunity valuing all members of the school equally, regardless of race, class, gender and culture and we encourage religious tolerance through understanding. (Castlebar School, Ealing, prospectus accessed 20 October 2005)

- To be aware of the world in which they live and to realise they have both obligations to society as well as rights within it. We therefore see social interaction as an important factor in their education. (Marlborough Primary School, Wiltshire, prospectus accessed 21 July 2005)

- We aim to produce understanding citizens of the 21st century who recognise the need to participate in a caring and responsible way for the sustainability of our world. (St Mary's C of E (Aided) Primary School in Staffordshire, prospectus accessed 21 July 2005)

- The provision of philosophical and moral discipline and training through the visual arts and to maintain a state of intellectual and artistic development across all ages ... a belief in the importance of each individual's integrity, and the importance of the expression of that individuality. (Room 13 Scotland, accessed 2 October 2006)

Whilst words like *their, creative, obligations, produce, discipline* and *human achievement* may not have come directly from children, there is a sense that the realities of the children's world may have influenced these aims. There is perhaps a greater emphasis on enhancing and explaining the lives of children here and now, not simply preparing children for a future (adult) world.

What, then, are the beliefs and values which might underpin the establishment of a curriculum which promotes cross-curricular links and activities? Some suggested principles may be linked under the five main categories:

1. Learning.
2. Knowledge.
3. Teaching.
4. Children.
5. The world.

The principles listed under these headings are not meant to be comprehensive, but are the expression of a personal ideology based upon 30 years in teaching. As such they are fully open to criticism, major alteration, rejection and many additions. Use the suggested principles to prompt discussion about the principles *you* would argue for in your school. Each principle is intended to provoke a discussion resulting in whole-school agreement and implementation. Each can also be used to examine one's personal beliefs and attitudes towards education.

Beliefs about learning

Illustration 6.4   *Deep learning comes from deep thinking – these year 2 children show signs of both*

As already discussed in Chapters 3, 4 and 5, current work in neurology, pedagogy and psychology has added much to our understanding of the biology and observable features of learning. However the word 'beliefs' in the subheading is not accidental. Ultimately, as professionals in education, we have to decide what we believe to be right and true about learning. Hopefully, these beliefs will not be uncritical but based upon experience, our own research, reflection, conversation, knowledge of research and the theoretical perspectives of others. Some current beliefs can be summarized for discussion in the following list.

- There are many different ways of thinking and understanding ... each child has their own way of being bright (Krechevsky, in Sternberg and Williams, 1998).
- Generative topics and challenging experiences provide motivation to question, problem-solve and find answers (Blythe, 1998).
- Learning is a consequence of thinking (Perkins, 1992).
- Emotional, practical and personal engagement are essential to learning (Damasio, 1994; Goleman, 1996).
- Group work, particularly in promoting conversation and other means of communication, is an effective way to promote learning (Vygotsky, 1978; Bruner, 1968; John-Steiner, 2000)
- Modern technologies are powerful ways of promoting, sustaining and deepening learning. The resources that support intelligent behaviour do not lie only within the mind and brain. They typically occur distributed throughout the environment and social system in which we operate (Perkins, 1995).
- Learning goes on in quiet, reflective and solitary moments too (Claxton, 1998, 2003).
- Deep transferable learning is best facilitated by a general sense of 'positive emotion' (Fredrickson, 2003).
- Applying the skills and knowledge of the subject disciplines are effective ways of making sense reduce of experience (Gardner, 2004).
- Children can learn how to learn through introduction to metacognition and aids to thinking (Mortimore, 1999).
- Intelligence is partly learnable (Shayer and Adey, 2002).
- Enjoyment is an important part of the development of positive attitudes towards learning, to self and community (Csikszentmihalyi, 2002; Damasio, 2003).

Such beliefs about teaching and learning can be linked into four categories: beliefs about *individual* learners, beliefs about working in *groups* or community, beliefs about the importance of *environment* and beliefs about subjects or *the disciplines*. These four aspects of pedagogy might be seen as the professional framework of beliefs which can be used to guarantee the liberation of the individual spirit.

Illustration 6.5 *Each individual expressing their own response to freedom.* Courtesy Scottish Children's Parliament

Such beliefs do not become principles until they are part of some kind of accepted moral position. So after discussing individual beliefs and attitudes it is necessary to decide if they can be turned into a fixed statement about teaching, upon which all stakeholders can agree. Thus a belief that each child may have their own way of being intelligent might be turned into the principle: 'We will act on the understanding that all children have different ways of showing intelligence'. Beliefs about the importance of enjoyment in learning may be expressed in the principle: 'We will seek daily opportunities to promote enjoyment of learning'. In their briefest form the agreed beliefs about education above might be expressed as the following principles.

We will:

- help each child discover his or her strengths and interests
- use relevant, powerful and challenging experiences to motivate learning
- attempt to promote high-level thinking in all learning situations
- ensure learning is practical and physical
- seek out emotional/personal links between desired learning and learner
- make frequent use of genuine group work
- find opportunities for solitary and reflective activity
- use modern technologies to support and encourage learning
- endeavour to create a sense of security and well-being in all
- help children learn to learn
- promote enjoyment of the learning process
- ensure all children have opportunities to achieve.

Illustration 6.6   *Drawing focuses the eyes and also the mind so that both visual and linguistic skills improve. (Brice Heath and Wolf, 2005)* Creative Partnerships, Kent

Understandings about knowledge

For most teachers the only opportunity to think at length about their knowledge comes during their Initial Teacher Education. Even the training of teachers is so dominated by 'school experience' and assessments against standards that too little time is devoted to understanding knowledge. Knowledge is different from information. A library or the Internet is full of information but this inert mass of data cannot become knowledge unless it is somehow internalized, organized and made relevant to the individual. Knowledge is not absolute but a matter of choice and degree; we never have 'the knowledge', rather we move towards what our culture says it is. It helps, however, if a teacher feels they are more knowledgeable in at least one area, than most people (Grainger, Barnes and Scoffham, 2006). The following list is again somewhat arbitrary and personal, but can form the basis of that important discussion on 'What is knowledge?'

- Knowledge outside the classroom is cross-curricular and organic in nature. It is not confined to single subject disciplines (Gardner, 2004).
- Knowledge is not absolute, but a matter of degree (Perkins, 1995).

(Continued)

- Knowledge may be constructed through education, and what constitutes 'useful' or worthwhile knowledge can or should be agreed upon by those involved in it (Gardner, 1999b; Matheson and Grosvenor, 1999).
- Subject disciplines are essential to good teaching (Gardner, 1999a, 2004; Matheson and Grosvenor, 1999).
- All subject disciplines are equally valuable in understanding the world and no one subject or group of subjects should have special status (NACCCE, 1999; Robinson, 2001).

Again turning such understandings into whole-school principles may mean shortening them into shared rules which might underlie planning and teaching behaviour. The list might therefore start as follows.

We will:

- look at the world in cross curricular ways
- get to know the school locality very well
- be open to change
- involve all in deciding what we should know
- use subject disciplines as useful ways of 'chunking' knowledge
- treat all subject disciplines with equal value.

Attitudes to teaching

'Everyone remembers a teacher', said the Teacher Training Agency (TTA) advert. Many of the celebrities in the annual National Teaching Awards remember enthusiastic, encouraging, inspiring, caring, fascinated individuals who clearly enjoyed teaching. Much research confirms the powerful impact specific teachers had on the development of individual interests and careers (see, for example, Csikszentmihalyi, 1997, pp. 174–6). Perhaps understandably, little research has been carried out in the sensitive area of the damage teachers and schools have done to the confidence and self-image of pupils. Anecdotal evidence and emerging empirical research (see, for example, Riley, 2006) suggests that many teachers are fully aware that at times they feel driven to humiliate and emotionally harm children.

As in all areas of life, teaching is very much influenced by attitude. Attitude to teaching itself is the key to decisions about what and how we teach. But the teachers' attitude to themselves, their own self-image, is equally important. Research has suggested that simply ascribing words such as creative,

Illustration 6.7   *Teacher and pupil working together to display ceramic tile prototypes generated from looking very closely at a medieval building*

original, expert or caring to individual teachers often makes a very significant difference to their feeling of worth and their confidence as teachers (Barnes and Shirley, 2005). The need to feel we are 'making a contribution' is as important for the teacher as it is for the child. School leaders need to be fully aware not just that their staff is the crucial resource, but that each individual's personal sense of well-being is essential to the proper functioning of the school (Barnes, 2001).

A greater focus upon well-being would transform staff development programmes. Currently most staff development time is taken up by addressing new government or local authority initiatives, revising administrative requirements, preparing for or following up inspections, or making school self-evaluations or pupil assessments. Necessary though these may be, staff development time exclusively devoted to these things does little to develop staff as people. In contrast, the implementation of a planned and focused progression of personally engaging learning activities for staff is likely to transform both atmosphere and achievement in a school by positively changing adult attitudes. If five days per year were assigned to building up the intellectual, cultural, spiritual, physical and social lives of each member of staff, I would suggest that current rates of teacher retention and recruitment would markedly improve.

Among the attitudes school leaders, teachers and others involved with children could consider developing are the following.

Illustration 6.8 *Teachers planning creative activity for themselves in a staff meeting*

- The confidence to encourage 'safe risk-taking', playing with ideas, using the imagination (Claxton and Lucas, 2004).
- A belief in the importance of making the time and opportunity to reflect on successful and not so successful lessons.
- The determination to avoid restrictive formulas with regard to teaching and learning.
- An enthusiasm for developing creative teaching behaviours (Grainger, Barnes and Scoffham, 2004).
- The expectation that teachers will plan genuine opportunities for creative thinking and action.
- An expectation that teachers will seek opportunities to develop their own creativity and interests as part of their staff development (Barnes, 2003).
- A belief in the importance of formative assessment in adding to challenge and taking children forward (Robinson, 1999).
- An awareness that their own subject knowledge can and should be constantly improved.
- An understanding that working together with staff with other areas of expertise enriches teaching and the experience of children.

Changing such attitudes to workable principles may mean using more child-friendly language to express them. It also makes very clear what the individual teacher is 'signing up to' by being part of the team.

Illustration 6.9   *A teacher dances a sea shanty with a group of children: enjoying their world with them*

In this school, teachers will:

- plan fun activities which really interest
- work with children to make the school a better place
- work with children to improve life in the community and local environment
- help children risk new ideas/uncertain answers
- give children time to think and dream
- make space for unique answers
- be creative themselves
- help children achieve their plans and dreams
- include all children
- constantly be adding to their own knowledge
- work with each other to make lessons more engaging.

Attitudes towards children

If teachers' clear and positive attitudes to themselves are an important part of strong cross-curricular planning, then positive, even idealistic, attitudes towards children are also necessary. Idealism does not have to deny the everyday realities of working in real, overcrowded, underresourced classes and communities, it simply attempts to look beyond and above present realities to a positive and possible future. As well as being optimistic, maybe it is also the teachers' job to nurture the kind of idealism which many of them expressed during their job interviews. This idealism may be essential to maintaining the positive frame of mind which so often characterizes good teachers. Such optimism can be summarized in the following attitudes:

- a belief in providing frequent and multiple opportunities for children to discover what interests them as individuals – to develop passions
- a belief in the importance of education as meaning-making in a social setting
- an understanding that the child's world is different from the adult's and that this needs to be taken into account when planning activities, curricula and environments.

Put clearly as guiding principles for a whole school these attitudes might read as follows.

We will:

- provide the basic knowledge and skills children need to make a positive contribution to their world now and in the future
- help children see themselves as budding experts in a chosen area of knowledge
- help children see themselves as creative beings with original thoughts
- help children find personal meaning in school activities
- help children understand love and caring as central attributes of being human
- understand that the world of our children is different from that of adults
- support children in feeling good about themselves
- look from the child's eye view and value it.

Illustration 6.10 *Power, population and global warning, what are the answers? Children asked such questions as part of the HEARTS project at Dungeness nuclear power station*

Illustrations 6.11(a) and 6.11(b)   *The Asian Tsunami: natural disaster or avoidable loss of life? Three survivors from Bandar Ache.* Courtesy Simon Adams

An informed adult view of the world of the twenty-first century

The emphasis on children in preceding paragraphs is an attempt to help redress the current adult-centred balance of primary education. It would be wrong to assume, however, that adult views, beliefs and knowledge should be ignored or sidelined. We have seen too (Chapter 1) that, through the Internet and television, today's children are much more in touch with global issues than in the past. Thompson and Giedd's research (Chapter 3) into the maturing brain has reminded us that adult minds are in some ways very different to those of children. Adults may more easily see consequences, look into the future and plan strategies. At our best, we adults can offer the wisdom of experience, a wider perspective, and a more balanced and broad-based approach to knowledge and experience. There are as many adult views of today's world as there are adults, and such views range from the permissive and liberal to the fundamentalist and conservative. In popular culture we can see them colourfully represented in reality television programmes such as Channel 4's *Wife Swap*, by the more outrageous inhabitants of the '*Big Brother* house' or by the 'Grumpy old men/women' of Channel 4's recent series.

Whilst a long discussion about what different commentators think the world will be like in five decades' time would be too digressive, it is clear that one of the expectations of teachers is that we prepare today's children for life in the world of the future. A combination of adult science, adult imagination, adult forecasting, adult research and adult experience suggests that problems such as international and cultural conflict water supply, unequal distribution of resources, AIDS, global warming, overpopulation, unfettered technological and scientific advance are themes which will colour the twenty-first century. Issues like these do and *will* impact upon our children's lives. It is probably essential that today's teachers have a view on these issues and are asked to address them at some level within the teacher education curriculum and the curriculum children follow when in primary school.

As a starting point for discussion, the Royal Society of Arts (RSA, 2005, website) has usefully published its list of the 15 'global challenges' for the twenty-first century. These could form a valuable starting point for discussion about the world for which we are educating children. Each item requires a principled response; beneath the adult language each raises an issue upon which children in our classes will already have a view. Each question can at a practical level, be understood by a 3-year-old, each can be philosophically considered by a 14-year-old. Perhaps these or the United Nation's millennium goals (UN, 2000, website) could form the starting point for whole-school agreement on the big ideas behind school conversations, curriculum, and culture.

The RSA's '15 global challenges' arose from their 'Future Gazing' Report in 2005 (RSA, 2005, website). What are the implications for education, the curriculum and our attitudes to children?

1. How can sustainable development be achieved for all?
2. How can everyone have sufficient water without conflict?
3. How can population growth and resources be brought into balance?
4. How can genuine democracy emerge from authoritarian regimes?
5. How can policy-making be more sensitive to global long-term perspectives?
6. How can the global convergence of information and communications technologies work for everyone?
7. How can ethical market economies be encouraged to help reduce the gap between rich and poor?
8. How can the threat of new and re-emerging diseases and immune micro-organisms be reduced?
9. How can the capacity to decide be improved as the nature of work and institutions changes?
10. How can shared values and new security strategies reduce ethnic conflicts, terrorism and the use of weapons of mass destruction?
11. How can the changing status of women help improve the human condition?
12. How can transnational organized crime networks be stopped from becoming more powerful and sophisticated global enterprises?
13. How can growing energy demands be met safely and efficiently?
14. How can scientific and technological breakthroughs be accelerated to improve the human condition?
15. How can ethical considerations be more routinely incorporated into global decisions?

Summary: what has all this got to do with cross-curricular learning?

The twenty-first century is set to be a century of challenges, like every other century before it. The big difference in this millennium is that these challenges cannot be kept local. Our global economy, instant global communications and global pollution have meant that whatever happens in one place quickly affects every other. If they want it, ordinary adults, and particularly teachers, are now in a position to exert some influence over the interrelated future of this world. To do so effectively, teachers and children need to be very clear about (a) what they value most and, (b) what parts of our society, environment and wider world they feel we can effectively influence. The answers to these questions and those like the UN's or the RSA's global challenges could and should underpin all our education decisions.

This book suggests that a cross-curricular approach is the approach most suitable to addressing core values in the learning context of children's own lived experience. I have selected and examined four key areas where the formulation of shared values in a school is a pressing need: learning, knowledge, teaching and children.

Each of these areas is subject to a number of often contrasting beliefs and attitudes. A school's first priority is to work towards turning a set of shared beliefs and attitudes into a set of agreed *principles*, which will inform all central decisions about staffing, resources, curriculum, time management and classroom organization. Such principles will also guide school self-evaluation and parents' and children's views on the achievements and qualities of the school. A school's statement of principles, or its fundamental aims, should be the result of an in-depth and frequently revisited and ongoing conversation between all stakeholders. In many ways this conversation is the most important policy decision that the school can make. The discussion on school principles should:

- involve parents, governors, children, volunteers and other adults working in the school, as well as teachers and the head teacher
- be regularly discussed and often revised
- be used to make internal evaluations of the success of the school
- be expected to be used by both stakeholders and external bodies to judge the quality of school.

The world is facing unprecedented challenges. Teachers are amongst the key individuals who can support our populations face these challenges. They must therefore have a clear understanding of global issues and a principled view on how to help tackle them. Teachers must start by becoming growing, learning, positive and interesting people themselves.

Key questions

- ✦ What do we stand for as school teachers and a school?
- ✦ What do we believe is important in framing our teaching?
- ✦ What has all this to do with the UN's millennium goals?

Further reading

Abbs, P. (2003) *Against the Flow*, London: Routledge.
Gardner, H., Csikszentmihalyi, M. and Damon, W. (2000) *Good Work: When Excellence and Ethics Meet*, New York: Basic Books.
Halpin, D. (2003) *Hope and Education*, London: Routledge.

CHAPTER 7

What Themes Are Suitable for Cross-Curricular Learning?

The brain learns best and retains most when the organism is actively involved in exploring physical sites and materials and asking questions to which it actually craves the answers. Merely passive experiences tend to attenuate and have little lasting impact. (Gardner, 1999a p. 82.)

Active involvement in *any* subject can be suitable for cross-curricular learning. Themes as disparate as a child's visit to relatives in Tyneside or Tobago, the death of a loved hamster, the discovery of a spider's web in the playground or a birthday trip to the adventure playground, can all generate deep learning. Any topic presented with enthusiasm and careful planning can help children crave answers, and successfully forge links between different areas of their knowledge. The keys are personal significance and limited subject focus, but how do we know a child is learning?

External features – postural, facial and attentional characteristics – are probably the most useful indicator that a child might be learning. We have seen that Ferre Laevers (1994) argues that physical signs of *involvement* are the first we should look for (see also Chapter 9). His and others' work on the indicators of thinking and learning has suggested that signs of genuine involvement in learning might include:

- facial expressions of enjoyment, concentration and motivation
- bodily posture of positive tension
- relaxed relationships with peers and other co-workers
- a performance which matches or exceeds the known capabilities of the child
- a reluctance to be distracted.

In addition, and in the light of our earlier emphasis on principles (Chapter 6) we should also be fully sensitive to whether the kind of learning which was happening might be described as:

Illustration 7.1   *This Ethiopian boy shows many of the signs of full involvement as he participates in a festival.* Richard Marsh

- worthwhile
- meaningful
- good
- right or
- helping develop 'big' concepts like beauty, truth, justice, and so on.

Deep and surface learning

Recent reports from research into changes in higher education (HE) (for example, Wilde et al., 2006) document concern that today's students, whilst hardworking and having good oral and presentation skills, often lack self-direction. The report suggests that many HE tutorial and admissions staff are worried at about students' lack of 'deep understanding' of the core ideas of individual subjects and the links between the subjects or themes. Wilde et al.'s report specifically bemoans what it calls an 'instrumentalised and surface approach learning' which, they argue, has become dominant since increased accountability and assessment practices have impacted on schools' curricula and administration. The terms *deep* and *surface* learning are descriptions applied by Marton and Saljo (1976) and colleagues in the context of researching adult learners, but such a distinction between different kinds of learning could be argued to apply to learners of all ages.

Marton argues that deep learning involves:

- looking for meaning in what was to be learned
- relating new information to previously internalized knowledge

Illustration 7.2 *Focus, energy, involvement and meaning combine powerfully and memorably in many school productions and concerts.* Courtesy of Scottish Children's Parliament

- making numerous links between their own lives, memories and experiences, and the new material to be understood
- understanding, applying and retaining knowledge.

Surface learners tend to rely more upon:

- memorizing
- focusing on reproducing specific facts
- understanding disconnected information
- rote learning techniques
- the instrumental purposes of education in achieving a certain goal.

They are also poorly able to remember, apply or explain what they have learned. Many of us rapidly become surface learners if we are threatened with an imminent examination or are made anxious in some other way.

Research into deep learning suggests that those who strive or who are helped to make *meaningful* connections between themselves and new knowledge, retain and are able to transfer their understanding more effectively. This approach to learning was implicit in the Plowden Report (DES, 1967) and the work of the progressives described in the Introduction to this book. A combined interest in fostering knowledge for its own sake and seeing a broad and balanced education as an essential ingredient of resilient communities usually underpins the principles of schools attempting to enrich the curriculum.

Meaningful projects

In the 1970s and 1980s, in our patronizing way, many teachers chose topics we 'knew' children would be interested in. Topics such as 'Pirates' or 'Buried

Treasure' were popular with teachers. We argued that all children liked pirates, lots of their films and books were about them and we had all read and enjoyed *Treasure Island* as children and seen the television serializations as well. Whilst there were stunning examples of very motivating, memorable and successful 'topics', I believe we were mistaken in many of our choices. Certainly in my classes, children quickly saw through the pirate maths and pirate RE, pirate poems and pirate geography, they tired easily of measuring planks to walk upon, and '57 doubloons add 25 doubloons', was still just 'sums'. Whilst the complex 'Topic Webs' we constructed were often impressive and should have won prizes for ingenuity, they shoe-horned subjects into spurious themes and the deepest thinking was the teacher's. Indeed, provoking *thought* in children was possibly the last thing on the teacher's mind and any sense of relevance came more by luck than judgement. Children were more engaged than in the days of simple 'chalk and talk' but perhaps we omitted to ask whether such work led to significantly raised standards. When teachers today say that current cross-curricular approaches are 'going back' to the topics of the 1970s and 1980s I worry, because there was a great deal wrong with them. How, then, do we arrive at relevant and contemporary themes and projects that avoid these pitfalls?

I would suggest at the outset the following guidelines could apply:

1. Consult the children about the theme and key questions.
2. Plan a shared and powerful experience related to the theme.
3. Choose only subjects which clearly add understanding to the experience.
4. Plan subject skills, knowledge and progression required in each of those subjects.
5. Aim at a state of *flow* in children.
6. Finish with a performance of understanding.

Use the whole school community as a resource. You have also seen in Chapter 2 how some schools use key workers from the community to develop speedy and more deeply rooted learning in children. Working with adults who are not teachers can help some children develop a sense of the everyday relevance in their school activity. But a teacher's growing professional and personal understanding of the daily lives of children will tend to generate themes which are more easily seen as relevant and meaningful to children. The aim is to generate the kind of responses expressed by children in terms like these:

Its just like I have discovered a new world of music that I never knew existed. (Alisha, Key Stage 3 pupil talking about a sound composition project)

We were sitting there actually *enjoying* learning. (Year 7 pupil talking about a history project enlivened by an artist)

'I'm going to spend my birthday money on getting the equipment to set things up at home.' (Pupil talking about a pin-hole camera project)

1. Consulting children

Gaultier a Key Stage 2 boy said: My dream school would be a school which would let me explore the world and tell me human knowledge ... at the start of the year the children will choose the topics they are most interested in (there are no compulsory timetables). Five professors will help the children in each place, quoted in Burke and Grosvenor, 2003, p. 62)

Illustration 7.3   *Music can open up a new world of positive and inclusive experience for children*

Illustration 7.4   *Group composition of music exercises intellectual, social, creative and technical skills in equal measure*

Illustration 7.5   *Children's power in action. Here children grill decision makers on aspects of national policy.* Courtesy of Scottish Children's Parliament

Recent thinking on citizenship in schools draws contemporary attention to the importance of pupil participation (for example, Alexander, 2001; Potter, 2002; Wrigley, 2005). The UN *Convention for the Rights of the Child* (UNCRC) Article 12 (UN, 1989, website), makes it clear that children should be consulted on *all* decisions affecting their lives. The recent establishment in the UK of the Children and Young Persons Unit (CYPU), a Children's Commissioner (for example, Children's Commissioner, 2005, website) and other policy implications of *Every Child Matters* , means that the idea of the children's voice being heard can now become mainstream. A preliminary research document to the Children Act of 2004 makes the following points in its summary:

- Taking account of what children say is what makes their involvement meaningful ...
- Acting on children and young people's views brings positive outcomes in ... increasing young people's sense of citizenship and social inclusion and enhancing their personal development. (Kirby, Lanyon and Synelaw, 2003 p. 9.)

So what kinds of themes do children choose? Teaching students are often surprised at the social awareness children display when school councils or children's parliaments ask for projects on:

- conservation of the rain forest
- protecting our local environment
- the earthquake in Pakistan
- fair trade
- health and happiness
- freedom and feeling safe
- poverty
- cleaning up our town
- our links with ... (a school in the developing world).

Commercial companies have taken up this moral and politically aware theme amongst our young people. The International Primary Curriculum (IPC, 2006, website), for example, offers popular units:

- the oil industry
- rulers and governments
- current affairs and the media
- sustainability
- fit for life
- artists' impressions of the world.

Recent national and local authority developments which will inevitably influence children's curricular choices include:

- the adoption in many schools of 'circle time' (Moseley, 1996), aimed at developing empathy, relationship skills and personal values
- the growing local authority and school management interest in emotional literacy (Goleman, 1996; Morris, 2006, website)
- school councils where elected representatives have a meaningful role in school decision-making (School Councils, 2005, website)
- pupil representatives on some governing bodies (in secondary schools at least)
- children's commissioners and children's parliaments.

Some schools have always included children centrally in their decision-making with regard to the curriculum. In Steiner schools, for almost 90 years, parents of each class have regularly met as a body to discuss the curriculum their children follow and general concerns about their children's physical, spiritual, moral and intellectual development. Whilst the curriculum follows a prescribed and adult-led route, the realization of the themes is strongly

Illustration 7.6 *Circle time has become a feature of many schools where the extra curricular interests and concerns of children may be expressed*

tailored to the holistic needs of the growing child and the personality of the class. Thus for example, they study *volcanoes* and *revolutions* at the same time as their bodies and relationships are in the upheavals of puberty.

However, children also continue to love the traditional. A recent survey revealed that colourful and exciting topics of the past, such as the following, are still popular:

- Egyptians
- castles
- Greek legends
- space
- light
- bubbles
- our pets
- Kenya.

When I asked the head of a case study school (Barnes, 2005d) what their curriculum themes would be for 2006, she answered that staff did not know because they had not yet asked the children. Some schools decide upon themes well in advance to ensure curriculum balance or to guarantee consideration of issues relevant to school context, policies, aims or philosophy. Others use published schemes or state education policies as starting points. Each of these sources of ideas for projects has its strengths. It is also legitimate for adults to make decisions about what it is important to learn because schools are seen as society's way of inducting the child into itself. However, today's children need to feel involved in the choice of theme and that the choice is meaningful to them. In a culture which increasingly raises children's awareness of their rights, the school which denies children's participation at the curriculum level is in danger of adding to the atmosphere of disaffection we encountered in Chapter 1.

2. Planning a shared experience

We all love trips, and we can learn much more from going out and seeing things. Numeracy hour and literacy hour can be boring . LET US OUT!
(Kimberley, 11, quoted in Burke and Grosvenor, 2003, P. 75)

Current trends towards individualized learning may run the risk of divorcing us from our physical, social and sensory selves. The new digital curriculum introduced by the BBC in January 2006 is targeted 'on establishing an inter-active dialogue *directly* with learners *while leaving scope* for parents, carers and teachers to mediate the resources' (BBC, 2005, website, emphasis added). This digital curriculum catering for up to 50 per cent of National Curriculum coverage throughout the UK, not only potentially leapfrogs contact with the teacher but also lesson-time interaction with the rest of the class. Some of our newest schools and 'academies' already boast of their independent worksta-tions which replace classrooms. It is possible, even common, to access the whole curriculum without personally experiencing the real world or getting dirty hands. Having the technology to ensure an education based in cyber-space is possible, but it may not be good.

Personal, social and physical experiences are great teachers. The strength of active, real-world and interpersonal learning is that it *will* inevitably be inter-preted in many different ways and mean something different to each individ-ual. Such variation in response can be harnessed to promote creative outcomes to problems or dilemmas arising from themed study. Active, communal and physical experiences may ultimately be preferred by children because their social, physical and sensory coordination develop first (see Chapter 3). Certainly shared, dynamic and bodily activity more effectively use the exquis-itely combined faculties of touch, smell, taste, feeling, movement and hearing which gave the human animal certain advantages over other animals, in the past there were evolutionary rewards for these preferences.

If we add our range of sensory accomplishments to the huge species-advantages of language, self-conscious thought and culture, then arguments for learning together, in real-life and relevant contexts, becomes difficult to refute.

Most objects and sounds which surround us generate personal memories and associations. These 'objects' (including categories of place and people), form part of the memory bank we unconsciously 'call-up' whenever appro-priate. If your class shares time at the circus, lakeside, theatre, car park or supermarket, each member will bring a different mind to the experience. Shared experiences can include:

- a public event (such as a carnival, charity fair, parade, Olympics, festival, political or state visit)
- any fieldwork within the school grounds or building
- fieldwork in the school locality or in some contrasting locality (such as on a school activity holiday)

Illustration 7.7   *Student teachers expressing the features of a medieval wall in their own dance composition*

- a visit (to a museum, supermarket, theatre or nature reserve)
- a special visitor (such as a grandparent, local nurse, poet, builder or gardener)
- a themed week (such as a 'Science, Technology or Maths week' or 'Africa week') or day (for example, 'Red Nose Day')
- a performance (such as a play, opera, dance, gymnastics, a musical or concert)
- a collection of objects (from a school collection, museum, a school dig or a visiting expert)
- a school event (such as sports day, open day, Victorian day or anniversary)
- a combined construction project (such as building an adventure playground, sculpture garden or 'robot wars' vehicle)
- a reflective activity (such as meditation, quiet day, a church/temple or mosque visit)
- the writing of a class story, set of poems or book based upon aspects of the local environment or using detailed knowledge of a local place as the setting.

Some schools start their cross-curricular theme with a shared activity; others choose to aim for such an event at the end of a term's interdisciplinary work. Any shared event will communicate *something* to participants. Your professional skill is shown in the ability to make something useful from the predictable diversity of response. The 'teacher as choreographer' makes a dance of theirs and individual responses to experience and crafts them into a meaningful expression of community and cultural values.

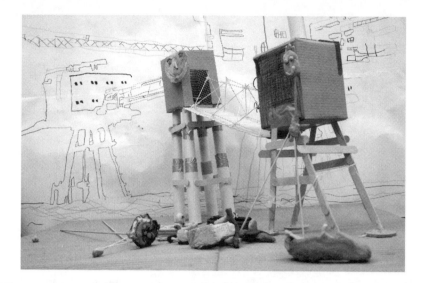

Illustration 7.8   *Children of 12 and 13 constructed these models of mid English channel forts where their 'marooned' artist was to live.* Courtesy Creative Partnerships, Kent

The provision of strong, emotionally engaging experiences has become the stock in trade of initiatives such as creative partnerships, cultural and community groups, and the various science and PSHE theatre projects touring the country. In a single local authority district, a sample of secondary and primary schools have recently based their curriculum around:

- a conceptual artist marooned for six months on a First World War mid-English Channel fort (Illustrations 7.8 and 10.4)
- the creation of a pair of 'sound mirrors', one in northern France and the other in Kent (see Illustration 8.10 in Chapter 8)
- a cultural, song, games, dance and drama project based on links with a school in Sierra Leone
- the residency of an artist in school for two years
- the building of a new school entrance in an Infants school (Illustration 8.5)
- a new school play area in a junior school
- the creation of a community cinema within a community secondary school
- the musical, *Jesus Christ Super Star* performed to sister high schools in the USA and eastern Europe as well as to its own community
- the production of a Shakespeare play
- the building of a geodesic dome in the school quadrangle
- the creation of a recording studio in a cupboard for trying things out
- live links, by letter, email and video with a school in Tanzania

- a massive community operatic and dramatic 'event' involving 20 primary and secondary schools, community clubs and organizations in a single district.

Children's voices best capture the impact of such powerful experiences:

> The Sierra Leone project was one of the best parts of school in my life. My overall highlight of my time with Usufu was one game, one song and one dance ... when we performed the dance to the rest of the school they were all jealous of us and at the end of the dance the children clapped till their hands were red. (Chris, Key Stage 2 pupil, quoted in Creative Partnerships Kent, 2005 p. 23)

> ... the cupboard lets me learn in my own way, in my own time, by my own choices, its like you are given the helmet to put on yourself, or they put the helmet on *for* you. The helmet that's given to you is your own choice. You can leave it away or you can take it ... that's natural learning and the other is forced learning.(Josh, Key Stage 3 pupil)

3. Choosing only subjects which add understanding

The cross-curriculum models of the 1970s and 1980s often foundered on the contrived inclusion of *all* subjects on every Topic Web. In today's best cross-curricular practice only three or four subjects are necessary to bring a balanced understanding to a theme. A serious danger of interdisciplinary work is that the boundaries between the subject disciplines become less distinct.

Recent research into a cross-curricular project

A school in the USA chose the year 1492 (When 'Columbus sailed the ocean blue') as its theme for a term. Apart from the obvious history focus (What was it like then? What happened? Why? How do we know?), pupils studied from the perspective of science (What is true? How have living things changed over the last 500 years? How do plants adapt to change?) and, finally, using a geographical lens children looked at diverse ecosystems which represented contrasting parts of the country in 1492 (they made a series of maps, discussed human–environment interactions and specifically the impact of humans since 1492). Using storybooks, the Internet, non-fiction publications, practical experimentation, fieldwork, the application of mapping and diagrammatic skills the different perspectives of scientist, historian and geographer were explored. The linking theme of a single year drew children into much wider debates and understandings of the ways in which historians develop interpretations, scientists develop explanations and geographers develop descriptions. The researcher (Roth, in Wineberg and Grossman, 2000) reflecting upon this project noted, however, that science learning within the theme was not as deep as social studies learning.

My own research (Barnes and Shirley, 2005) suggests that in delivering cross-curricular themes teachers should:

- identify and focus on clear, appropriate, subject-based learning objectives
- continually monitor the depth of understanding by informal assessment during the activities (also Blythe, 1998; Stone-Wisk, 1998).
- avoid compromising subjects in efforts to 'fit them' to a theme
- be prepared to drop the theme for a period in order to teach subject specific skills and knowledge
- give children early opportunities to *apply* newly learned, skills and knowledge when returning to the theme (Stone-Wisk, 1998)
- strive to generate a genuine questioning stance in the children (also Blythe, 1998; Stone-Wisk, 1998).
- be prepared to intervene in any group activity in order to help raise standards and meet challenging objectives.

4. Planning skills, knowledge and progression

The national curricula of England, Wales, Northern Ireland and the National Guidelines for Scotland are permissive and flexible documents. On careful reading they are not as content-heavy as many complain, but allow considerable leeway in terms of delivery. The QCA and NNS and NLS documents, whilst heavier in knowledge and skills content, are not statutory but provide useful guidance and frameworks to work within if needed. The great benefit of the various statutory curricula is their attention to progression and measures of achievement within each subject. The various attainment levels are clearly progressive in complexity and depth, and provide very helpful guides as to age-appropriate achievement. If you are planning the learning within a theme, after deciding on the shared experience children will have, the Attainment Targets and their levels are good places to start. There is a strong interrelationship in language and concepts between the levels whatever the subject.

Working from subject-specific statements of attainment and the generic concepts in Table 7.1, the teacher can devise clear, measurable objectives for each lesson. Through constant interaction, concentrated feedback, open-ended (and occasionally closed) questioning the teacher can ensure achievement is raised. With clear objectives either directly stated to the children or elicited after the activities ('What do you think I wanted you to learn from this?') the teacher can ensure that subject skills and knowledge are not lost in what Roth calls the 'bland broth' of interdisciplinary study (in Wineburg and Grossman, 2000). Looking above and below the average level for the age using the generic concepts in Table 7.1 the teacher may plan for differentiated support and appropriate progression within each subject represented.

Table 7.1   Generic National Curriculum levels 1–5

Attainment level	Generic concepts	Typical generic activities
Level 1	Literal	See, experience, respond, describe
Level 2	Organization	Arrange, compare, contrast, classify, put into own words
Level 3	Evaluation	Make choices, give reasons, ask questions, find and use, present
Level 4	Inference	Work out, explain, select, combine, make educated guesses
Level 5	Appreciation	Justify, generalize, look for qualities, modify, establish own conclusions

Note: The author is grateful to Jane Heyes and Brompton Westbrook Primary School for this analysis

5. Aiming at a state of flow in children

The school I'd like … could slow down a little. (Hugh, 6, quoted in Burke and Grosvenor, 2003)

Csikszentmihalyi's concept of *flow* brilliantly summarizes that sense of complete involvement we teachers often see when children are fully engaged in an activity over which they feel they have some control. The state of flow is described as the sensation we feel when ideas, thoughts and life itself seem to run freely. Csikszentmihalyi's research suggests that when we reflect on this feeling, the following features of flow are most frequently described:

- complete involvement in an activity for its own sake
- confidence that our skills match the challenge we have been set
- awareness that time seems different from ordinary experience
- less self-consciousness
- less fear of failure
- current worries fade
- feedback comes immediately mostly from the self
- we can say we feel most alive, and have most sense of meaning.

Intrinsic motivation, as we have seen in Chapter 4, is often observed in the school playground, participation in the school play or concert, or engagement in certain practical, sporting and creative sessions. In combining feelings associated with play, physical activity, challenge, inquisitiveness opportunity for creative connection-making, relaxed and friendly relationships with newly acquired knowledge and skills that flow is most likely to occur.

Illustration 7.9 *This child is gently being helped to become part of the class through sensitive handling and participation in rhythmic, group physical activity.* Photo: Cherry

---

Flow in action

In a school serving a deprived 'raw, rough and unsociable' area of the bankrupted city Berlin a group of 250 young people, were asked to join a project to learn and perform a ballet to Stravinsky's *Rite of Spring*. Sir Simon Rattle, a famous conductor, and choreographer Royston Maldoom led this social project, expressly designed to change minds and counter disaffection through involvement in a cross-arts project. These young people had never had contact with western classical music, never danced and many were battling severe social, emotional and health problems of their own, and some were very reluctant to participate. The story of their transformation from low aspirations and negativity towards a more hopeful, positive, confident and sensitized life is told in the film *Rhythm Is It* (Sanchez and Gruber, 2005, website). At one point in the film choreographer Maldoom says, 'Don't think you are just doing dancing. You can change your life in a dance class!' The film ends with extracts from the final rehearsal and performance in which one can observe flow in action in the faces and bodies of the children. The film portrays the combination of real, hard and painfully earned skill, and a high challenge which two months before had seemed insurmountable, which clearly results in some transformed and liberated lives.

The state of flow seems more likely in school children when they: are involved with other people genuinely questionning, come from homes with plenty of books, space of their own, and when they have fewer electronic entertainments. As we have already seen, Csikszentmihalyi also observes it is most common when people are engaged in creative and active pursuits. These observations are powerful arguments for a curriculum which operates outside the limits of the normal classroom in the real and multidisciplinary world outside.

6. Finish with a performance of understanding

In terms of principles for the teacher to consider, the most effective means of monitoring and formatively appraising work done across several curricula is the *Performance of Understanding* (Perkins, in Blythe, 1998). In this kind of assessment procedure children create some kind of demonstration of the degree of their understanding. Assessment generally and specific attention to the performance of understanding are the subject of Chapter 9.

Themes

It is clear that there are as many relevant and fascinating themes as there are objects, places, feelings, ideas and living things in the universe. There can be no definitive list. The essence of a theme that will generate learning is one which both teacher and children can feel enthusiastic about and can therefore sustain commitment to. For cross-curricular work to be successful in raising standards through motivating children, there is no alternative to thorough planning, ongoing assessment and continued attention to specific objectives within focus subjects. The short lists below are themes which have recently and successfully been used in schools since the publication of the primary strategy: *Excellence and Enjoyment* (DFES, 2004, website). I have chosen to identify themes which perhaps suggest one major focus subject in order to emphasize the fact that key learning objectives within the subjects need to be restricted within each theme so that subject learning is not 'watered down. A Foundation Stage or Key Stage 1 theme with a science focus such as 'Why won't my seed grow?' (de Boo, 2004) will lay the foundations for science later on in school by helping children handle, tend and think about seeds and growth, but, true to good early years practice, children will also sort and classify, count, draw, construct, make musical instruments listen to and invent stories. The Knowledge and Understanding of the World or Key Stage 1 science objectives may be 'to identify the features of living things', 'to be able to relate the life process of a plant' or 'to identify similarities and differences in natural things'. The teacher will know the expected range of levels of understanding by looking at the level descriptions and thus be able both to differentiate and encourage children to higher levels of achievement. Each of the *non*-science activities will also have a levelled objective (for example 'sort objects and talk about sorting', 'initiate communication with others' or 'be aware of the needs of others'.) Through these and other relevant objectives, teachers and teaching assistants will be helping children grow in the areas of creativity, communication, mathematics, personal, emotional and social development.

Some themes with a science focus

Systems

Models

Turn on the light

Patterns of change

Interactions

Colour

Bubbles

Why won't my seed grow?

Why is water important?

How many legs?

Some themes with a geography focus

Our street/our neighbours

Improving a derelict site/school playground

Weather

A building site

A basket of fruit from …

A day out in the town/country/seaside/India

A linked school in a distant locality

Finding our way/maps and mapping

A local river, lake, dam or coast/geographical processes

Getting there/transport systems

My footprint/sustainability and me

My home/systems that serve us

Where's in the news?

Some themes with an RE focus

People

Journeys

Celebrations

Stories

Special places

Symbols and signs

Judaism, Sikhism, Buddhism, Islam, Christianity, Hinduism

What's in the news?

What is beauty?

What is truth?

What is good?

What is bad?

Some themes with a history focus

Change

My birthday

My family

A particular building

Grandma Brown's visit

Florence Nightingale and Mary Seacole

The Olympic Games

The Gunpowder Plot

In an artist's/engineer's/scientist's shoes

Our school

The 1851 Great Exhibition

A visit to the museum

A mystery object

Final questions for those thinking of topic themes

Perhaps you might consider the following questions before coming to a firm decision on a theme.

1. Consulting the children

- Does this theme fit with the school's wider aims?
- How will I make it relevant and meaningful to the children?
- How can I involve children in decisions?

2. Planning a shared experience

- How can I involve and enhance community links though this project?
- What are my overarching goals for this theme? In what big ways do I want the children to be different at the end of this topic?
- What shared experiences can we plan?

3. Choosing only subjects which add understanding

- What two or three (maximum four) curriculum subjects best throw light on this theme?
- What are the curriculum needs this term/year/week?

4. Plan subject skills, knowledge and progression required

- What level of skills and knowledge in each subject do I need to help children demonstrate?
- What experts from the community can I obtain to help me?

5. Aiming at a state of flow

- What can I do to generate a state of flow in the children during aspects of this theme?
- How can I make this project personally meaningful to the maximum number of children?
- How can I generate genuine questions?

6. Finishing with a performance of understanding.

- In what ways can the children demonstrate the depth of their learning?
- How can I help children show that their learning is transferable to other situations and settings?

Further reading

Chen, J. (ed.) (1998) *Project Spectrum: Early Learning Activities*, New York: Teachers College Press.

Blyth, T. (ed.)(1997) *The Teaching for Understanding Guide*, New York: Jossey-Bass.

Arthur, J., Grainger, T. and Wray, D. (eds) (2006) *Learning to Teach in the Primary School*, London: Routledge.

CHAPTER 8

How Should We Plan for Cross-Curricular Activity?

We must plan carefully to ensure that every child gains the maximum from our teaching. Planning inevitably includes paperwork, but arguably the most important aspects come well before anything is written. Thoughtful conversations should come first. Such conversations need structure and direction but should lead to:

- a coherent and consistent philosophy
- a secure and supportive ethos
- a warm ambience
- safe and stimulating spaces for learning.

Group decision-making between teams of teachers, key workers, curriculum advisers and, increasingly, children and parents will follow. When and whilst these first critical decisions are made, you should constantly consider how to make them relevant to children and community. Finally, and still before the paperwork, you need to think about the balance between generating motivation and fulfilling the demands of national requirements. This chapter shows how those National Curriculum expectations (with particular attention to the key skills) can become a meaningful, lively and even satisfying part of your planning. It emphasizes the idea of powerful experiences and supports some of its conclusions with reference to current research and practice in beacon schools.

The chapter contains some more formal and paper-bound examples of long-, medium- and short-term planning which take account of the principles discussed earlier in this book. Definitions of types of planning are necessary before we use them.

The *long-term plan* covers a complete key stage. It assures the school, parents, curriculum coordinators and governors that curriculum coverage and challenge can, and will, be maintained. It also gives an overview showing the direction of learning, the big issues tackled and how learning, curriculum and community are interrelated.

A *medium-term plan* shows detail of what a termly theme or cross-curricular module might look like. It attempts to put into practice the strong principle reiterated throughout this book, that a *restricted* number of curriculum subjects should be the focus of each term's cross-curricular learning. A medium-term plan should show the proposed relationship between *key questions* and attention to specific subject-based skills and knowledge. It must show progression towards a questioning stance and the development of ever-deeper understanding.

The *short-term plan* is not a lesson plan but details of a week in which certain generic and related questions of lifelong importance are addressed. It shows specific attainment targets and levels to be addressed in greater detail in order to maintain momentum.

A *lesson plan* is obviously a detailed guide to what will happen within an actual lesson and can include;

- the key question
- new and subject-based vocabulary
- the learning intention(s)
- specific links with the everyday lives of children
- links with previous learning and activity
- creative thinking opportunities
- sample differentiated questions for teacher–pupil interaction
- notes on classroom organization
- specific skills to be taught
- specific activities/experiences
- formative assessment opportunities
- targeted children
- opportunities to apply new learning
- links to future learning.

Making links

Throughout the CGFS and the UK National Curricula we are reminded about linking subjects. 'Stepping stones', areas of learning, programmes of study and general teaching requirements are wide open to imaginative and school-specific interpretation. In its first pages the English National Curriculum recites the now familiar mantra regarding education being a route to, 'spiritual, moral, social, cultural, physical and mental development, and thus the well-being, of the individual'. It clearly states that the curriculum orders are intended to:

> ... enable us to respond positively to the opportunities and challenges of the rapidly changing world in which we live and work. In particular, we

need to be prepared to engage as individuals, parents, workers and citizens with economic, social and cultural change, including the continued globalization of the economy and society, with new work and leisure patterns and with the rapid expansion of communication technologies. (DfES/QCA, 1999, p. 10)

Most curricula are flexible enough to support the cross-curricular planning and creative thinking implicit in recent government-sponsored guidance. If words like those above are not mere rhetoric they must result in a highly flexible, constantly revised curriculum, sensitively tuned to contemporary lives and communities. Even without revision, most national and local curricula allow for the kind of challenging curriculum experiments we saw represented in Chapter 2. Criticisms of curricula are common, but perhaps it is more productive to take a different *attitude* to existing guidance and link learning more precisely to the lived worlds of children themselves.

In many ways the writers of the *Curriculum Guidance for the Foundation Stage* (DfES/QCA, 1999a) blazed the trail towards broader, richer, more creative approaches to the curriculum. The QCA, in its response to *All Our Futures* (NACCCE, 1999) and its government review in 2006, the Department of Culture Media and Sport (DCMS) through sponsorship of research, Sport England, Arts Council and Creative Partnerships and the Healthy Schools campaign (DoH/DfES, 2005) have all spread a similar message. *Every Child Matters* and the resulting proposals relating to personalized learning and the re-conceptualizing of schools as multipurpose 'children's centres,' perhaps heralds the development of a new mindset towards education. Recent government documents seek broader definitions of learning, concentrating on lifelong, transferable, personally tailored, significant, confidence-building, global and community-specific features. It is up to teachers and others in schools to take control of this agenda for the betterment of humankind.

There is evidence that schools are moving towards accepting a role where staff and pupil well-being have equal importance with curriculum content. This balance is particularly well served by cross-curricular and creative approaches to teaching and learning. The government White Paper on education, *Higher standards, better Schools for All* (HM Government, 2005, website) explicitly expresses the importance of the pliant, personalized and positive approach: 'Children and young people learn best with a curriculum which enthuses and engages. We are already seeing increasing curriculum flexibility and helping schools to make the most of this.'

To be effective and sustainable, a curriculum should link effortlessly to an established and school-based framework of shared values and assured relevance. A rationale which is clear to all stakeholders, which genuinely values all and aims to ensure personalized progression seems much more likely to raise standards.

When a teacher helps make a subject personally relevant to children, they help the individual child discover physical, personal and emotional links

Illustration 8.1 *Secondary School children making links between history, creative writing and movement. They are planning a series of freeze frames based upon one*

with their own lives. Working in this way, we attempt to make the existential connection which Peter Abbs (2003) found so lacking in his geography teacher and which possibly millions still fail to find in their daily exposure to education. Many of you will instantly recollect the teachers who have really 'spoken' to you and have somehow imbued their subject with a sense of personal meaningfulness. It is planning for this *emotional* identification with subject or theme which neurological, psychological and pedagogical research leads me to believe is a prerequisite for deep learning.

Planning for relevance

Planning for relevance does not just mean the teacher chooses a topic which he or she thinks is significant in the child's world. Neither is it always as simple as finding an appropriate entry point from everyday life. Teachers may be correct in their choices, but those choices must be made to *feel* meaningful within the minds of the learners before they enter into a learning contract with the teacher. Experienced teachers have become masters at this kind of negotiation. I gathered the following set of short examples during a single working week:

- A teacher in east Kent made *longshore drift* relevant to her Year 8 geography fieldwork class, by getting part of the class to dance the zig zag movement of the pebbles on the beach as she described their movement.

Illustration 8.2   *Student teachers finding relevance in an old wall*

- A class teacher in Rotherham used his class's ringside seat at the demolition of the old school building as an excuse to bring old members of the community into the new school building to be interviewed.
- A Year 3 teacher made transparency and opacity relevant by asking groups of children to make trendy sunglasses for the class teddy bear.
- A teacher in Whitby significantly improved the creative writing of all her pupils by asking them to include their detailed observations of her precise movements as she wandered furtively between the ruins of an old monastery the day before.

The learning gained from such activity is a product not simply of good teaching, but of detailed attention to the emotional setting of learning. Relevance can be *created* by planning child-centred spaces for learning and ensure a wholesome social and moral atmosphere. The emotional and intellectual content can also be planned for relevance by setting up meaningful links and structuring each learning experience with the child centrally in mind. In doing this the teacher can make even the most unpromising pile of stones meaningful and generative. (Illustration 8.2)

Planning spaces for learning: examples from the Foundation Stage and Key Stage 1

The *Curriculum Guidance for the Foundation Stage* was seen as cross-curricular from the start. The language of this document avoids reference to separated subjects and speaks of 'areas of learning' to underline this. The promotion of a strong self-image and strong self-esteem are specifically mentioned as aims for the curriculum. The CGFS accepts that real, relevant and personally engaging experience interpreted through several areas of learning is most likely to promote such confidence. The guidance also charges teachers with helping develop children's

- personal, social and emotional well-being
- positive attitudes and dispositions towards their (own) learning
- social skills
- attention skills and persistence.

These aims are listed before the required developments within the prescribed 'areas of learning'. The clear spotlight upon the social, emotional and personal aspects of learning underscores the point that the *ways* and the *reasons* children learn are at least as important as what they will learn.

Planning for the most effective learning experience starts with the careful and detailed consideration of the spaces in which they learn. This has been a preoccupation of those who plan learning spaces for the children of Reggio Emilia in northern Italy. In pre-schools of Reggio, great attention and considerable resources are devoted to the fine detail of the children's environment. The fabrics, the design and materials of coat hooks, the colour of furniture, lighting, placing of services such as the school kitchen, or the views from windows are all carefully considered. There is a distinct child-centredness to all these decisions, immediately evident in the child-friendly levels of window sills, door handles and taps, as well as the powerful use of light, colour, fabrics and soft edges.

Jerome Bruner has worked with Reggio's pre-schools and has isolated three essentials for the pre-school child learning space. These principles for learning spaces could be profitably applied throughout education. For Bruner, learning space must be:

- *mine, thine, and ours* (it 'needs to provide places for each individual who occupies it … but must be communal as well')
- *in and of the broader community* (it should be in the physical community and its activities should arise from the community)
- *a learning community* ('a place to learn together about the real world, and about possible worlds of imagination … where the young discover the uses of mind, of imagination, of materials, and learn the power of doing these things together'). (Bruner, in Ceppi and Zini, 2003, p. 137)

The exquisite learning outcomes of such attention to detail are well known and provide ample evidence of the ease of generating high levels of achievement in child-centred conditions (see Reggio Emilia, 2006, website).

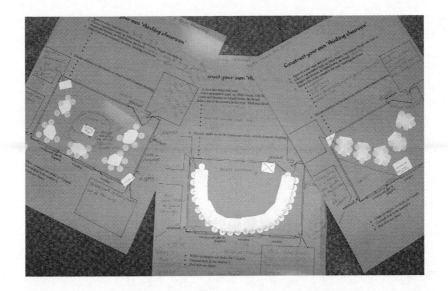

Illustration 8.3   Student teachers' plans for a 'Thinking Classroom'

Clearly, in Reggio, generous local funding and the economic profits of fame have worked together to construct exciting places and learning tools for the children. Reggio Emilia 'principles', however, are applicable in any economic setting. The first principle is to put the child at the heart of the decision-making process. Implications of this have recently been explored in an English context by Shirley Brice Heath in a community infants school in Hythe, Kent. Here Nursery, Reception, Year 1 and Year 2 children worked on a project to redesign and oversee the building of a new reception area for their school. The 3–7-year-olds worked with architects, an artist and interior designers to plan and follow through plans for a truly child-centred entrance and route way through their school (Brice Heath and Wolf, 2004). Through frequent planning and orientation meetings, questionnaires and a major exhibition of their plans and ideas, children and architects arrived at a brief for the rebuilding and redesign of large areas of the school. The official brief to the architects and designers was to explore, 'how good design can improve the quality of life in schools by listening to the voices of the consumers. It inspires pupils by putting them in the driving seat, giving them control and responsibility as clients' (Brice Heath and Wolf, 2004, p. 9). But the children's brief to the architects was in the form of a mighty exhibition. Designer Ben Kelly who worked with the children recounted

> We posed questions to them and their response was this exhibition; that's how they overcame the practical problems of communication. They communicated in the way that young children do best, by chucking a load of stuff out from within themselves; drawings, paintings, models, collages, written stuff, tons and tons of it – all over the walls! Their brief/exhibition was incredible. It had such vigour, life and enthusiasm. It really was

Illustration 8.4   *Children proudly introduce their display in the entrance they designed with architects.* Courtesy Creative partnerships, Kent

stimulating. It was the key that unlocked the process. (Brice Heath and Wolf, 2004, p. 14)

Children's decisions about space for both learning and celebrating their learning were taken seriously by adults and the results were far in excess of expectations. Profound discussions about morality, security, culture, beauty, life and death were common in this context. Children decided, for example, that they did not want their reception area to be boring, 'just about sitting', they wanted to move people around and they wanted to showcase the art they were so proud of. They planned a display system and 'Barbie pink' carpeted route way around their displayed work which was in many ways to be the heart of the school. Interestingly, adults took on the playfulness of children in their design and the children took on some aspects of the seriousness of adults. The deep implications of these genuine and meaningful interactions between adults and children may be summarized in a single comment from Jack: 'We learned to make things. My favourite was the bucket lights [yellow ceiling lights made to look like sand castle buckets from the nearby beach] – they looked cool. When I walk into this reception area after it's built, I think I'll feel famous' (Brice Heath and Wolf, p. 19). Such a sense of specialness, accomplishment, and meaning which results from involvement in creative acts, could be argued to be every child's birthright. (Illustrations 8.4, 8.5)

The Hythe project was cross-curricular in every way. Children were involved in this project for a whole year before the building was complete. They richly developed their language at both its most practical and most

Illustration 8.5   *Infants' school entrance designed with 'big art' and buckets as light shades by the 5 – 7year old pupils.* Courtesy Creative Partnerships, Kent

symbolic levels. They used and extended their art to make objects which truly became a valued part of their environment and developed a range of design/technology skills and principles. Additionally they learned that even at 4 years of age they could generate real change for the better in their community. It is not difficult, however, to translate this ambitious project into the more prosaic context of every primary classroom. What about the following questions which any class could fruitfully be involved in addressing?

- How could we rearrange the classroom furniture so that we can combine private space to work quietly on our own and opportunities to work together?

- How can we decorate the walls to make this classroom really reflect us as people?

- How can we improve the view from our classroom window?

- How can we address one of the millennium goals (see p. 161) in this classroom this term?

- We have £200 to spend on some new furniture/equipment/resources for this room this year what shall we buy?

- How can we find out what local people *really* want in the redevelopment of part of the school grounds?

Such questions are real, open, and can be used genuinely to elicit the views and more importantly real-world actions and products of children's thought. Answers which generated action would involve children and adults together in a co-learning situation in which a range of skills and knowledge from design and technology, art, language, mathematics, science or geography might be taught and quickly and *meaningfully* applied. Genuine and thoughtful solutions would change the children's environment. They would be arrived at through compromise, empathy, problem-solving, creative thinking and a host of other cross-curricular skills. But answers to such questions might also communicate important messages that ordinary folk *can* change things, and that we can agree on principled ways of improving our community.

Planning the emotional and intellectual context

The Foundation Stage curriculum

The CGFS (Curriculum Guidance for the Foundation Stage) is very direct regarding how teachers and other adults must plan for real experiences from which children learn. Essentially such learning experiences should feel like play. Planning for generative play is a key and wholly natural way for all children to learn. To make learning likely, however, adults need to consider structures to plan within. In teams teachers of pre-school and reception class children should consider:

1. How to provide the physical and emotional security which allows for safe risk taking and encourages a positive view of mistakes.
2. How to introduce the element of challenge into the planned play activity.
3. How they are going to support the play without intervening too much.
4. How to extend the activity and the learning.
5. How to ensure that spontaneous play is likely.
6. How to add to the child's language world. (See Illustration 8.6)

These generic thoughts aside, the most effective spaces and situations for challenging and generative play are often outside the classroom. The city-centre nursery school in Chapter 2, the kindergartens of Germany, Switzerland and Scandinavia, the Forest Schools of Denmark and the playgrounds of the Reggio Emilia pre-schools each use the semi-natural world of playground, woodland, fields, nature trails and parks nearest them as major resources. Rain or shine, within these outdoor environments, children may be asked to find their way, travel, imagine, collect, classify, build, record or express within wider themes such as:

- Getting bigger
- Going on a bear hunt
- Life around us
- People who help us
- Shelters

Illustration 8.6   *Six year olds effectively linking art, language and science by working with an artist on careful looking and drawing.* Courtesy Creative Partnerships, Kent

- Feeling happy; feeling sad
- Finding the way home.

Within the classroom the world of the imagination may take children much further away. Questions such as

- What do angels look like?
- What do I look like when I'm peaceful?
- How do we think the internet works?
- How do television pictures get to us?
- What would the world look like if I was a bird/germ/giant/ant? can extend the thinking, socialization and motor skills of every child.

Long-term planning for a Key Stage 1 curriculum

As education becomes more formal and local or national accountability becomes more complex, planning gets more complex too. Long-term planning needs to take account of:

1. National/local curriculum subjects – designed to help children understand their world *now.*
2. The cross-curricular strands – designed to help children make a positive impact upon *the future.*
3. Educational research – intended to support teachers in combining these personal and societal objectives.

In England many teachers of children 5–7-years-old retained an element of the cross-curricular in their planning. The National Curriculum *key skills* and *thinking skills* intended to direct the general approach to planning have often been less evident at this stage. The pressures of time and 'initiative overload' have meant that classroom teachers have little time to read about research and current education thinking. If, however, we aim to take account of individual differences in learning and help each child become a self-regulated learner, then these cross-curricular skills are very helpful. So our planning should include all National Curriculum subjects, incorporate the cross-curricular strands but also respond to research. First we should be quite clear about what subjects, strands and research we are talking about:

The National Curriculum subjects in England

- Art
- Design and Technology
- English
- Geography
- History
- Information and Communications Technology
- Mathematics
- Modern foreign languages
- Music
- Physical education
- Religious education
- Science.

The cross-curricular strands

The key skills in the English National Curriculum provide six interdisciplinary threads which can run through the education. The thinking skills and cross-curricular aspects weave between them to construct a network which can potentially unite the whole learning experience of children. The DfES 'Creative learning journey' (DfES, 2006b, website) amongst others, attempts to use goals closely related to those in the Foundation Stage guidance to link subjects. Other schemes use the National Curriculum's 'key skills', thinking skills and 'cross-curricular aspects' to achieve integration of the disciplines.

Research suggests that a connected curriculum will only be effective in promoting learning if it rests on the bedrock of a supportive, secure school community (Ahmad et al., 2003). Successful schools plan in teams and maximize the relevance of their curriculum to local community and the lives of children. They use the rich physical, human and cultural resources of their locality, and plan a series of powerful shared experiences for children to interpret in individualized ways with their newly learned skills.

The key skills are:

- Communication
- Application of number
- Information technology
- Working with others
- Improving own learning and performance
- Problem-solving.

The thinking skills are:

- Information processing
- Reasoning
- Enquiry
- Creative thinking
- Evaluation.

The other cross-curricular aspects to be taken into account are:

- Financial capability
- Enterprise education
- Education for sustainable development
- PSHE/Citizenship
- Statement of values.

Research in teaching and learning

Ten key points summarize the thrust of current developments in education research:

Ten suggestions from research cited elsewhere in this book

1. Create a positive, secure and comfortable atmosphere.
2. Ensure a range of practical, creative and analytical activities for each child.
3. Have clear goals, challenges and individualized targets pitched a little above current ability.
4. Use a manageable number of relevant subjects to throw light on the topic.
5. Build emotionally significant links to the life of each child, engaging all the senses and using tools and objects to support and promote thinking.
6. Involve developmentally appropriate progression in skills, knowledge and understanding.

7. Work within structures and a wider framework which includes concepts, subject skills, knowledge and attitudes.
8. Emphasize individual and cooperative thinking and learning throughout.
9. Provide supportive assessment procedures which build security and include time and tools for reflection.
10. Offer a wide range of opportunities to discover engagement, enjoyment and other positive emotions.

Department for Education and Skills research also suggests that the best schools aim at personalized learning and effectively address emotional health and well-being for all. These schools develop philosophies which value and aim to develop resilience, problem-solving, emotional intelligence, differences and cooperation between individuals and groups (DfES, 2003). Assessment in such a setting is not a bureaucratic or competitive add-on but enriches and deepens each child's encounter with learning.

Combining, subjects, key skills and education research: what would this curriculum look like in practice?

Starting planning with the key skills and incorporating National Curriculum subjects as they become relevant to understanding real experience, might make a long-term plan look very different. First, consider the links each key skill makes with the subjects.

Communication

Reading, writing, speaking and listening would be encouraged in meaningful contexts across all school experience. Other powerful forms of communication through play, pictures and symbols, through music, numbers, dance and mime, and in facial expressions and body language would also be centrally represented. Schools could maximize alternative modes of communication by offering children a wide range of different methods to present their learning. Understanding in PE might be better communicated in movement or a game, geographical understanding might be clarified by a map, table, diagram, drawing or journey, history by an exhibition of artefacts or music by a composition.

Application of number

Number might well be one of the languages through which children understood a more general curriculum theme. In topics centred on design and technology, art and PE we may practically apply concepts of weight, measurement, symmetry and balance. In a geography and history project, distance, graphs, statistics, scale and time are key to understanding the wider world. A theme illuminated by the perspectives of music, RE, MFL, English or science may need number to help children understand sonic, spiritual, linguistic and natural patterns around them.

Information technology (IT)

The challenge is not simply to use IT, but to ensure it supports the progressive development of skills, knowledge and understanding in each subject. For example a Year 1 class might use digital cameras to record significant aspects of their locality and then classify them into four categories: 'natural life', 'our historic environment', 'working in our village' and 'what's changing?' The degree and development of their local understanding could easily be recorded from the discussions, selections and poster presentations which accompanied this activity.

Working with others

School is the only place where most children regularly relate to a range of age mates, so group work on real-life, curriculum-based challenges can be a key opportunity to build new relationships and develop emotional literacy. Empathy, the capacity to relate, leadership or 'followership', and coping with disagreements and disappointments are all part of the experience of working on combined projects. Most great strides in human culture have not resulted from lone efforts but have arisen from the creative collaboration of groups (John-Steiner, 2000). Group investigations, games, murals, model-building, musical improvisations and compositions, and problem-solving in teams will develop social skills and provoke more effective and creative solutions. (Illustration 8.7)

Improving own learning and performance

Reflection is not simply a pleasant and calming activity but has profound effects upon learning and performance. Five-and 6-year-old children in a Cognitive Acceleration study (Shayer and Adey, 2002) were asked questions which provoked thinking at a level not usually associated with their age. In a practical science session on materials, teachers asked questions such as:

- What do you think we are going to have to think about?
- What could you do if you have problems?
- How do you know that?
- What might make this easier?

Illustration 8.7 *A team of two discuss their design and technology solution with a creative practitioner.* Courtesy Creative partnerships, Kent

- How are we going to do this?
- What might happen if ... ?
- I wonder what it would be like if ... ?
- Are there any other ways this can be done?
- What else do we need to think about?

These metacognitive questions are all ways of ensuring improved performance by deepening thinking and apply to all subjects.

Problem-solving

Imagine a Reception class on the beach. Each group is set a problem: 'How can we tell the children in our French sister school what its really like here? There's only one problem, we can't use any words because they couldn't understand us.' The children discuss the problem then share their solutions with the rest of the class: painting paintings, collecting shells and stones, recording the sound of the waves, taking photos and making up some music.

Illustration 8.8   *Six year old children thinking about the problem of composing a class musical composition based around the castle chamber they are sitting in*

On their return to class there were other problems. 'How are we going to send all this stuff to them?' and 'What can we do with it?'

In such an example, a genuinely expressed, convincing problem is shared by teacher and pupils and will generate both a desire for and the means to find a solution. (Illustration 8.8)

A curriculum map

Combining subjects, key skills and recommendations from research is a complex and perplexing challenge. One way of facing such a task is for staff in a Year group or Key Stage to work together to produce a curriculum map. This document is intended to plot progression and coverage at both subject and skills level in the context of an integrated curriculum.

Table 8.1 comprises long-term plans for the cross-curricular experience of a Year 1 or 2 class covering three half-terms. It deliberately excludes standard lessons in core subjects which would run more or less independently of the plan. It uses the school and school locality as the focus of this work. The curriculum map attempts to combine experience of the key skills and the thinking skills in activities which automatically address many issues itemized in the Citizenship/PSHE and values guidance. The main feature, however, is that it depends upon three powerful, shared experiences. These experiences are understood through the eyes of several different subjects by class, groups and individuals. Appropriately levelled coverage of the whole curriculum is addressed, by mapping out equal time allocations for foundation subjects and making decisions on the percentage of cross-curricular time to be given to the core subjects, RE and PSHE/Citizenship.

Providing structured learning experiences: examples of medium-term planning for 7–14-year-olds

Similar curriculum planning principles apply to older children too. Deciding upon the *time* to be devoted to cross-curricular approaches may need to come first. Some primary and secondary schools are experimenting with the abandonment of a timetable altogether for periods, so that children can respond to an experience in a variety of negotiated ways. Some place all their cross-curricular work into one themed week: a science week, Europe week, arts week or cross-curricular mathematics week. Some give a day per week to the cross-curricular application of subject-based skills. Others have the more integrated approach exemplified by the case studies in Chapter 2. In each setting general principles like those discussed in Chapter 6 and guidelines regarding the choice of topic suggested in Chapter 7 will apply. Regardless of the actual time allocated to cross-curricular work, I would suggest that the following common features should be considered:

- limiting subjects
- powerful experiences
- key questions
- balance between skills, knowledge, thought and action.

Limiting subjects

Whilst it is probably possible to bend every subject to fit a chosen theme, we have seen that this can be confusing and counterproductive. Limiting the subjects to two, three or a maximum of four, has been discussed in previous chapters, but in medium-term planning, specific detail of the programme of study and attainment targets for each subject should be included.

Powerful experiences

Children (and probably most of us) learn most easily through actually being *physically* involved in exploring sites, materials and ideas. It is incumbent upon schools to create and control those experiences for children to produce

Table 8.1 Long-term plans for cross-curricular experience of a Year 1 or 2 class covering three half terms

Key Experience 1 A visit to the site of the new bypass

	What's the problem? (Problem-solving skills)	How can we organize it? (Working with others)	How's it going to help children's learning? (Improving own learning)	How are we going to include opportunities for maths? (Application of number)	How am I going to help my children see themselves as thinkers? (Thinking skills)	How am I going to use IT? (Information technology)	How are we going to present our understanding? (Communication)
Art – making close-up drawings of small aspects of the site and then making them into giant abstract paintings)	We've got to plan an exhibition of our half term's work on the new road	Group sculpture Group installation Group display	Reflection: What do I think worked best? Critical evaluations looking for ways to improve	Framing pictures, allocating resources by weight (e.g. clay) Scaling up and down Sale of mouse mats made from paintings	Creative thinking: How can I make this drawing into a giant painting?	Word Art for titles, Modified Photography/ video as background information for display	Planning the exhibition to make most sense of the exhibits, e.g. positioning, background information, design features
Design and technology – making the bypass less ugly	We've got to make a model of our ideas for making the bypass less ugly	Group projects based upon a model of the new road	Identifying refinements/ applications Thinking about different people's points of view	Scale drawing Measuring components Measured designs	Reasoning and enquiry thinking: What do different people think? What would improve this place?	Digital camera Website information on road building	Preparing and delivering a brief
English – using the road to generate a debate/writing a road story	We've got to work out the pros and cons of building a bypass around our village	Play Questionnaires Group evaluations Debates Role-play	What would happen if … ?, Are there any other ways this can be done? What will it be like when … ?	Using numbers to make the arguments, numbers of people affected, traffic, animals etc.	Information processing Evaluation thinking: What do we think about this issue?	Word processing Stimulus material from the web	Role-play Debate Dramatic reading of stories

(Continued)

Table 8.1 (Continued)

Key Experience 2 Work in the school locality for the school website

	What's the problem? (Problem-solving skills)	How can we organize it? (Working with others)	How's it going to help children's learning? (Improving own learning)	How are we going to include opportunities for maths? (Application of number)	How am I going to help my children see themselves as thinkers? (Thinking skills)	How am I going to use IT? (Information technology)	How are we going to present our understanding? (Communication)
Geography – discovering what the locality is like now	We have to prepare an introduction to our local area for the school website	Field work Role-play an issue related to change in the locality Group map-making	What do different kinds of people think of living here? What are the problems? What are the benefits?	Mapping Traffic survey Using maps at different scales Making graphs	Creative thinking: How can we represent this area on a map? Enquiry thinking: What do we like/dislike about our locality?	Current information from the www CD-ROM/GIS satellite images and packages e.g. Digital worlds	Mapping, planning poster
History – finding out about the locality in the past	We have to make a history, page for the school website	Class discussion on issue in history e.g. separate girls' and boys' entrance,	Imagine what it was like then Consider different perspectives	Presenting of numerical data Comparing dimensions of school hall/ classrooms with old plans	Information processing: deciding on which information to include and which to leave out	Making links to Census and other historical information on the web, collect and evaluate different sources	Designing a museum exhibition Presentation of historical information
Mathematics – presenting the facts and figures about the locality	We've got to present statistics about the local area for our project	Teams challenged to make the clearest graph	What are we going to need to think about if this graph is to be clear?	Applying number to real situations	Creative thinking: new presentation ideas Information processing	Using calculators, different measures, collecting data	Number patterns Graphs Diagrams

Table 8.1 (Continued)

Key Experience 3 Work in the school grounds to find the variety of life around school

	What's the problem? (Problem-solving skills)	How can we organize it? (Working with others)	How's it going to help children's learning? (Improving own learning)	How are we going to include opportunities for maths? (Application of number)	How am I going to help my children see themselves as thinkers? (Thinking skills)	How am I going to use IT? (Information technology)	How are we going to present our understanding? (Communication)
Modern foreign language – making the school website attractive to people from other countries	Designing a welcome page for visitors from other European countries	Role play in a foreign language	Appreciating the perspective of outsiders	Counting in foreign languages, simple mathematical problems in French, Spanish or German	Evaluation: Why might this be a good thing?	Translators Foreign sites Background information on the web CD-ROM packages	Foreign language days French restaurants
Music – making music to accompany a mini-beast film.	Our film needs music which help people understand the life and wonder of tiny creatures	Group composition, children work in groups to make music for slugs, ants, woodlice, centipedes, etc.	How can we make this more surprising, how can we use patterns, silence, symmetry in our music? How could we improve it?	Beats in a bar Number patterns in music (Gamelan) Drumming patterns Repeating patterns	Creative thinking: using sound to represent animate objects	Digital keyboards Altered environmental sounds Using CD, mini disc, video DVD on insect life. Making own video	Musical composition Listening to the music of others, e.g. Vaughan Williams' 'The wasps' Evaluation of music
Physical education – making a mini-beast dance, movement or body sculpture	We have to make a dance or movement on the theme of insects	Group planning and performance of dance /movement routines. Group decisions on body sculpture	Negotiating movement/dance decisions, evaluating/ planning improvements.	Numbered sequences E.g. Dance movements. Sale of tickets to performances	Creative thinking: using body movements and shape to suggest mini-beast movement and life.	Use of music examples from the web or CD/ Video of skills/ stimulus Make DVD of final product	Dance Body sculpture movement

(Continued)

Table 8.1 (Continued)

	What's the problem? (Problem-solving skills)	How can we organize it? (Working with others)	How's it going to help children's learning? (Improving own learning)	How are we going to include opportunities for maths? (Application of number)	How am I going to help my children see themselves as thinkers? (Thinking skills)	How am I going to use IT? (Information technology)	How are we going to present our understanding? (Communication)
Religious education – asking the big questions	Thinking about the significance of the natural world. Expressing feelings in poems, lists, music or painting	Paired discussion, Why do you think God made insects? Are there any things we can't see?	Thinking about the purpose/ sustainability/ quality of life issues. The seen and unseen world	Significant numbers, 3, 7, 12 Numbers in nature	Reasoning: asking the why question Evaluation: asking why this is valuable?	Stimulus for reflection Other cultures views on insects (e.g. Bushmen and the Mantis). Record reflections for DVD	Reflective writing, poetry prayer
Science – finding out about classification, mini-beast life and sustainability	We want to find out more about mini-beasts' habitats, life cycles, food and how we can classify them	Individual group responses to various Science problems: classification, preferred habitats, life cycle, food	Making and testing hypotheses	Fibonacci series Numbers in natural objects; (petals, leaves, sea shells) Classification. Moral considerations	Information processing reasoning, enquiry and Evaluation: all involved	Variety of life. Take close-up photos and video footage of insects in their habitat	Experiment presentation

Illustration 8.9 *A First World war 'sound mirror' designed to detect the presence of approaching enemy aircraft, captures the attention of a pupil.* Courtesy Creative Partnerships, Kent

the most positive and personally productive learning outcomes for each individual. This can be done by planning not just for the physical and social environment the children work in, but the experiences they will learn through (Illustration 8.9). Planning generative experiences should not be

Illustration 8.10   *An impromptu classroom display after a reception class walk in the playground.* Photo: *Cherry Tewfik*

contemplated by an isolated teacher. They are better planned in a team if possible. The progression of experiences a child has in his or her school career needs careful mapping throughout the key stage and beyond. Some experiences will be revisited, such as a second or third workshop with a theatre group or a trip to the local church, forest or mosque. As in Forest Schools, multiple visits will each have a different focus. A curriculum based around experiences will clearly need a whole-school approach and adults planning it might consider the following suggestions.

Planning the experiences

Plan a range of six generative experiences per year for each year group and through discussion, ensure each experience requires a contrasting spread of subject disciplines to examine, explain and express it. Such experiences can be physical, social, creative, cerebral, emotional or practical, but they will all have personal and emotional meaning. Damasio's almost casual observation that 'few if any objects in the world are emotionally neutral' (Damasio, 2003, p. 56) reminds us that we should use the objects which surround us. These 'objects' include other people, buildings, pebbles, teacups, trees, mountains, rubbish sacks or grains of dust, and all are packed with personal references and relevance which can be used as the 'way in' to individual involvement. Taking this view would suggest that visits and visitors, stimulus objects, sounds and events might form the bulk of such experiences.

Potent experiences can occur in the mind too. Well-presented opportunities to read or write, make or listen to music, watch or participate in performances, produce or appreciate art, invent or play games or quietly reflect, need to be planned into the child's experience. The character and setting of such events should also arise from, and contribute to, the school's agreed set of core values. Planning a series of *generative experiences* (Perkins, 1992) is in many ways the most important set of curriculum decisions teachers and other adults can make. The same 'happening' will not be generative for all children – some will be unaffected by an experience that adults feel sure would interest all children – so a range of passive, active, interior, exterior, creative and practical encounters should be planned.

One Year 8 class in Birmingham were taken to the top of the Malvern Hills for an enriching and inspiring geography field course. Their teacher reported on her return that they were totally unmoved, disinterested and unfocused. When the next week the same group were taken to their own shopping street for well-prepared and detailed fieldwork on the shops and services there, the class reported that it had been their best day's work ever. When asked to explain, a female student said, 'We were really happy you had taken the trouble to find out lots of stuff about our place'.

Asking key questions

With older age groups it is often a good idea to unite the thinking and learning under a single overarching question which will give explicit purpose to learning (see Blythe, 1998). Such key questions should address the issues which preoccupy people at any intellectual level. Both the university professor and the young child are interested in the big questions of life: Who are we? Where are we going? What's the meaning of it all? Peter Abbs (2003) would suggest that any questions which touch upon the existential would be likely to draw the child in to active participation in his or her learning; for example:

- What is my responsibility to the environment?
- What are my dreams for the future?
- Who is my neighbour?
- What does it mean to be alive?
- What is war like?
- How does learning about other cultures help me understand about myself?
- What does it mean to 'come of age' and how does it differ across time, culture and gender? (See Richhart, 2002.)

Howard Gardner (1999b) has devoted a whole book to examining the curriculum implications of three questions: What is beauty? What is truth? What is good/evil?

Balancing experience, skills and knowledge

Experiences cannot be fully understood or expressed without interpreting them through the skills and subject knowledge of the appropriate disciplines. Questions cannot be very satisfactorily answered unless there is a precise vocabulary with which to answer them. Any engaging, sustainable and relevant curriculum, therefore, should have a balance between subject craft-skills and knowledge, on the one hand, and opportunities for personal expression, on the other. The proposed six-or seven-week themed units are seen as taking up half the week each week. This allows eventually for full immersion in the skills and crafted products of experts who have responded to similar themes.

For the first three weeks and after their visit to a Second World War 'experience' in a local museum for example, children may be plunged into a range of poetry and prose about war. In other sessions they may learn about several musicians' responses to war and the timbres, structures and motifs they used to communicate. They might also make detailed analyses of the various forms of evidence upon which historians base their judgements about the Second World War. Only after such immersion and periods of direct skills and knowledge teaching, will children be in a position to make informed decisions about their responses to the overarching question: What is war like? Only after knowing something of the craft-skills which writers, historians and musicians apply to the theme of war can learners satisfyingly apply those skills themselves. Such an approach is self-differentiating. In applying newly learned skills, children may ask for support or more information; teachers may sense new opportunities to present factual information or re-teach from alternative starting points. In the second three weeks, learning is increasingly focused upon the children's personal and emotional responses to what they have learned.

Perhaps earlier in their school career children might be led to ask, 'What is so important about water?' Teachers may have decided to use the skills of science, geography and RE to answer this question. The timetable for the term might look like this:

Table 8.2   A medium teem plan for a 'Why is water so important' topic

Monday	Core Literacy/English	Core Numeracy/maths	RE (Water theme)	Geography (Water theme)
Tuesday	Core History	Literacy/English (Water theme)	Cross-curricular (Water theme)	Cross-curricular (Water theme)
Wednesday	Core Numeracy/maths	Core Design and technology	Core PE	Core Art
Thursday	Science (Water theme)	Science (Water theme)	Creative Literacy/English (Water theme)	Core Music
Friday	Core Literacy/ English/MFL	Ongoing Investigative Numeracy/maths	Cross-curricular (Water theme)	Cross-curricular (Water theme)

Such a timetable is flexible enough to allow for the essential visit, visitor or responses to specific issues arising from the visit. In the example above, science, geography, RE and English are the focus subjects, but other curriculum subjects are still represented every week. In the following term substantially more time may be given to mathematics, history and PE. In the subsequent term art, design and technology and modern foreign languages may have the floor. A timetable like this is not very radical and fits easily within established approaches. More adventurous schools may wish to devote more time to the theme, but half a week each week for six weeks is sufficient to build successfully upon the generative experience for each child.

Short-term (weekly) plans

The plan in Table 8.3 gives further detail on the key skills to be developed in a single week in three chosen curriculum subjects. The week is an imagined follow-up to a visit to a waterworks not far from the school. Engaging activities included group discussion of a particular challenge, fieldwork in the school

Table 8.3 Medium-term plan for a Year 5 subject programme

Powerful experience		Working visit to a waterworks/river/lake					
Key question		Why is water so important?					
	Week A	Week 1	Week 2	Week 3	Week 4	Week 5	Week 6
Science *Subject questions*	VISIT	In what ways do we use water? What was going on at the water works?	What is the water cycle?	How does water work in my body	How does water move around my house?	How does water affect the plant world?	How do plants affect the water supply?
Subject skills and knowledge	VISIT	Brainstorm, asking questions/ follow up Suspension of earth/sand Water filtration/ separation Water filters	Reversible Changes of state of water Temperature Evaporation Observations records Diagrams and drawings condensation	Teaching about water in the body Water for good health Keeping clean Water and micro organisms	Observation, diagrams, domestic context of water Gravity and the movement of water around the house Scientific language Water and hazards Cleaning water	Effect of water on growth of plants Water taken into plants roots, into stem and to leaves Water and adaptation	Need to protect plants Food chains and plants Forests and rainfall
Geography	VISIT	What happens to water when it falls as rain on the school?	What happens to the water that falls on our streets and landscapes?	What is a river?	What part do rivers play in our lives?	What part does a river play in the life of a locality in Egypt/India/ Tanzania?	What about world/local water shortages? What about wealth and water? Is distribution fair? How can we help conserve water around the school/ at home?

(Continued)

Table 8.3 (Continued)

		Working visit to a waterworks/river/lake				
Powerful experience						
Key question		*Why is water so important?*				
	Week A	Week 1	Week 2	Week 3	Week 4	Week 5	Week 6

	Week A	Week 1	Week 2	Week 3	Week 4	Week 5	Week 6
Skills and knowledge		Using photographs Fieldwork Downhill movement	Mapping fieldwork Data collection Presenting data about locality Water disposal/supply systems	Map work (1) (symbols) Diagrams Fieldwork Field sketching Features of a river	Map work (2) (interpretation) Locality/case studies Questions Functions of a river	Atlas work Map work Using photos Distant place case study Detailed study of Nile transport	Plans Geographical enquiry on water shortages, the Internet Conservation improvements Change in the environment
Religious education		What has water got to do with religion?	Water as a symbol/metaphor	Water in religious stories	How is my life like a river?	Water haikus	Water makes you think about …
Skills and knowledge		Religious stories	The use of metaphor and parable	Reflection on meaning in stories	Reflecting on own feelings	Capturing feelings and emotions (self and others)	Role play on fairness

Table 8.4 Short-term plan on the key skills to be developed in a single week in three curriculum subjects

Year group and session	Year 5 week 2 (after visit)		
Focus subjects	*Science*	*Geography*	*PSHE and Citizenship*
Term theme	*Why is water so important?*		
Overarching question(s) for whole theme	*What is my responsibility to the environment?* *How does scientific method help me understand my world?*		
Understanding goal(s) for week's sessions	*1. In what ways is water important?* *2. What is it and where does it come from?* *3. What can I do to help conserve water?* *4. Why should I conserve water?*		
Session 1 (after visit)	*Pool everything class knows about water and how it is used. Answering question 1. Keep a log of water use in 24 hours. Discuss appropriate format. Discuss conservation (question 3)*	*Where is there natural water near the school? Where does it come from, where does it go? What happens to rain water when it falls on the school? Answering question 2*	*Working in groups Discussions leading to answer question 4. Presentations or debate related to class work*
Programme of study reference	2a. Ask questions which can be investigated scientifically 2b. Consider sources of information including first hand experience	6c. Water and its effect on landscapes and people. Water as a precious and finite resource (see Follow-up lesson below)	2a. Researching and discussing topical issues problems and events
Attainment level	Lev. 4. Recognize that scientific ideas are based upon evidence Decide on an appropriate approach to answer the question from a science point of view	Lev. 4 Recognizing and describing physical processes Describing geographical patterns relating to water in the local environment	Developing a sense of moral responsibility, Begin to understand that their own choices and behaviour can affect local national and global issues

Table 8.4   *(Continued)*

Focus Subjects	*Science*	*Geography*	*PSHE and Citizenship*
Assessment	Encourage children to be thorough and provide detailed examples Accuracy and detail of records in logs	Accuracy and detail of annotations on school photo or river maps	Degree of participation, sensitivity to others, patience
Differentiation	*Open questions:* What would happen if … ? What are the links between … ?	*Open questions:* How else might … ? What do you guess … ?	*Open questions:* What sorts of things can we do here and now? What might the impact of … be?
Research and subject skills	Keeping a log Personal experience Comparing and presenting findings	Using a photograph, using maps Recognizing and interpreting water symbols	Group discussion/ debate. Rules of debate

grounds, the keeping of a 24-hour log of water use for homework and within school, the group presentation of findings from research and debate. There is a consciousness of the big theme ('My responsibility to the environment' and 'The significance of the scientific method'), but the weekly understanding goals focus on the smaller steps towards answering the overarching questions.

A lesson, or short-term, subject plan

The sample lesson plan below shows the level of detail required to ensure learning of skills, knowledge and attitudes in a single subject. It describes how new skills and knowledge will be introduced on the back of the visit. It also shows how children will be led towards applying their newly gained knowledge to a fresh situation. The concept of 'dipping in and out' of the topic are well illustrated in this geography plan, which combines teaching key geography skills out of context and then giving children the opportunity of applying them *in* context.

FOLLOW-UP LESSON AFTER VISIT TO FIELD STUDY CENTRE

KEY GEOGRAPHICAL QUESTIONS	• *Where is there natural water near the school?* • *Where does it come from where does it go?* • *What happens to rain water when it falls on the school?*
NATIONAL C. REFERENCE	6c. Water and its effect on landscapes and people
PREVIOUS LEARNING	*Class had visited a small nature reserve run by the local electricity substation. This consisted of a number of small lakes and a river with a nature trail around them. The class were taught the words: lake, stream, channel, source, flood plain, bed, erosion*
GEOGRAPHICAL VOCABULARY	*Condensation, evaporation, weathering, spring, channel, slope, pollution, flood, deposition*
CLASSROOM ORGANIZATION FIELD WORK	• Trip outside to playground to annotate photo • Observe action of water on sand pile
INTRODUCTION: LINKS WITH DAILY LIFE	• *Remind class about visit to the lakes and confirm level of understanding of water cycle* • *Compare the lakes with the school building in the rain. What happens to the water in the lakes? What happens in the school grounds? How does it get dirty? What happens to the dirt? Why do they think there were no houses near the lake? Elicit:* **puddles, evaporation, condensation, run off, slope, flood, rainfall, pollution** *in the answers*
DEVELOPMENT (New skills and knowledge)	**Teach about flooding and deposition using the pile of sand in the playground** **Teach (using diagrams) about similar signs of erosion on the river bank** **Teach (using data collection sheet) about weathering using observations on the school building and playground as examples**
APPLICATION to topic theme	*Show: how water defines aspects of settlements, how water adds variety to life (natural and our own), how change happens constantly in processes of erosion, deposition and weathering and how people respond to it.*
ASSESSMENT	Children construct a poster called 'Water and Change'. They can use the school, the playground, the lakes or another place where water features prominently to express the term *change*
CREATIVE THINKING POSSIBILITIES	**Decisions about: examples of change, visual and verbal means of communication and conversations about priorities. How can we conserve water more effectively in our daily lives?**

✦ How can we help generate an atmosphere where conversations about children's learning are common?

✦ How can we minimize on the paperwork whilst maximizing the quality learning experience for the children?

✦ How can we ensure that understanding is expressed in visual, graphical, movement, artistic, creative, aural, numeric and interpersonal *as well as* linguistic ways?

✦ What is the advantage in planning in teams?

Further reading

Gardner, H. (2000) *The Disciplined Mind*, New York: Simon and Schuster.

Jeffrey, B. and Woods, P. (2003) *The Creative School*, London: Routledge.

Wineburg, S. and Grossman, P. (2000) *Interdisciplinary Curriculum: Challenges to Implementation*, New York: Teachers College Press.

CHAPTER 9

How Can We Assess Cross-Curricular and Creative Learning?

In this chapter I want to argue that *summative* assessment, that is, assessment which sums up the learning in a specific unit or over a particular period, is not a useful tool for cross-curricular or creative learning. It may be useful within pure subject-based contexts and is definitely helpful in transitional contexts. *Formative* assessment, or assessment for learning, however, can very easily and helpfully be used in all creative and cross-curricular activity. I also discuss *peer assessment* as a valuable and highly motivating assessment tool which often gives as much benefit to the assessor as to the assessed.

The idea of *presenting* understanding before a final performance will be examined in closer detail with the suggestion that such presentations are potentially a key growth point in any medium-term scheme of work. Children grow in understanding through their own presentations. They become aware of the gaps in their own understanding, they receive more easily the advice of their peers with whom they have shared the challenges and problems, and they grow in confidence.

The most important and lasting of assessments are those we make on ourselves. In periods of deep and positive engagement in learning, one of the attributes which most sustains our concentration is the feedback we get immediately from others or we give ourselves. This vital component of flow has been frequently observed in relevant cross-curricular learning activity. This chapter ends by a reminder of other aspects of flow which are observably generated in the types of thematic and creative work examined in this book.

Is it worth assessing?

Teachers continually assess. We are not always aware of it, but we assess as we ask questions and listen to answers. We assess as we sense the atmosphere of a room full of pupils or when we visit tables on various tours around the class. And we assess as we listen to the questions, comments and chatter of children engaged in work or play throughout the school day and beyond. Assessment has always been part of the teacher's role, though it has not always been against progressive, planned, articulated and monitored learning objectives. From the earliest days of formal education we know that teachers kept detailed mark books and made school reports: summative assessments of individual progress in reading, writing, tables, arithmetic, Latin, general knowledge. From such school assessments we can see, for example, that Isaac Newton, Albert Einstein, Winston Churchill and John Lennon were clearly destined for a lifetime of failure!

More frequent, stringent, statutory, uniform and formalized assessment has become a noticeable feature of all teaching since the 1980s. This new push for assessment was intended to measure relative success at learning, promote further learning, check the appropriateness of teaching and keep children 'on task'. With the advent of SATs, voluntary SATs, booster classes in English and maths and, of course, published league tables of school results, English children are amongst the most assessed in the world. Modern assessments serve a variety of purposes. They give an update on a child's progress to parents and carers. For governors they give confidence that the school is fulfilling its legal responsibilities. They also serve to inform of school progress (in the core subjects only) against other similar schools or its own previous record. For school principals, heads or subject coordinators they may serve to monitor the success of a particular teacher in delivering the core subjects. If you are an OFSTED inspector you may use records of assessments to assess curriculum coverage, age-appropriate expectations and ensure an adequate degree of accountability on the part of the teacher. Whilst assessments are expected in all foundation subjects and RE, the assessments most consulted during inspections are, of course, the core subjects of English, mathematics and science. None of the official functions of assessment matter very much to most children, and yet assessment intended to promote *further learning* can be a most productive and positive part of a teacher's interaction with the child.

The kind of curriculum put forward in this book relates to the personal growth and fulfilment of children and the part education can play in it. Illich, and many since his day, remind us that personal growth is ultimately not a measurable entity. But there are some things that can be productively measured along the way so that we teachers can be assured we are supporting children in their journey.

Summative assessment

Teachers and parents need to know whether teaching has been successful in adding to the child's understanding. We need to know whether their style, pace, chosen content or time allocations should be changed to generate more

Illustration 9.1   *Children participating in a 'big conversation' with Scotland's Deputy Minister for Children and Young People and the Children's Commissioner for Scotland.* Courtesy of Scottish Children's Parliament

success next time. In order to be sure that a crucial learning objective has been met, some form of assessment must be carried out. But none of these legitimate needs of teachers require summative assessment. Summative assessment is a *final* measurement of a child's achievement, perhaps before entering a new school, a new phase or perhaps a new class. It is literally the summing up of a child's learning at a particular point. Because there is no redress from a truly summative assessment, it is not a particularly helpful spur to future learning. Neither are summative assessments necessarily accurate measurements of success in life, if, for example, one considers the dismal school reports on notable characters such as Richard Branson, Agatha Christie, Susan Hampshire or Whoopi Goldberg. Summative assessments add little to our understanding of creative or cross-curricular learning activities in schools.

Formative assessment

Formative assessment is assessment intended to take the child forward on their learning journey. The concept of formative assessment or 'assessment for learning' has been current for many years. British schools paid lip-service to its importance throughout the 1990s, when the National Curriculum was being launched. However, the NACCCE report in 1999 (paras 200–11) noted its relatively minor importance in school procedures and argued for a more privileged place for formative assessment (Recommendation 5). In the same year as the NACCCE investigations were being conducted, researchers Black and Wiliam (1998) found that, at its best, formative assessment could achieve the following:

- raising children's attainment
- increasing their self-esteem
- giving them a greater stake in their learning
- enabling a greater prospect of 'lifelong learning'.

In an 18-month project on formative assessment, led by educationalist Shirley Clarke, teachers were introduced to now familiar terms such as 'learning intentions', 'success criteria' and 'pupil self-evaluation' (Clarke, 2001, website). Even after only a term of serious application teachers felt able to credit the *assessment for learning* techniques she had introduced, with the following benefits:

- Children liked knowing the learning intentions and success criteria.
- Most teachers saw benefit in sharing the learning intentions and success criteria.
- Seventy-five per cent of teachers said that children understood tasks better.
- Almost all teachers said that sharing learning intentions and success criteria had had a positive effect on their teaching.
- Just under half of lessons involved successful use of self-evaluation questions.
- Most teachers said children were no longer afraid to make mistakes and were more able to admit to difficulties.
- Half of the teachers said that children of all abilities are able to access self-evaluation questions.
- Two-thirds of children had some perception of the true point of self-evaluation.
- Of the teachers who tried pupil self-evaluation, almost all said it had a positive effect on their teaching.

Findings like these are highly relevant to assessing cross-curricular activities in the classroom. The personally meaningful, less formal and open-ended nature of much cross-curricular learning, lends itself well to the idea of self-evaluation and the creation of a positive atmosphere which accepts mistakes as a vital part of learning. There are many ways of managing formative assessment: the informal feedback of the concerned teacher as he or she moves around the class offering help, posing questions and listening to observations, the formal marking of class work or the informal testing of certain factual knowledge in order to identify barriers to learning. However, each of these can be something of a 'bolt-on' assessment, not truly integrated with the, hopefully, vital activity of the topic of study. The concept of the performance of understanding was devised by David Perkins, Tina Blythe and their associates at Project Zero (Project Zero, 2006, website), the educational research arm of Harvard's Graduate School of Education.

Performances of understanding

The performance of understanding as a form of formative assessment was mentioned briefly in Chapter 7 when suitable themes for cross-curricular learning were discussed. This is a term coined by Professor David Perkins and expounded upon by Tina Blythe in her book, *The Teaching for Understanding Guide* (Blythe, 1998). Simply expressed, performance of understanding is a curriculum opportunity for a child or a group of children to demonstrate the depth and degree of their learning by applying it in a new situation. This 'performance' is not literally a dramatic or musical performance (though it might be), but a chance publicly to show learning. It may be:

- a collection
- a construction
- a dance
- a debate
- a demonstration ...
- a diagram
- a led discussion
- a map or plan
- a meal
- a mime
- a newspaper article
- a piece of music
- a play
- a poem
- a poster
- a reading
- a recital
- a song
- a talk
- a walk or guided tour
- an annotated drawing
- an annotated drawing
- an essay
- an exhibition
- an experiment
- an exposition.

or any combination of these and other ways of communicating understanding, but the essence of the performance of understanding is that the 'performer(s)' have not previously expressed their understanding of the topic in this way. (Illustration 9.2)

A class in a performing arts school in Kent has been carrying out cross-curricular learning related to the earthquake on the Kashmir/Pakistan border. The theme was planned to cover six weeks (see Table 9.1 below). Using the skills and learning the relevant knowledge in geography, they were introduced

Illustration 9.2   *A performance of Understanding. Children explaining their responses to a 'health and happiness' workshop in Scotland.* Courtesy Scottish Children's Parliament

through maps, videos, newspaper reports, diagrams and photographs to the landscape, weather and economic conditions in the area. They were also given a direct teaching session on what causes earthquakes. They studied the normal daily lives and religion of a community living there through both RE and geographical perspectives. Their PSHE lesson with newspapers told them a great deal about conditions there directly after the earthquake and in the cold months of winter 2005–06 and they thought about different ways of reporting such news. A friend of the school, who was born near the affected region of Kashmir, spoke to the class about his life there and answered questions during another PSHE/Citizenship lesson. In another geography lesson they considered in detail what conditions must be like in the community they studied and used an email link with a charity to get up-to-date information on the aid effort. They have learned about Kashmiri cooking and culture from a local cultural group and some parents.

Since the school was based in a large area of open countryside with considerable grounds, rural science and gardening formed a significant part of the curriculum. The children decided to use their work and talents to grow food for sale to friends and parents in order to raise money for their identified project connected with the disaster. This was to extend aspects of the theme and the associated learning through the next term.

The final taught week of this very relevant and emotive theme consisted of children planning and mounting a charity collection for the victims of the natural disaster. The teacher was on hand as adviser, but had little idea of what aspects children would choose as the focus of their final week presentations to parents. The charity event eventually planned included four themed PowerPoint presentations on a village in Kashmir from a group of four children, who used their own maps, photographs found on the Internet and information

Table 9.1 The Kashmiri/Pakistani earthquake. A six week plan leading to a fund-raising event

Week 1 theme	Week 2 theme	Week 3 theme	Week 4 theme	Week 5 theme	Week 6 theme
Introduction With video/newspapers Children's comments and questions	Physical geography Maps Diagrams	What happened to the villages? What life is like now for the survivors	What religion tells us about natural disasters/helping our neighbour	Kashmiri culture. Food, clothing, music, dance	Fund-raising week for the Kashmiri earthquake
Demonstrating subject understanding	*Demonstrating subject understanding*	*Demonstrating subject understanding*	*Demonstrating subject understanding*	*Demonstrating subject understanding*	*Performance of understanding*
Geog. Cit. Asking geographical/ citizenship questions	**Geog.** Constructing maps Understanding diagrams and photographs	**Geog.** Making intelligent guesses based upon geographical understandings. Suggesting possible improvements and solutions	**RE** Asking spiritual questions Understanding spiritual dimension **Cit.** Our role in disaster relief The role of aid agencies	**D/T** cooking, designing menu **Music** Recognizing pattern, pitch and applying knowledge to own compositions	**Geog** PowerPoint presentations on geog. of Kasmir **RE** Play on caring for hungry and homeless. **Cit.** Kashmir in the news; The facts **D/T** Kashmiri menu, planned and served.

from aid agencies. Kashmiri cakes and rice were cooked, presented and served by an appropriately dressed group of six children. A further five decided to mount their own exhibition on the current state of affairs in the region using their own maps, material sent by an aid agency, collected newspaper cuttings and re-presented information from the Internet. A group of six chose to perform a short play based upon an Islamic tale about helping the hungry and homeless, but set it in the mountains of Kashmir. Three other children created a detailed and accurate mountainous backdrop. Finally a group of five children decided to write and duplicate a newspaper-style fact sheet for parents and guests to take home with them. This was extended in subsequent terms to bring news of the money-raising fruit and vegetable sales.

During the preparation week before the final day of performances, each group was asked a number of times to rehearse what they were going to do/say/show to the rest of the class, and the class was encouraged to offer advice or ask questions which resulted in improvements. This process of refinement significantly raised the stakes and markedly improved standards through peer assessment. On the last day, each activity refocused attention on the main theme (and in the process generated a great deal of money for the cause) but throughout the week teachers were able to use the various demonstrations of subject understanding to help them assess the level of learning of each individual against National Curriculum levels.

These assessments were in no way summative; they were intended to have a positive effect upon present and future learning. During this last week of the project, teachers were able to act less like instructors and more like coaches. In this role they were able actively to point to possible improvements or ask formative questions during the mounting of exhibitions, painting of scenery or cooking of food. During and after the event they were able to involve the children themselves in their own self-assessment:

Children's peer assessment questions

- What went well? Why do you think it went so well?
- What did you enjoy most? Why?
- Whose work do you think communicated best? Why?
- What did you like about [N's] presentation?
- What would you do to improve your presentation, if you had another chance?
- What still puzzles you about what [N] said/showed?
- Has the project as a whole left you with any questions?

During the final week and after the event, teachers had multiple opportunities to make records of the level of subject understanding displayed by individuals. Teachers noticed the questions children asked of other groups, their responses to the suggestions of others, individual application within their own group and the level of subject understanding shown in rehearsals and performance. On average

Illustration 9.3 *Peer assessment in action. Children passing focused and positive comments to other participating groups after a practical workshop. Courtesy Scottish Children's Parliament*

one teacher assessed six children a day, and on some days subject coordinators were invited to make subject specific assessments. The organizing teacher made a further 15 assessments during the final performances. The collected observations and records during this themed term demonstrated a host of individual achievements which will be referred to in end-of-year reports. They were used to ensure that each class member was given opportunities in the next term to build upon new learning or to guide them to demonstrate new skills in other subject areas.

Presentations and peer assessment

In teaching the arts there is a well-known cycle of activities known as the *Processes of the Arts* (Robinson, 1990). This cycle may start at any point, but includes activities generic to the arts, such as exploring, forming, presenting, evaluating and performing. The concept of *presenting* is considered quite distinct from performing and I believe this distinction may usefully be applied across the curriculum well beyond the arts. Presenting in Robinson's model consists of taking time out of an activity to show colleagues what has been formed, learned, understood *so far*. There is no pretence that this is a performance; it is certainly 'work in progress' and has an important peer assessment function. When a group or individual has the chance to demonstrate its, his or her subject understanding in a consciously provisional setting, where everyone knows it is 'not finished yet', a real opportunity to 'raise the game' presents itself. (Illustration 9.3)

In cross-curricular settings like that outlined above (and in Chapter 2) each group in the class will have been engaged in related activities. Hopefully, the class ethos is one of mutual support, confidence and a relaxed attitude to mistakes; each group will understand the issues confronting the others. When they hold up *their* work in progress for comment, giving feedback, learning from others' insights and receiving feedback from others assumes a personally engaging, relevant and wholly formative character. Many children have reported that it is in these situations they learn most – their peers have become their teachers. Indeed, David Perkins makes such 'distributed cognition', that is, thinking shared across the group, the central theme of his views on learnable intelligence (Sternberg and Williams, 1998). (Illustration 9.4)

Illustration 9.4 *Student teachers presenting their understanding of place for their peers to comment upon*

Table 9.2   A simple format for (individual or group) peer assessment

Assessment focus	Examples
Say two things you really liked about the presentation.	• I really liked the way you started that piece off with a very simple tune and then changed it in little ways each time we heard it. • I especially liked the way you told us how you thought about a castle servant's life.
Ask about two things which puzzle you.	• Why did you decide to paint on the frame as well? • What made you think of using water for power instead of air? • Did you think of using any other instruments? • Why did you finish in that way?
Offer one point of advice	• Next time you present this, I think you should … • Have you thought of …? • Do you think you could …?

Here are two haikus on the subject of barriers, which started with observations in the school playground. They were composed by 8-year-olds. How would you formatively assess them? What would you pick out as particularly good? What would you want to ask? Do you have any advice?

Soft silky cobwebs

Attached upon the great wall

Silky carpenter's lodge. (Figure 9.1)

Joshua   Wednesday 20th
July 2005.

Soft Silky cobwebs
attached apon the great wall,
Silk - carpenter's lodge

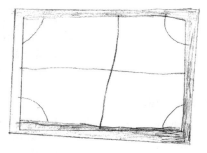

Figure 9.1   An 8-year-old responds to the tiny detail of his immediate environment

(Continued)

(Continued)

Green nettles that sting

Grow very deep in the grass

Waiting to hurt you. (Figure 9.2)

Figure 9.2   Haiku by an 8-year-old girl on the same theme

Self-assessment

The benefits of presentation do not end with peer appraisal. Presentation can be a non-threatening way of provoking *self-criticism*. In publicly presenting understanding so far, the presenters themselves are more likely to be made aware of the gaps in their own understanding. Presenting itself can become a form of learning, feedback coming instantly from the individual self or the 'group self'. This links back to Csikszentmihayli's concept of flow, one of its universal characteristics is 'rapid feedback', which often follows naturally from a self wholly engaged in an activity. Indeed, as you look at the examples of cross-curricular activities in the previous section or Chapter 2, you might see that *all* the conditions of flow are likely to be present.

- *Time seemed altered* for many of the children as they became engrossed in activities they had chosen within the theme.
- Skills were introduced to the children either during cross-curricular sessions or in subject-specific lessons. These were then applied in the cross-curricular context.
- Playground, home or relationship *worries* apparently *diminished* during cross-curricular activities in a number of the case studies quoted.
- It appeared from observing the faces and interactions of children during case study observations that they were *less self-consciousness*.
- The *confidence* of children during presentations and performances was one of the features most remarked upon by parents and teachers.
- The intense engagement of children in activities observed and described suggests that they were being enjoyed for *their own sake*. There was frequently a sense that individual children became *'lost' in an activity*.

Cross-curricular learning will, of course, only generate flow under circumstances where it takes place within the supportive and secure environment already fully discussed. It will only flourish when curriculum challenges are carefully planned to put specifically introduced skills and knowledge into action. Full engagement for the vast majority is only likely when a theme or activity has taken on some kind of existential importance to the children. But, under these circumstances, cross-curricular activity itself may generate its own formative assessment of a highly personal and meaningful kind. Such reflexive self-assessment will also prepare the child's mind to receive kindly assessments and additional challenges from others.

Written reflections of a Year 6 child after a cross-curricular project in the school environmental area

I felt really calm in the environment area, although I have been there loads of times before I hadn't really paid so much attention to everything ... My favourite activities were the object focus and when we laid [*sic*] down and looked up at the sky through the eyes of our object. I felt really quiet as I studied my chosen object, and we all know that doesn't happen very often! It felt kind of nice and relaxed and peaceful, but the time went really quickly and I could have spent longer out here ... I feel that we are working so well together ...

Illustration 9.5   *This year 1 child is talking to his Teaching Assistant about the practicality of his plans for a new playground. Flow is evident in his concentration and commitment*

Assessing engagement

Looking for the outward signs of flow is a good way of assessing the degree of engagement, and therefore learning, in a child. Much of significance can be missed if teachers fail to look at the faces and postures of their children at work (Barnes, 2005f). Student teachers should make consideration of the facial and bodily expressions of involvement a conscious part of their evaluations. We should all make ourselves continually aware of the non-verbal signs children are giving us. Belgian educator Ferre Laevers has been influential in formulating a useable five-point scale to measure the physical signs of such involvement (the Leuven Involvement Scale, LIS). According to this scale a child's degree of participation can be measured as shown in Table 9.3.

Table 9.3   Measure of a child's degree of participation

Level 1	No activity, the child mentally absent and stereotypic repetition of elementary movements
Level 2	Actions with many interruptions
Level 3	Actions more concerted, but concentration seems lacking and motivation and pleasure are lacking.
Level 4	Moments of intense mental activity shown by times of concentration beyond the routine
Level 5	Total involvement expressed by full concentration, signs of enjoyment and absorption. Any disturbance or interruption is experienced as frustrating.

Source: adapted from Laevers (1994)

Linking this work with the research of Ekman and others into facial expression, teachers and others working with children, quickly come to recognize the range of facial expressions of engagement. Responding unconsciously to such facial and bodily nuances is probably part of our biological inheritance, but bringing that understanding into the consciousness and attempting to generate particular expressions of engagement or enjoyment could significantly add to the effectiveness of teaching.

Key questions

+ How can we make assessment meaningful and a useful learning tool?
+ How can we promote distributed cognition as part of the daily experience of children in school?
+ What should be the balance of flow experiences and more mundane activities in class?
+ Should subject skills and knowledge be assessed in a different way from their cross curricular application?

Further reading

Krechevsky, M. (1998) *Project Spectrum: Preschool Assessment Handbook*, New York: Teachers College Press.

Laevers, F. (1994) *Defining and Assessing Quality in Early Childhood Education*, Leuven: Leuven University Press.

Sternberg, R. and Williams, W. (1998) *Intelligence, Instruction and Assessment: Theory into Practice*, Mahwah, NJ: Lawrence Erlbaum.

Chapter 10

Key Issues for Debate

This chapter can be used to inform staff meetings, discussions and planning meetings. It is intended to provoke discussions which will have an impact upon future ethos, management, planning, delivery, learning and personal experience in school.

Teachers do not have to choose between *either* subject disciplines *or* thematic methods, but should have *both*. Cross-curricular approaches to teaching and learning are not the universal panacea for the current educational, personal and social challenges facing us. Sometimes using de-contextualized didactic approaches may be necessary to maintain a sense of challenge, favour certain subject skills and knowledge and ensure measurable progression. Alongside cross-curricular and creative modes of teaching and learning, instruction and coaching in skills and knowledge within the *separate*d disciplines are often important. A similar sense of balance should be evident in all discussions aimed at finding an appropriate curriculum for the twenty-first century.

Cross-curricular approaches have been argued to provide greater motivation for children. But, motivation may come from many sources and inspire children differently, and apply differently in various societies and systems. We need generously to allow for cultural and personal differences and avoid seeking one-size-fits-all answers. We saw in Chapter 1 that change is rapid and apparently inexorable, but the fact of inevitable change does not mean that everything has to change. As discussed in Chapter 6, there may be some absolutes, some principles which can transcend the technological, societal and organizational revolution. At a time in history when one culture attempts to spread its brand of democracy to the rest of the world, concepts of power, who holds it, its negotiability, ability to be shared and its appropriateness for children, are hotly debated. Individuality, creativity, globalization, the 'litigation and surveillance culture', changing roles of school and other institutions and the behaviour of young people are rarely out of the news. What follows is a personal response to some of these issues; deliberately provocative, obviously open to question, but an attempt to mark out areas for productive debate in staff rooms, seminar groups and school councils.

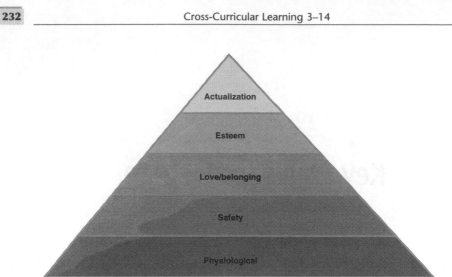

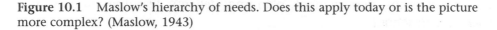

Figure 10.1   Maslow's hierarchy of needs. Does this apply today or is the picture more complex? (Maslow, 1943)

Motivation

As I visit class after class in different schools in widely contrasting parts of the UK and the world, I feel increasingly confident to suggest that motivation is the key to efficient, satisfying and lifelong learning. Research for the Organization for Economic Cooperation and Development (OECD) pinpoints motivation as the main factor in learning (OECD, 2003).

Although devised in the first half of the last century, Maslow's notion of a *hierarchy of needs* remains an interesting model to describe various sources of motivation (Maslow, 1943).

Observing classes of 7–16-year-olds over the past six years in rapidly developing regions such as south India, Indonesia or East Africa, I see and hear from children that the most common source of motivation towards learning stems from a desire for a life economically more secure than that of their parents. In the developing countries of the world and in the poorer sections of developed economies, physiological and economic security needs dominate. Learning for many children in the developing world is an instrumental activity providing them with the basic skills, knowledge and certificates successfully to compete for jobs in an increasingly tough and global jobs market. The ideological model of education predominant in these countries is close to 'classical humanism', with emphasis upon the authority of the teacher, a didactic and subject-based approach to teaching, and learning generally more reliant upon memory, repetition and an easy facility with language. Education in these contexts is seen as a means of liberation from poverty. Whilst love, belonging, self-esteem and self-actualization appear abundantly present in the lives of the vast majority of observed children, these can be argued to come from wider cultural and family contexts; they are not dominant features of the school agenda in the developing world. Existing within cultures which typically value such qualities as trustworthiness, spiritual interpretations, respect for elders and hard work, schools might appear to be places where peers are trusted, there is little bullying and children's own sense of life satisfaction is high. Globalization, in the form of Internet, Sky TV, the Discovery Channel, mobile phones and World Bank-sponsored curriculum revision, is now, however, changing attitudes, educational practice and philosophy in these countries, (see Layard, 2005; Wrigley, 2005). For many in the developing world, probably the majority, the sense that education is the route towards 'betterment' remains a powerful motivation. Such strong motivation easily overpowers any sense that the teaching and learning methods might be boring, de-contextualized, lacking opportunities for practical application and repetitive.

A very different story presents itself in some developed economies. Ask a similar age group of children in the UK or USA about school and aspects pertaining to their general well-being in school, and the results may reflect the following figures from the World Health Organization (2004):

- Forty-three per cent of English 11-year-olds (35 per cent in the USA) report having been bullied in the past few months.

- Sixty-three per cent of 11-year-old English boys (45 per cent in the USA) admit to having been involved in physical fighting in the previous year.

- Only 50 per cent of English (USA, 60 per cent) 11-year-olds agree that their peers are 'kind and helpful' (this compares with 82 per cent in Scotland and 87 per cent in Macedonia).

- Forty per cent of 11-year-old boys in England (USA, 38 per cent) feel 'pressured by schoolwork' (this compares with 5 per cent in the Netherlands).

- Only 15 per cent of English (USA, 18 per cent) children at 13 could say they 'liked school a lot' (this compares with 60 per cent in Macedonia) (WHO, 2004, website).

Such statistics suggest that a significant percentage of our children are unlikely to be well motivated by the education, relationships or ethos pervading in their schools. The physiological, physical and security needs of western children may generally be more fulfilled than those of their Indian counterparts, but based on WHO report findings it could be argued that the westerners have greater needs on Maslow's esteem, love and actualization levels. Psychologist Viktor Frankl noted a decade ago that the feeling of meaninglessness had become rife since the 1950s (Frankl, 1992). Such an analysis could have wide educational implications. Perhaps government, and all institutions directly impacting upon children's lives, should do significantly more to develop opportunities for self-actualization and meaning-making. Where else *should* schools start than by attempting to build trusting relationships within the communities they influence? The construction of self-esteem, the redevelopment of community, support for family and an understanding of what it is to love, trust and belong may be fundamental to deep learning itself.

Questions for discussion:

- Do you think motivation is an important feature in learning? Give some examples.
- Are there any specific kinds of activity which you have noticed motivate most children in your class/Year 7/Year R?
- What can we learn about motivation from observing children's play?
- How do we go about motivating the unmotivated child?
- What should government do to promote life satisfaction in children?
- What can we do?

Managing change

There are many barriers to the establishment of creative and cross-curricular approaches. First, many teachers may feel comfortable with the present, typical balance of literacy and numeracy hours in the morning and the QCA schemes of work in the afternoon. When the QCA guidance and schemes of work for national curriculum subjects (QCA, 1998a, 2000) were published, there was a general sigh of relief from many overloaded teachers. This guidance quickly became an unofficial national curriculum and there is evidence that significant numbers of teachers and student teachers felt themselves to be professionally deskilled by being encouraged to depend too heavily on de-contextualized and externally prepared formulae (PWC, 2001; Smithers and Robinson, 2001, website).

If teachers are to establish a more creative curriculum, then they must first feel that they are capable of being creative themselves. A current lack of opportunity to invent their own lessons and schemes of work, or respond quickly to children's unplanned-for interests may have deprived some teachers of the sense that their job traditionally required a great deal of creative thinking. In a secondary school context a syllabus dominated by exams and Standard Assessment Tasks makes curricular risk-taking even more difficult. As a result many teachers may not feel creative practitioners at all – the very idea of a creative curriculum, teaching creative thinking and teaching for creativity may seem threatening.

The QCA schemes were intended to support teachers in presenting a complex curriculum seen as difficult to fit into the time available. However, just before the schemes were published, QCA in a publication, ironically named *Maintaining Breadth and Balance* (QCA, 1998b, p. 3), told primary schools that they 'no longer had to teach the full programmes of study in the six foundation subjects'. The result was a loss of breadth and balance and a steady decline in time, thought and energy devoted to some foundation subjects in primary schools. Inevitably standards in these foundation subjects suffered and training teachers noted significantly diminishing opportunities to observe practice in them (see Barnes, 2001; Rogers, 1999, 2003). Since 2000 various official attempts have been made to address a situation where literacy and numeracy dominate school time and the foundation subjects, science, RE, ICT, PSHE and citizenship are squeezed into the remaining spaces. Perhaps the most helpful is *Designing and Timetabling the Primary Curriculum* (QCA, 2002b) which offers case study examples of how schools with differing aims fulfilled them though creative and sometimes cross-curricular approaches to the timetable.

A climate of change presents many transitions. These transitions can be made into positive opportunities and can centrally involve the curriculum. One such example in the UK is the difficult transition between Key Stages 2 and 3. Some imaginative schools in both key stages are developing a 'Bridging curriculum', where primary and secondary school staff and children work together on a theme shared by Years 6 and 7 pupils (see Davies and McMahon, 2004). Shared themes, often focused around science (probably because of a secondary school's superior science resources), cushion the sometimes worrying transition between schools at 11 years but also serve to raise teaching and learning standards, ensure progression and enhance the status of learning over teaching.

The rapid and accelerating changes of the twenty-first century and their implications are well analysed by writers such as Ken Robinson (2001) and Susan Greenfield (2003), but few analyses look to the curriculum for an answer. Yet a well-designed curriculum delivered by committed and community-conscious teachers and other adults is a powerful force. As the caring society's backup or in the absence of other support mechanisms, the curriculum can help children cope with either the multifarious categories of change or the rates of change we all experience. Founded upon an honest appraisal of the needs of the community, an intimacy with the families involved and a desire to make positive the ethos of the school, an empowering and meaningful curriculum can be contrasted. Good relationships, good planning, a strong sense of personal/emotional relevance, authentic challenge and a recognition of the child's world will help children understand and engage with an otherwise bewildering world. They and we have little idea of what world we will live in 20 years hence, but what we *can* do is to help children develop:

- a sense of personal, family and community meaning and belonging
- a heightened and positively-framed sensitivity and care for the self, others and environment
- an ability to understand their own emotions and how to handle, harness and read them in the self and others

Illustration 10.1 *A child describes the link between health, happiness and music; 'Health is the arm movement and happiness is the music, like a set of drums.'* Courtesy Scottish Children's Parliament

- a positive view of their ability to learn new things
- a positive view of others, valuing their diversity and uniqueness
- an appreciation of what their culture sees as beautiful, good, true and right
- a method of working which is cooperative, patient, fair and fulfilling
- a knowledge of the distinctive contributions of each subject discipline to understanding their world
- an understanding that a holistic view of experiences, emotions, places, things, patterns, processes and ideas requires the application of multiple disciplines and viewpoints
- a realization that they are creative beings, able to produce inventive and unique solutions to problems which confront them
- a confidence and accuracy with many technologies and in handling information from a wide variety of sources.

These could be argued to be the kind of personal skills needed regardless of what the future holds. They are also a series of competences which can be seen as a preliminary marker towards the (re?) establishment of a set of socially accepted absolutes which might transcend change.

Questions for discussion:

- How can we adapt the curriculum in our school to take account of changing technologies?
- How can we support children in thinking about their role in the future?

Illustration 10.2 *Power reinterpreted from a different camera angle.* Robert Jarvis

- What kind of changes can we see happening around us, in our own area at the moment? How do they relate to more global issues?
- How can we counter the feeling that individuals are powerless in the face of change?

Power

Power relationships are changing in western societies. The deference with which in former times we treated royalty, the church, the police, the judiciary, the famous and the wealthy is constantly challenged by press, and often by individuals. Awareness of rights and the possibility of litigation have come to characterize many aspects of daily life. Whilst huge power remains vested in politicians, newspaper magnates, senior civil servants, captains of industry, and even health and safety executives, power is also increasingly placed in the hands of many more poorly paid mortals. Transferring power in a school context has been touched upon in our discussion of schools councils and children's participation. When pupils took control of information-gathering activities in the HEARTS project (Chapter 2) their motivation, application and concentration increased. There are many arguments for the frequent shifting of power within a school setting (see for example, Davies, 2000; Freire, 1994; Illich, 1971; Jeffrey and Woods, 2003) Clearly in many circumstances and for safety's sake, ultimate power may have to reside with adults, but there are plentiful opportunities in a school day where children can at least *feel* they have the power to influence things. In this regard, one teacher education student likened the effective teacher to 'a cunning dictator' who contrives to make his people feel they have freedom and power whilst actually retaining most himself. But power sharing can be more genuine than this.

Illustration 10.3   *Children's response to the question, 'What can adults and children do together?'* Courtesy Scottish Children's Parliament

Cross-curricular practice often depends upon group work and self-directed activity, in both cases children may need to be taught to handle power. Modelling sessions in which children *practise* making decisions, taking a lead or dealing with disputes are invaluable just before the onset of genuine group problem-solving. A class debate about the responsibilities of power need not be theoretical if this Personal, Social and Health Education (PSHE) and Citizenship theme is followed by a real class meeting to decide on the class theme or how to meet a particular challenge.

Questions for discussion:

- How do we shift the locus of control whilst retaining responsibility for the health and safety of children?
- What are the health and safety implications of shifting power towards children?
- How do we give children the impression of choice whist we continue to make decisions about curriculum content?
- What differences have new technologies made to children's sense of power and control?

Creativity

Cross-curricular learning and creativity go hand in hand; this is recognized by the QCA (2002a, 2005, website) and in the practice of thousands of teachers. Mixing a group of children and two subject perspectives together to make sense of a single event, theme or object should be a recipe for unusual insights, original questions, unique perspectives and products. There are almost endless possibilities in the mix because, as we have seen, each child brings to any situation his or her own set of memories, links and associations, and each of these link in a different way to his or her understanding of the subjects involved. As I have made clear, the teaching of distinct bodies of subject knowledge and skills is irreplaceable. The robustness and rigidity of this disciplined understanding can in many ways be the best provoker of creativity, 'Structure ignites spontaneity', says Nachmanovitch, who continues in a musical context: 'In ragas, or solo jazz play, sounds are limited to a restricted sphere, within which a gigantic range of inventiveness opens up. If you have all the colours available, you are sometimes almost too free. With one dimension constrained, play becomes freer in other dimensions' (Nachmanovitch, 1990, p. 85).

Creativity is not necessarily a matter of blindly letting go or weakly allowing 'free expression'. The NACCCE report makes it very clear that in its view sustained creative achievement 'involves knowledge of the field in question and skills in the media concerned ... [and to] recognise the mutual dependence of freedom and control at the heart of the creative process' (NACCCE, 1999, para. 49).

Psychological and neurological research already cited reminds us that what we call creativity cannot be situated in a single area of the brain or found in a single set of experiences. Creativity may be stimulated by the accidental coming together of two thoughts, materials or people, and cross-curricular approaches will make such accidents more likely. As Margaret Boden suggests:

> Creativity is best construed not as a single power which you either have or do not, but as multidimensional. Creative processes involve different mental functions, combinations of skills and personality attributes ... they involve special purposes for familiar mental operations and the more efficient use of our ordinary abilities, not something profoundly different. (Boden, 1990, p. 250)

Creative acts are judged so by acceptance by a particular field of judges and this applies, as Pope says, 'at every level from considering Nobel Prize nominations the scribbles of four year olds' (Pope, 2005, p. 68). But whilst Csikszentmihalyi generally speaks of creativity within one domain of understanding, Pope reminds us that much of the most startling and influential creativity goes on, in the margins *between* domains, in interdisciplinary or cross-cultural exchanges which result in hybrid forms. Such exchanges happen in nature of course, but in human cultures some of the most creative forms have come at the overlap of cultures; think of medieval Venice, ninth-century Spain, Moghul India, jazz in the southern states of the USA, or the fusions of ancient cultures in Ptolomy's Egypt.

Thematic work may provoke opportunities for the overlap of ideas in a school setting too. Creative solutions to a well-defined brief from the teacher might involve a mathematical sequence applied to a musical challenge, a geographical process described using a dance, scientific understandings like the movement of water created through painting or a technological problem solved through reference to an historical solution.

My own research (Grainger, Barnes and Scoffham, 2006) has suggested the importance of teachers recognizing and naming creative acts amongst children as they work on such projects.

One class of 8-year-olds was designing and constructing a handbag which was to be filled with objects which showed what their head teacher, Ms Masters, was interested in. Their teacher consistently identified original responses in the children:

'Talking to other people helped Linda have more ideas didn't it?'

Sarah: 'Jordan has just written what *he* likes.' [to put in his model of Ms Masters' bag]
Teacher: Is that what you think he thinks? I think he's got very good reasons for drawing a Dalek *as well* as liking them himself.'

'What is that telling us about Ms Masters?'

'That's a really good idea, Taylor, combining two ideas in one.'

'Who would like to come up and share just a little bit of what they are doing?'

'Raise your hand if you have thought of anything new or different today.' (Barnes, 2005c)

Recent research for Creative Partnerships has shown that establishing a general and creative frame of mind both in teachers and children, is a key aspect of promoting creative thinking and creative activity. A background atmosphere where creativity was frequently (and precisely) honoured had distinct effects on the children's view of their own and others' creativity. They had little problem in naming aspects of their teacher's creativity and spoke confidently of their own. Being aware of one's own creativity is good for confidence but also seems to be related to a sense of well-being, prolongs concentration and promotes warm, positive relationships and is associated with an enhanced sense of meaning (Csikszentmihalyi, 1997; Pope, 2005).

Questions for discussion:

- How can we promote creativity in the adults in our school?
- How can we sustain the sense of growth in our own learning?
- How could we gain more job satisfaction?
- How can we create the conditions in which these things are likely to be the experience of children too?

Illustration 10.4   *After finding out about wind direction and air pressure these 13-and 14-year-olds send messages to a 'marooned' artist in the middle of the English channel as part of a Creative Partnerships initiative.* Courtesy Creative Partnerships, Kent

Behaviour

Some teachers are concerned that group work and the freedom to interpret instructions, or activity outside the classroom using many different materials and modes of learning is bound to provoke poor behaviour. It is difficult to counter this perception unless such work is carefully planned and implemented. In the HEARTS project (Chapter 2) most students expected behaviour challenges amongst their 12-year-olds, but after two full days of the project over 80 per cent remarked upon the good behaviour of children in this open-ended setting. Additionally, almost 50 per cent of the student teachers used the words 'enthusiastic', 'collaborative', 'relaxed' and 'new ideas' to describe their feelings about the behaviour of the children. More than 70 per cent used the words 'enjoyed' or 'engaged' to describe children's attitude to learning in this context. Planning and helping children find personal relevance was crucial to the success of this cross-curricular activity, just as it is for *any* school activity, but further I would argue that involvement in cross-curricular and creative activities has been responsible many times for *producing* good behaviour. In the case of the HEARTS project, finding relevance did not involve identifying direct links with children's everyday lives, but discovering tiny aspects of an unfamiliar environment which connected in one way or another to the memories of each separate individual. For one it was fossils, another a fairy story, another an angry friend and yet another a film they had seen, but for all, that link had a kind of existential importance; the link was a recognizable part of their autobiographical self.

Illustration 10.5 *These 6-year-olds are discovering personal links to a medieval castle by meaning making their own descriptive and atmospheric music whilst on their visit*

Just as productive group work needs teaching, so does behaviour; it is not always 'caught' as we might hope. But high expectations and clear, simple ground rules for safe, caring behaviour, or precise time limits are easy to demonstrate and even practise before practical activity. Identifying, describing and honouring 'good' behaviour as it happens keeps children aware of these expectations.

Added to general subject planning and specific learning objectives, one of the most powerful motivators to good behaviour is success at something which is perceived as truly challenging. The teacher or team should therefore plan and work to generate enthusiasm for a genuine challenge which seems just a little *beyond* the grasp, for the greatest sense of achievement and focus.

Questions for discussion:

- Is behaviour best improved by rules or a stimulating curriculum?
- How can we help children become aware of and responsible for their own behaviour?
- How can we positively involve family, community and child in discussions about behaviour?

Globalization

We have become very aware of the global dimension in our lives. In 2005/06 alone, war in Israel and Lebanon, world trade agreements, Live 8, G8 summits, the increasing membership of the European Union, the impact of the Asian tsunami, terrorist outrages, hurricane Katrina and the Pakistani/ Kashmiri earthquake made us all recognize our interdependence. It is difficult to ignore the impact of pandemics, global technologies, global terrorism, the global economy, global climate change and global pollution. Yet despite guidance from the Development Education Association (for example, DEA, 2001), the global still plays very little part in our National Curriculum programmes of study, the QCA schemes of work or school prospectuses. The UK government recently reminded us of the importance of the global dimension by publishing *Putting the World into World Class Education* (DfES, 2004) in an attempt to build partnerships between schools across the globe, learn in a global context and established three (noticeably economy-driven) aims:

1. Equipping children for life in a global society and work in a global economy.
2. Engaging international partners to achieve their goals and ours.
3. Maximizing the contribution of education to overseas trade and inward investment.

The global can play a big part in the kind of thematic activity already outlined in this book. The global dimension does not have to be as overtly British-economy serving as the government's three aims, it can be used to develop a more sensitive and informed understanding of the life and death issues facing the vast majority of the world population.

One school on the Kent coast, established a link with a primary school in Tanzania and their link forms the core of thematic work for several weeks of combined geography, PSHE/Citizenship and English work. Children write letters with real questions they know will be answered, they research and present comprehensive details about the actual locality of their partner school; its weather statistics, its population, maps of the village, plans of the farms and detail about daily life of a few actual families. This year they

(Continued)

(Continued)

worked with a teacher who had visited the area. In groups of five they took on family roles and used the plans of six fragmented and steeply sited farms to discuss what the family could do with £50 given by the local church organization for improvements. They were able to check out what actually happened in subsequent letters, but this activity gave the children a remarkably deep and lasting insight into the issues facing $\frac{4}{5}$ of the world's population. It will not surprise readers that the same school raised £1000 this year to send to the Tanzanian school for new equipment. (Glen Sharp)

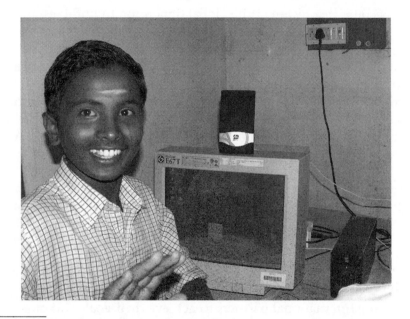

Illustration 10.6   *This village child in south India has access to the rest of the world through the Internet*

Questions for discussion

- What global links do we already have?
- How can we make the global significant to the children in our school?
- How can the global be made an integrator in our curriculum?

Litigation and 'the surveillance culture'

Advice on school policy and legislation regarding safety on school visits is contained on the government teachernet website (DfES, 2005a, website). It reflects the increasing concern for children's safety after a number of well-publicized and very tragic accidents involving children on school visits. The fear of litigation and the extra paperwork, detailed 'risk assessments' along with the requirement of particular ratios of adults to children and the need for individual parental permission, has resulted in an understandable reduction of school visits. *None of the requirements are unnecessary, all are the result of carefully considered and responsible practice and none should be disregarded.* However, schools which continue to make fieldwork a major priority have found that establishing such procedures as

- clear and uniform school-based guidelines
- adequate and school-provided preparation time
- accessible and easily understood paperwork
- the advice of experienced practitioners
- the preparation of individual 'class visit packs' containing essential medication, mobile phone, first aid kit and permission slips significantly lessens the load on teachers.

The parliamentary Education and Skills Committee appears in full agreement that education outside the classroom is a valuable and motivating thing in itself: 'Outdoor learning supports academic achievement ... as well as development of "soft skills" and social skills particularly in hard to reach children ... neither the DfES nor Local Authorities have done enough to publicize the benefits of education outside the classroom ...' (summary, Education Outside the Classroom, 2005). The same committee agreed that the bureaucracy associated with school visits is a major problems but found no evidence that school visits are inherently risky. The committee recommended a 'Manifesto for Outdoor learning,' (DFES, 2005c, website) with structures and a personality to champion outdoor learning across all curriculum areas. It also recommended that unions currently advising their members not to go on school trips reconsider their position.

Related to the lack of trust inherent in the development of a litigation culture, has been the gradual rise of surveillance activities in our schools as well as our high streets. Whilst I offer little criticism of schools with closed-circuit television (CCTV), now common throughout the western world through public perception of increased risk to children, the recent development of stringent curriculum surveillance can have negative and unforeseen effects on teaching and learning quality. As ordinary teachers are increasingly observed by heads, curriculum coordinators, parents, governors and inspectors, they are likely to choose the 'safest' and least disruptive options for their teaching. They are less likely to take the risks we have been exploring throughout this book. Cross-curricular teaching *is* risky; sometimes a well-prepared topic does not catch the imagination as hoped for. Group work, open-ended questions and situations, or creative lessons will often be nosier and appear less controlled than a highly structured and inflexible 'off-the-shelf lesson'. But I have argued that this risky, noisy, exciting and unpredictable education is vital to the healthy future of our individuals and our society.

Questions for discussion:

- What kind of curriculum/lessons best build positive attitudes to lifelong learning?
- What kind of curriculum/lessons help children develop transferable skills for use in a variety of future circumstances?
- What kind of curriculum/lessons assists children in forming positive views of themselves?
- What kind of curriculum/lessons teach social and emotionally intelligent skills necessary for work in teams in later life?
- What kind of curriculum/lessons help children learn independence, understand how to use initiative, cultivate flexibility, rehearse prioritizing and discover their own creativity?
- What kind of curriculum/lessons can prepare children for an uncertain future of inevitable and yet unimaginable change?

Changing role of the school

Even before the publication of *No Child Left Behind* or *Every Child Matters* (ECM) it was clear that the very nature of schools was fast changing. Community learning centres are not a new idea and Children's Centres where medical, social and educational needs were catered for have been piloted in a number of authorities in the UK, the rest of Europe and the USA. Many schools are already effectively operating variations of the 8.00 a.m. to 6.00 p.m. day with breakfast clubs, after-school clubs and the like. Since ECM the pace of change has quickened. In the UK newly designated 'Directors of Children's Services' and coordinated local authority responsibility for all aspects of childhood mean that each school has to consider a widening of its role in the community. Alongside these changes, contradictory but economically driven moves appear to threaten the very communities ECM wants to sustain. School closures continue because of falling rolls or low numbers, thus removing some schools from the heart of small and fragile communities. Policing, the administration of primary health care and social services continue to suffer from the inexorable pressures to economize by being organized in bigger but less locally accountable units. Finally, *increasing* poverty and an increasing gap between the haves and the have nots in the developed world, but especially affecting the lives of young people, seems to be adding to the list of social, health and educational problems confronting them.

Information and communications technology now makes it possible for each child to have a separate and isolated education. Education can conceivably be totally individualized. By 2008 the BBC will be able to deliver 50 per cent of the National Curriculum for 5–16-year-olds over the heads of teachers in an 'interactive dialogue directly with learners' (BBC, 2005, website). Such education is

Illustration 10.7 *Infant children's plans for their school entrance realized by a team of architects who worked with them.* Courtesy Creative Partnerships, Kent

possible, but is it right? Against this technological and political background schools will inevitably become more complex organizations with multiple functions beyond the simple passing on of knowledge. Schools will be increasingly charged with developing independence and this may even result in the need to abandon the idea of the timetable.

There are warning signs that teachers will bear the brunt of many of these new initiatives. However, there is a fear that many of the activities envisaged for the children's centres will not use teachers for their core knowledge – a professional understanding of children and their learning – but, rather, as entertainers, childminders or janitors. To ensure that children continue to get the best from their teachers, teachers themselves need to be more fully aware of the unique, precious and professional knowledge they possess. The knowledge they gain is not possessed by any other professionals, it should not be underestimated, neglected or watered down. Neither should teachers feel trapped into propping up systems and approaches they know from experience, do not work. Human beings are social and cultured animals, we only consider ourselves mentally well when we are generally happy with the relationships we form with others. Whilst society continues to see education as a social, communal, culture-driven affair, teachers will be the key adults in children's lives after their carers. At their best, teachers are made distinctive by the insights they accumulate about young people's learning. At its best, teachers' contribution to the well-being of each individual and of society can be expressed in the following statements:

1. Teachers are the only professionals who serve their clients *en masse.* They understand and use many different methods of presenting information so as to match different styles of learning within a single class. They know how simultaneously to engage children from a wide range of backgrounds.

2. They know how to organize activities in groups so as to ensure social, emotional and personal development at the same time as intellectual development.

3. They know how to control large groups of young people without fear, how to motivate them without bribery, how to excite them without losing control, how to take risks without danger and how to praise without lying.

4. Teachers understand the importance of motivation in learning and the variety of ways of persuading children that they want to learn.

5. They understand about simultaneously stretching the most and the least able child in the same class *and know that those two children may be interchangeable in different learning situations.*

6. Teachers are unique in knowing, understanding and in many ways representing the whole range of sub-cultures within the communities they serve. They know how to arrange educational experiences so that at one and the same time they generate meaningful learning *and* avoid offence to both the most liberal and most conservative members of society. They know and understand how different extremes of society feel about things that matter to them.

7. They experience daily the close relationship between physical and mental well-being and learning. They see the multitude of ways family break-up, a house move, the loss of a friend or an eraser can affect a child's learning. They also regularly witness the impact of deprivation or wealth.

8. Teachers are at the front line of applying government policy to generate change in society and economy through the curriculum, yet they are rarely directly consulted.

Teachers rapidly become experts in children's learning and the kind of curriculum which motivates them. They need to be listened to in building the new approach to the curriculum required for a world of children's centres, new technologies, new definitions of family, new challenges and very old moral dilemmas. No other professional has the teacher's wealth of research knowledge on how to make links between the disciplines, manage children in groups, how to fire an individual's imagination, how to rebuild a child's self-esteem and how to construct an environment which promotes in them the desire to learn. Both the child's and the teacher's well-being depend on balance of attention to the disciplines, the group, the individual and the environment for learning. Good teachers have been

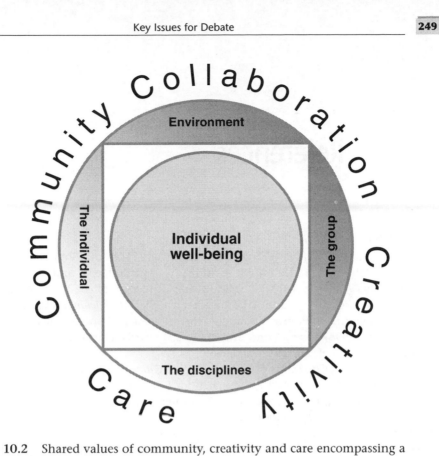

Figure 10.2   Shared values of community, creativity and care encompassing a curriculum founded on a balance between individual and group, the disciplines and environment, will result in greater chances of individual well-being for both teacher and child

balancing these factors for ever. With these and many more unique and undeniable qualities it is amazing that teachers continue to be so maligned in the press, threatened by inspection, replaced by under-qualified assistants and put upon by politicians. In the changing world of the school, teachers' unique and professional range of skills and knowledge must be fully and sensitively utilized. Ask teachers about the curriculum which will best serve today's children for now and their future, and I believe the majority will respond with a variant of the creative and cross-curriculum.

References

Abbs, P. (2003) *Against the Flow*, London: Routledge.

Adey, P. and Shayer, M. (1994) *Really Raising Standards*, London: Routledge.

Ahmad, Y., Dalrymple, J., Daum, M., Griffiths, N., Hockridge, T. and Ryan, E. (2003) *Listening to Children and Young People*, Bristol: University of the West of England.

Alexander, R., Rose, A.J., and Woodhead, C. (1992) *Curriculum Organisation and Classroom Practice in Primary Schools: A Discussion Paper*, London: DES.

Alexander, R. (1998) Basics, cores and choices: towards a new primary curriculum, *Education 3–13*, vol. 26, no. 2, pp.60–69.

Alexander, T. (2001) *Citizenship Schools: A Practical Guide to Education for Citizenship and Personal Development*, London: Campaign for Learning/UNICEF.

Alexander, T. and Potter, J. (eds) (2005) *Education for a Change: Transforming the Way We Teach our Children*, London: Routledge-Falmer.

Antidote (2003) *The Emotional Literacy Handbook*, London: David Fulton.

Arnsten, A. and Li, B. (2005) Neurobiology of executive functions: catecholamine influences in prefrontal cortical functions, *Biological Psychiatry*, vol. 57, no. 11, pp. 1377–84.

Arthur, J., Grainger, T. and Wray, D. (2006) *Learning to Teach in the Primary School*, London: Routledge.

Bandura, A. (1994) Self-efficacy, in V.S. Ramachaudran (ed.), *Encyclopedia of Human Behaviour*, vol. 4, pp. 71–81, New York: Academic Press.

Barnes, J. (1994) The city planners of St Peters, *Remnants*, Journal of English Heritage Education Service, no. 24, Autumn, pp. 1–4.

Barnes, J. (2001) Creativity and composition in music, in C. Philpott and C. Plummeridge (eds), *Issues in Music Education*, London: Routledge.

Barnes, J. (2003) Teachers' emotions, teachers' creativity – a discussion paper, *Improving* Schools, vol. 6, no. 1, pp. 39–43.

Barnes, J. (2004) Case study notes, 4 November.

Barnes, J. (2005a) On your mind, *Nursery World*, vol. 105, no. 3965, pp. 12–13.

Barnes, J. (2005b) Strangely familiar: authentic experience, teacher education and a thought provoking environment, *Improving Schools*, vol. 8, no. 2, pp. 199–206.

Barnes, J. (2005c) Case study notes, 28 November.

Barnes, J. (2005d) Case study notes 14 December.

Barnes, J, (2005e) Research notes 26 May.

Barnes, J. (2005f) You could see it on their faces: the importance of provoking smiles in schools, *Health Education*, vol. 105, no. 5, pp. 392–400.

Barnes, J. (2006a) Strangely familiar: cross curricular and creative thinking in teacher education, paper presented at International Conference on Imagination in Education, Vancouver, July.

Barnes, J. (2006b) Constructing an approach to school development through experience and biography, unpublished PhD thesis, Canterbury Christ Church University.

Barnes, J. and Hancox, G. (2004) Young, gifted and human: a report from the National Gifted and Talented Summer Academy, *Improving* Schools, vol. 7, no. 1, pp. 11–21.

Barnes, J. and Shirley, I. (2005) Strangely familiar: promoting creativity in initial teacher education, paper presented at British Educational Research Association (BERA) conference, 16 September.

Baron, R. and Byrne, D. (2004) *Social Psychology*, 10th edn, London: Allyn and Bacon.

Bell, D. (2004) The value and importance of geography, *Primary Geographer*, vol. 56, pp. 4–5.

Bentley, T. (2006) Towards a self creating society, presentation at 'This Learning Life' conference, Bristol, 21 April.

Black, P. and Wiliam, D. (1998) *Inside the Black Box*, Slough: NFER/Nelson.

Blake, W, (1789) *Songs of Innocence and Experience*, facsimile edn 1967, London: Oxford University Press.

Blakemore, S. and Frith, U. (2006) *The Learning Brain: lessons for education*, Oxford: Blackwell.

Blythe, T. (ed.) (1998) *The Teaching for Understanding Guide*, New York: Jossey-Bass.

Booth, T. and Ainscow, M. (2002) *Index for Inclusion: Developing Learning and Participation in Schools*, Bristol: Centre for Studies on Inclusive Education.

Bowlby, J. (1988) *A Secure Base: Clinical Applications of Attachment Theory*, London: Routledge.

Bransford, J., Brown, A. and Cooking, R. (1999) *How People Learn: Brain, Mind Experience and School*, Stanford, CA: National Research Council.

Brice Heath, S. and Wolf, S. (2004) *Visual Learning in the Community School*, London: Arts Council.

Brice Heath, S. and Wolf, S (2005) Focus in creative learning: drawing on art for language development, *Literacy*, vol. 39, no. 3, pp. i–i(1).

Bruner, J. (1968) *Towards a Theory of Instruction*, New York: Norton.

Bruner, J. (1996) *The Culture of Education*, Cambridge, MA: Harvard University Press.

Bruner, J. (2003) Some specifications for a space to house a Reggio preschool, in G. Ceppi and M. Zini (eds), *Children, Spaces, Relation: Metaproject for an Environment for Young Children*, Milan: Domus Academy Research Centre.

Bruner, J. and Haste, H. (1987) *Making Sense: The Child's Construction of the World*, New York: Methuen.

Burke, C. and Grosvenor, I. (2003) *The School I'd Like: Children and Young People's Reflections on an Education for the 21st Century*, London: Routledge.

Buzan, T. (2002) *How to Mind Map*, London: Thorsons.

Callaghan, J. (1976) Towards a national debate (The full text of the speech by Prime Minister James Callaghan, at a foundation stone-laying ceremony at Ruskin College, Oxford, on October 18 1976), *Guardian*, available at http://education.guardian.co.uk/print/0,3858,4277858-109002,00.html.

Catling, S. (2004) Primary student teachers' world map knowledge, in S. Catling and F. Martin (eds), *Researching Primary Geography*, London: Register of Research in Primary Geography.

Catling, S. (2005) Children's personal geographies and the English primary school geography curriculum, *Children's Geographies*, vol. 3, no. 3, pp. 325–44.

Ceppi, G. and Zini, M. (eds) (2003) *Children, Spaces, Relation: Metaproject for an Environment for Young Children*, Milan: Domus Academy Research Centre.

Claxton, G. (1998) *Hare Brain, Tortoise Mind,* London: Fourth Estate.

Claxton, G. (2003) *Building Learning Power,* London: TLO.

Claxton, G. and Lucas, B. (2004) *Be Creative,* London: BBC.

Collishaw, S., Maughan, B., Goodman, R. and Pickles, A. (2004) Time trends in adolescent mental health, *Journal of Child Psychology and Psychiatry,* vol. 45, no. 8. p. 1350.

Comenius, J. (trans. 1967) *The Great Didactic,* London: Russell and Russell.

Costa, A. (ed.) (1991) *Developing Minds: A Resource Book for Teaching Thinking,* vol. 1, Alexandra, VA.: Association for Supervision and Curriculum Development.

Craft, A. (2000) *Creativity across the Primary Curriculum,* London: Routledge.

Craft, A. (2005) *Creativity in Schools: Tensions and Dilemmas,* London: Routledge.

Creative Partnerships Kent (2005) *Footnotes to an Idea,* London: Creative Partnerships/ Arts Council.

Critchley, H. (2003) Emotion and its disorders, *British Medical Bulletin,* vol. 65, pp. 35–47.

Csikszentmihalyi, M (1997) *Creativity: Flow and the Psychology of Discovery and Invention,* New York: HarperCollins.

Csikszentmihalyi, M. (2002) *Flow: The Classic Work on How to Achieve Happiness,* New York: Ebury Press.

Csikszentmihalyi, M. (2003) *Good Business,* New York: Hodder and Stoughton.

Damasio, A. (2000) *The Feeling of What Happens: Body, Emotion and the Making of Consciousness,* London: Heinemann.

Damasio, A. (2003) *Looking for Spinoza: Joy, Sorrow and the Feeling Brain,* Orlando, FL: Harcourt.

Damasio, A. (1994) *Descartes' Error,* London: HarperCollins.

Darder, A. (2002) *Reinventing Paulo Freire: A Pedagogy of Love,* Oxford: Westview.

David , T. (1999) *Teaching Young Children,* London: Paul Chapman Publishing.

Davidson, R., Daren, C. and Kalin, N. (2000) Emotion, plasticity, context and regulation. perspectives from affective neuroscience, *Psychological Bulletin,* vol. 126, no. 6, pp. 890–906.

Davies, D. and McMahon, K. (2004) A smooth trajectory: developing continuity and progression between primary and secondary science education through a jointly planned projectiles project, *International Journal of Science Education,* vol. 26, pp. 1009–21.

Davies, N. (2000) *The School Report: Why Britain's Schools Are Failing,* London: Vintage.

Dawkins, R, (2003) *A Devils Chaplin: Selected Essays,* London: Phoenix.

De Boo, M. (ed.) (2004) *The Early Years Handbook: Support for Practitioners in the Foundation Stage,* Sheffield: Geographical Association.

De Bono, E. (1999) *Six Thinking Hats.* New York: Black Bay.

Department of Economic Affairs (DEA) (2001) *Global Perspectives in Education,* London: DEA.

Department of Education and Science (DES) (1967) *Children and their Primary Schools: A Report of the Central Advisory Council for Education (England)* (Plowden Report), London: HMSO.

Department for Education and Employment (DfEE) (1998) *The National Literacy Strategy,* London: DfEE.

Department for Education and Employment (DfEE) (1999) *The National Numeracy Strategy,* London: DfEE.

Department for Education and Employment/Qualifications and Curriculum Authority (DfEE/QCA) (1999) *The National Curriculum Handbook for Primary Teacher in England,* London: DfEE.

Department for Education and Skills (DfES) (2003) *Developing Children's Social, Emotional and Behavioural Skills: Guidance*, London: DfES.

Department for Education and Skills (DfES) (2004) *Putting the World into World Class Education: An International Strategy for Educations, Skills and Children's Services*, London: DfES.

Department for Education and Skills/Qualifications and Curriculum Authority (DfES/QCA) (1999a) *Curriculum Guidance for the Foundation Stage*, London: DfES.

Department for Education and Skills/Qualifications and Curriculum Authority (DfES/QCA) (1999b) *The National Curriculum Handbook for Primary Teachers in England*. London, HMSO.

Department for Education and Skills/Qualifications and Curriculum Authority (DfES/QCA) (2003) *Speaking, Listening, Learning: Working with Children in Key Stages 1 and 2*, London : DfES

Department of Health/Department for Education and Skills (DoH/DfES) (2005) *National Healthy Schools Status ; Guide for Schools*, London : DoH/DfES, Crown copyright.

Department of Health and Social Security (DHSS) (2004) *Promoting Emotional Health and Wellbeing, Through the National Healthy Schools Standard*, London: DHSS.

Dewey, J. (1897) My pedagogic creed, *The School Journal*, vol. 54, no. 3, pp. 77–80.

Dismore, H., Bailey, R., Wellard, I., Pickard, A., Grainger, T., Shirley, I. and Barnes, J. (2006) *Phase Two, Space for Sport and the Arts Evaluation: Final Report*, Canterbury: Sport England/Arts Council.

Ekman, P. (2004) *Emotions Revealed: Understanding Faces and Feelings*, London: Phoenix.

Entwistle, N. (2000) Promoting deep learning through teaching and assessment: conceptual frameworks and educational contexts, paper presented at Teaching and Learning Research Programme (TLRP) conference, Leicester, 11 November.

Faverjon, S., Silvera, D., Fu, D., Cha, B., Akman, C., Hu, Y. and Holmes, G. (2002) Beneficial effects of enriched environment following status epilepticus in immature rats, *Neurology*, vol. 59, no. 9, pp. 1302–3.

Feldman, D. (1976) The child as craftsman, *Phi Delta Kappan*, vol. 58, no.1, pp.143–9.

Fisher, R. (1999) *Head Start: How to Develop your Child's Mind*, London: Souvenir.

Fisher, R. and Williams, M. (2004) *Unlocking Creativity: Teaching across the Curriculum*, London: David Fulton.

Frankl, V. (1992) *Man's Search for Meaning*, London: Rider.

Fraser-Smith, N., Lesperance, F. and Talajic, M. (1995) The impact of negative emotions on prognosis following myocardial infarction: is it more than depression? *Health Psychology*, vol. 14, pp. 388–98.

Frederickson, B (2003) The value of Positive Emotions. *American Scientist*. vol. 91, 2003. pp. 300– 305

Fredrickson, B. (2004) The broaden and build theory of positive emotions, *Philosophical Transactions of the Royal Society: Biological Sciences*, vol. 359, no. 1449, pp.1367–77.

Fredrickson, B. and Branigan, C. (2005) Positive emotions broaden the scope of attention and thought–action repertoires, *Cognition and Emotion*, vol. 19, no. 3, pp. 313–32.

Fredrickson, B. and Tugade, M. (2004) Resilient individuals use positive emotions to bounce back from negative experiences, *Journal of Personality and Social Psychology*, vol. 80, no. 2, pp. 326–33.

Freire, P. (1994) *The Pedagogy of Hope: Reliving the Pedagogy of the Oppressed*, New York: Continuum.

Froebel, F. (1826) *Die Menschenerziehung (On the Education of Man)*, Leipzig: Weinbrach.

Gardner, H. (1993) *Frames of Mind: The Theory of Multiple Intelligences*, 2nd edn, London: Fontana.

Gardner, H. (1999a) *The Disciplined Mind: What All Students Should Understand*, New York: Simon and Schuster.

Gardner, H. (1999b) *Intelligence Reframed: Multiple Intelligence for the 21st Century*, New York: Basic Books.

Gardner, H. (2004) *Changing Minds: The Art and Science of Changing our Own and Other People's Minds*, Boston, MA, A Harvard Business School.

Gardner, H., Csikszentmihalyi, M. and Damon, W. (2000) *Good Work; Where Ethics and Excellence Meet*, New York: Basic Books.

Garrett, A., Carrion, V., Pageler, N., Menon, V., Mackenzie, K., Saltzman, K. and Reiss, A.(2002) fMRI response to facial expression in adolescent PTSD, paper presented at 49th Annual Meeting of the American Academy of Child and Adolescent Psychiatry, San Francisco, CA, 22–27 October.

Giedd, J., Blumenthal, J., Jeffries, N., Castellanos, F., Liu, H., Zijdenbos, A., Paus, T., Evans, A. and Rapoport, J. (1999) Brain development during childhood and adolescence: a longitudinal MRI study, *Nature Neuroscience*, vol. 10, pp. 861–3.

Gogtay, N., Giedd, J., Hayaski, K., Greenstein, D., Vaituzis, C., Hugent, T., Herman, D., Clasen, L., Toga, A., Rapoport, J. and Thompson, P. (2004) Dynamic mapping of human cortical development during childhood through early adulthood, *Proceedings of the National Academy of Sciences of the USA*, vol. 101, no. 21, pp. 8174–9.

Goldstein, L. (1997) *Teaching with Love: A Feminist Approach to Early Childhood Education*, New York: Peter Lang.

Goldstein, L. and Lake, V. (2000) Love, love, and more love for children: exploring pre-service teachers' understandings of caring, *Teaching and Teacher Education*, vol. 16, no. 7, pp. 861–72.

Goleman, D. (1996) *Emotional Intelligence*, London: Bloomsbury.

Goleman, D. (ed.) (1997) *Healing Emotions*, Boston, MA: Shambhala.

Goleman, D. (1999) *Working with Emotional Intelligence*, London: Bloomsbury.

Grainger, T., Barnes, J. and Scoffham, S. (2004) A creative cocktail: creative teaching in ITE, *Journal of Education in Teaching (JET)*, vol. 30, no. 3, pp. 243–53.

Grainger, T., Barnes, J. and Scoffham, S. (2006) *Creativity for Tomorrow*, Margate: Creative Partnerships, Kent.

Greenfield, S. (2003) *Tomorrow's People*, London: Penguin.

Greenhalgh, P. (1994) *Emotional Growth and Learning*, London: Routledge.

Gruzelier, J. (2003) Enhancing music performance through brain rhythm training, *Music Forum* (journal of the Music Council of Australia), October, pp. 34–5.

Guardian (2006) Alzheimer's drug could be widely sold to make everyone brainier, 27 January, p. 11.

Halpin, P. (2003) *Hope and Education*, London: Routledge.

Hanko, G. (1999) *Increasing Competence through Collaborative Problem Solving*, London: David Fulton.

Harland, J., Kinder, K., Lord, P., Stott, A., Schagen, I. and Haynes, J. (2000) *Arts Education in Secondary Schools: Effects and Effectiveness*, Slough: NFER.

Hayes, D. (2003) *Planning Teaching and Class Management in Primary Schools*, London: David Fulton.

Hicks, D. (2001) *Citizenship for the Future: A Practical Classroom Guide*, Godalming: World Wide Fund for Nature.

Higgins, S., Baumfield, V. and Leat, D. (2003) *Thinking Through Primary Teaching*, Cambridge: Kington.

HM Government (2004) *Every Child Matters*, London: DfES.

Howard-Jones, P. and Pickering, S. (2005) *Collaborative Frameworks for Neuroscience and Education: Scoping Paper*, Bristol: TLRP- ESRC.

Illich, I. (1971) *Deschooling Society*, London: Calder and Boyars.

Isen, A. (2002) A role for neuropsychology in understanding the facilitating influence of positive affect on social behaviour and cognitive processes, in C. Snyder and S. Lopez (eds), *Handbook of Positive Psychology*, New York: Oxford University Press.

Jeffrey, B. and Woods, P. (2003) *The Creative School*, London: Routledge.

Jensen, E. (1995) *Brain Based Learning*, Del Mar, CA: Eric Jensen.

Jensen, E. (2000) *Music with Brain in Mind*, San Diego, CA: The Brain Store.

John-Steiner, V. (2000) *Creative Collaboration*, Oxford: Oxford University Press.

Joubert, M. (2001) The art of creative teaching, in A. Craft, B. Jeffrey and M. Leibling (eds), *Creativity in Education*, London: Continuum.

Kawachi, I., Sparrow, D., Vokonas, P. and Weiss, S. (1994) Symptoms of anxiety and risk of coronary heart disease, *Circulation*, vol. 89, pp. 1992–7.

Khul, P. (2002) *Born to Learn: Language, Reading and the Brain of the Child*, North West Region, USA, Idaho, Early Learning Summit, 9–10 June.

Kirby, P., Lanyon, F. and Synelaw, R. (2003) *Building a Culture of Participation*, London: DfES.

Koestler, A. (1964) *The Act of Creation*, London: Penguin Arkana.

Laevers, F. (ed.) (1994a) *Defining and Assessing Quality in Early Childhood Education*, Leuven: Leuven University Press.

Laevers, F. (1994b) *The Leuven Involvement Scale for Young Children, LIS-YC, Manual*, Leuven: Centre for Experiential Education.

Layard, R. (2005) *Happiness*, London, Penguin.

Layard, R. (2006) *The Depression Report: A New Deal for Depression and Anxiety Disorders*, London: Centre for Economic Performance.

LeDoux, J. (1999) *The Emotional Brain*, London; Phoenix.

LeDoux, J. (2002) *The Synaptic Self*, New York: Viking.

Lee, A., Ogle, W. and Sapolsky, R. (2002) Stress and depression; possible links to neuron death in the hippocampus, *Bipolar Disorders*, vol. 4, no. 2, p. 117.

Luna, B. and Sweeney, J. (2004) The emergence of collaborative brain function: fMRI studies of the development of response inhibition, *Annals of the New York Academy of Science*, vol. 1021, no. 1, pp. 296–309.

Maguire, E., Gadian, D., Johnsrude, I., Good, C., Ashburner, J., Frackowiak, R. and Frith, C. (2000) Navigation-related structural change in the hippocampi of taxi drivers, *Proceedings of the National Academy of Sciences*, vol. 97, no. 8, pp. 4398–403.

Marton, F. and Booth, S. (1997) *Learning and Awareness*, Mahwah, NJ: Lawrence Erlbaum Associates.

Marton, F. and Saljo, R. (1976) On qualitative differences in learning I – Outcome and process, *British Journal of Educational Technology*, vol. 46, pp. 115–27.

Maslow, A. (1943) A theory of human motivation, *Psychological Review*, vol. 50, pp. 370–96.

Matheson, D. and Grosvenor, I. (eds) (1999) *An Introduction to the Study of Education*, London: David Fulton.

Morris, D (2004) *The Nature of Happiness*, London: Little Books

Morris, E. (2005) *Developing Emotionally Literate Staff: A Practical Guide*, London: Paul Chapman Publishing.

Morris, E. and Scott, C. (2002) *Whole School Emotional Literacy Indicator*, Frampton on Severn: School of Emotional literacy Press.

Mortimore, P. (ed.) (1999) *Understanding Pedagogy and its Impact on Learning*, London: Paul Chapman Publishing.

Moseley, J.(1996) *Quality Circle Time in the Primary School*, Wisbech: LDA.

National Advisory Council on Creative and Cultural Education (NACCCE) (1999) *All Our Futures: Creativity, Culture and Education*, London: DfEE.

Nachmanovitch, S. (1990) *Free Play: Improvisation I Life and Art*, New York: Penguin Putnam.

Organization for Economic Cooperation and Development (OECD) (2003) *Learners for Life: Student Approaches to Learning*, Paris: OECD Publications.

Office for Standards in Education (OFSTED) (2002) *The Curriculum in Successful Primary Schools*, London: OFSTED.

Office for Standards in Education (OFSTED) (2004) *A New Relationship with Schools: Improving Performance through School Self-Evaluation*, Nottingham: DfES Publications.

Overy, K. (1998) Can music really improve the mind? *Psychology of Music*, vol. 26, pp. 97–9.

Page, J. (2000) *Reframing the Early Childhood Curriculum: Educational Imperatives for the Future*, London: Routledge.

Pantev, C., Oostenveld, R., Engelien, A., Ross, B., Roberts, L. and Hoke, M. (1998) Increased auditory cortical representation in musicians, *Nature*, vol. 392, pp. 811–14.

Perkins, D. (1992) *Smart Schools*, New York: Free Press.

Perkins, D. (1995) *Outsmarting IQ: The Emerging Science of Learnable Intelligence*, New York: Free Press.

Perkins, D. (2002) *The Eureka Effect: The Art and Logic of Breakthrough Thinking*, New York: Norton.

Perkins, D. (2006) Whole game learning, presentation at 'This Learning Life' conference, University of Bristol , 20 April.

Piaget, J. (1954) *The Construction of Reality in the Child*, trans. M. Cook, New York: Basic Books.

Pinker, S. (1994) *The Language Instinct: The New Science of Language and Mind*, New York: Penguin Science.

Pinker, S. (2002) *The Blank Slate*, London: Penguin.

Plato (1955) *The Republic*, trans. D. Lee, London: Penguin Classics.

Plato (1970) *The Laws*, trans. T. Saunders, London: Penguin Classics.

Pollard, A. (1990) *Towards a Sociology of Learning in Primary School*, London: Rinehart and Winston.

Pollard, A. (1996) *The Social World of Children's Learning*, London: Cassell.

Pope, R. (2005) *Creativity: History, Theory, Practice*, London: Routledge.

Popenici, S. (2006) Imagine the future: role models and schools' captured imagination, paper presented at the International Conference on Imagination and Education, Vancouver, July.

Potter, J. (2002*) Active Citizenship in Schools: A Good Practice Guide to Developing Whole School Policy*, London: Kogan Page.

PriceWaterhouseCoopers(PWC) (2001). *Teacher Workload Study*, London: DfES.

Qualifications and Curriculum Authority (QCA) (1998a) *A Scheme of Work for Key Stages 1 and 2, Geography, History, Design Technology, Physical Education*, London: QCA.

Qualifications and Curriculum Authority (QCA) (1998b) *Maintaining Breadth and Balance*, London: QCA.

Qualifications and Curriculum Authority (QCA) (2000) *A Scheme of Work for Key Stages 1 and 2: Art and Design, Music*, London: QCA.

Qualifications and Curriculum Authority (QCA) (2002a) *Citizenship at Key Stages 1–4*, 1 January QCA/02/944, London: QCA.

Qualifications and Curriculum Authority (QCA) (2002b) *Designing and Timetabling the Primary Curriculum*, London: QCA.

Rhen, J. (1995) Deep and surface approaches to learning: an introduction, *National Teaching and Learning Forum*, vol.5, no.1, pp. 1–3.

Richhart, R. (2002) *Intellectual Character, Why It Is, Why It Matters and How to Get It*, New York: Jossey-Bass.

Riley, P. (2006) To stir with love: imagination, attachment and teacher behaviour, paper delivered at the International conference on Imagination in Education, Vancouver, July.

Robertson, I. (1999) *Mind Sculpture*, London: Bantam.

Robinson, K. (ed.) (1990) *The Arts 5–16: A Curriculum Framework*, London: Oliver and Boyd.

Robinson, K. (2001) *Out of Our Minds*, London: Capstone.

Rogers, R. (1999) *The Disappearing Arts*, London: RSA/Gulbenkian.

Rogers, R. (2003) *Time for the Arts?* London: RSA.

Royal Society of Arts (RSA) (2003) *Opening Minds: Project Handbook*, London: RSA.

Salovey, P. and Sluyter, D. (1997) *Emotional Development and Emotional Intelligence*, New York: Basic Books.

School Curriculum and Assessment Authority (SCAA) (1997) *The Arts and the Curriculum*, London: SCAA.

Seligman, M. (2004) *Authentic Happiness*, New York: Basic Books.

Seltzer, K. and Bentley, T. (1999) *The Creative Age: Knowledge and Skills for the New Economy*, London: Demos.

Sharp, P. (2001) *Nurturing Emotional Literacy*, London: David Fulton.

Shayer, M. and Adey, P. (2002) *Learning Intelligence: Cognitive Acceleration Across the Curriculum from 5–15 years*, Buckingham: Open University Press.

Shephard, L. (1992) What policy makers who mandate tests should know about the new psychology of intellectual ability and learning, in B. Gifford and M. O'Conner (eds), *Changing Assessments, Alternative of Aptitude, Achievement and Instruction*, London: Kluwer.

Shepherd, L. (1991) Psychometricians' beliefs about learning, *Education Researcher*, vol. 20, no. 8, pp. 2–16.

Silber, K. (1965) *Pestalozzi: The Man and his Work*, London: Routledge.

Slaughter, R. (1996) Mapping the future: creating a structural overview of the next 20 years, *Journal of Futures Studies*, vol. 1, no. 1, pp. 5–26.

Smith, A. and Call, N. (2000) *The Alps Approach: Accelerated Learning in Primary Schools*, Stafford: Network Educational Press.

Smith, F., Hardman, F., Wall, K. and Mroz, M. (2004) Interactive whole class teaching in the national literacy and numeracy strategies, *British Educational Research Journal*, vol. 30, no. 3, 395–411.

Steiner, R. (1919) *Education: An Introductory Reader*, London: Rudolf Steiner Press.

Sternberg, R. (1997a) *Thinking Styles*, Cambridge: Cambridge University Press.

Sternberg, R. (1997b) *Successful Intelligence*, New York: Plume.

Sternberg, R. (2002) Teaching students to be wise and not just smart, Keynote Lecture delivered 16 June at the 10th International Conference on Thinking, Harrogate.

Sternberg, R. and Williams, W. (eds) (1998) *Intelligence, Instruction and* Assessment, Mawah, NJ: Lawrence Erlbaum Associates.

Stone-Wisk, M. (ed.) (1998) *Teaching for Understanding*, San Francisco, CA: Jossey-Bass.

Swanwick, K (1994) *Musical Knowledge: Intuition, Analysis and Music Education*, London: Routledge.

Swanwick, K. (1999) Teaching Music Musically, London: Routledge.

Teacher Training Agency (TTA) (2003) *Qualifying to Teach: Handbook of Guidance*, London: TTA.

Thompson, P.M., Giedd, J.N., Woods, R.P., MacDonald, D., Evans, A.C. and Toga, A.W. (2000) Growth patterns in the developing brain detected by using continuum mechanical tensor maps. Nature, vol. 404, pp. 190–3.

UK Board of Education (1931) *The Primary School* (Hadow Report), London: HMSO.

Vygotsky, L. (1962) *Thought and Language*, New York: Wiley.

Vygotsky, L. (1978) *Mind in Society: The Development of Higher Psychological Pocesses*, Cambridge, MA: Harvard University Press.

Warnock, M. (1996) Foreword, in M. Bennathan and M. Boxall, *Effective Intervention in Primary Schools*, London: David Fulton.

Weare, K. and Gray, G. (2003) *What Works in Developing Children's Emotional and Social Competence and Well Being?* Norwich: HMSO.

White, J. (2002) *The Child's Mind*, London: Routledge.

Wilde, S., Wright, S., Hayward, G., Johnson, J. and Skerrett, R. (2006) *Nuffield Review Higher Education Focus Groups Preliminary Report, 09/02/06*. London: Nuffield.

Williams, S. (2005) Act 2 Scene 3, Track from Saul Williams Audio Compact Disc. Wichita 11 April.

Wilkinson, R. (2005) *The Impact of Inequality*, London, Routledge.

Wineburg, S. and Grossman, P. (eds) (2000) *Interdisciplinary Curriculum; Challenges to Implementation*, NewYork: Teachers College Press.

Wrigley, T. (2005) *Schools of Hope: A New Agenda for School Improvement*, reprinted edn, Stoke-on-Trent: Trentham.

Yates, K., Taylor, H., Drotar, D., Wade, S., Klein, S., Stancin, T. and Schatschneider, C. (1997) Research report pre-injury family environment as a determinate of recovery from traumatic brain injuries in school aged children, *Journal of the International Neurophysiological Society*, vol. 3, pp. 617–30.

Websites

Baird, A. and Fugelsang, J.(2004) The emergence of consequential thought, evidence from neuroscience, *Philosophical Transactions of the Royal Society*, published online November 2004, www.dartmouth.edu/~jonf/BaFug_RoySoc04.pdf (accessed 8 June 2006).

Barnes, J. (2005) Letter in Royal Society of Arts Education Newsletter, www.thersa.org/journal/letter.asp (accessed 8 June 2006).

BBC (2005) Digital Curriculum www.bbc.co.uk/info/policies/digital_curriculum.shtml (accessed 8 June 2006).

BECTA (2006) British Educational Communications Technology Agency website http://contentsearch.becta.org.uk/search/index.jsp?clear=y (accessed 12 June 2006).

Bread for the world (2005) www.bread.org/hungerbasics/international.html (accessed 28 August 2005).

Campaign for Learning (2006) www.campaign-for-learning.org.uk/ (accessed 12 June 2006).

Channel 4 (2005), *Supernanny*, television programme, www.channel4.com/health/microsites/S/supernanny/ (accessed 2 September 2005).

Childline (2004) children's charity, www.childline.org.uk/pdfs/review04.pdf (accessed 10 August 2005).

Childnet International (2003) Details of a Japanese conference on the child use of internet and mobile phone technology, www.iajapan.org/hotline/mobilepdf/proceedings.pdf (accessed 11 August 2005).

Children's Commissioner (2005) www.childrenscommissioner.org (accessed 14 June 2006).

Children's use of the Internet, (2006) http://internet-filter-review.toptenreviews.com/ (accessed 19 August 2006).

Clark, S. (2001) Assessment for learning in a Gillingham partnership, www.aaia.org.uk/pdf/Gillingham1.pdf#search=%22clarke%2C%20S%20assessment%20for%20learning%2C%202001%22 (accessed 12 August 2006).

Claxton, G. (2006) Building learning power, www.buildinglearningpower.co.uk/ (accessed 19 August 2006).

Collishaw et al. (2004) www.blackwell-synergy.com/doi/full/10.1111/j.1469-7610.2004.00335.x (accessed 21 June 2005).

Csikszentmihalyi, M. (2000) Lecture on flow theory, www.616.ips.k12.in.us/Theories/Flow/default.aspx (accessed 12 September 2005).

DfES (2002) Governors' reports and school prospectuses, www.teachernet.gov.uk/_doc/2170/GARSP%20primary.pdf (accessed 21 July 2005).

DfES (2004a) *Every Child Matters: Change for Children in Schools*, http://publications. teachernet.gov.uk/eOrderingDownload/DfES-1089-2004.pdf (accessed 28 August 2005).

DfES (2004b) *Learning and Teaching in the Primary School*, www.standards.dfes.gov.uk/ numeracy/publications/targeted_support/learn_teach_primary/pc_learnteach 034404_improve.pdf (accessed 7 June 2006).

DfES (2004c) *Excellence and Enjoyment*, primary education strategy, www.standards. dfes.gov.uk/primary/publications/literacy/63553/pns_excell_enjoy037703v2.pdf (accessed 23 March 2006).

DfES (2005a) Teachernet website, www.teachernet.com/ (accessed 14 June 2006).

DfES (2005b) Social, emotional and behavioural skills, www.standards.dfes.gov.uk/ primary/publications/banda/939949/ba_cpdcd174705modp.ppt (accessed 12 Jube 2006).

DfES (2006a) The standards site section on teachers as researchers, http://64.233.183. 104/search?q=cache:YvkfOKU3JAoJ:www.standards.dfes.gov.uk/ntrp/+teachers+as+ researchers+UK&hl=en&gl=uk&ct=clnk&cd=1 (accessed 10 June 2006).

DfES, (2006b) Creative learning journey, www.creativelearningjourney.org.uk/ introduction/commentary.html (accessed 19 August 2006).

DfES (2006c) 'Global Gateway' links with schools across the world, www.globalgate-way.org.uk/ (accessed 19 August 2006).

DfES/OFSTED (2004) Learners' personal development and well-being, p. 25, www.ofsted.gov.uk/publications/index.cfm?fuseaction=pubs.displayfile&id=3862& type=pdf (accessed 28 August 2005).

DH (2005) National Healthy Schools Standard, www.teachernet.gov.uk/management/ atoz/n/nhss/ (accessed 29 August 2005).

DH/DfES (2005) *National Healthy Schools Status, Guide for Schools*, www.un.org/ cyberschoolbus/briefing/labour/index.htm (accessed 12 June 2006).

Digital Worlds (2005) Geographical Information Systems package centred on school localities, www.digitalworlds.co.uk/primary%20curriculum.htm (accessed 23 March 2006).

Eco Schools project (2005) www.eco-schools.org.uk/ (accessed 26 August 2005).

Entwistle, N. (2000) *Deep and surface learning*, www8.caret.cam.ac.uk/pub/acadpub/ Entwistle2000.pdf (accessed 12 September 2005).

Fredrickson, B. (2004a) http://scholar.google.com/scholar?hl=en&lr=&q=cache: 3qKnvmO6jz8J:www.ruf.rice.edu/~gpotts/emotion/readings/Tugdale-04.pdf+ fredrickson+B.+%22positive+ emotions%22 (accessed 8 June 2006).

Fredrickson, B. (2004b) Royal Society Lecture, www.journals.royalsoc.ac.uk/ (rnrzkanhn20kaq4503ggbo45)/app/home/content.asp?referrer=contribution& format=3&page=1&pagecount=11(accessed 12 June 2006).

Frontline (2002) Article on the teenage brain, http://66.102.9.104/search? q=cache: 4vzYG0cqQDYJ:www.pbs.org/wgbh/pages/frontline/shows/teenbrain/etc/synop-sis.html+Giedd+couch+hardwired+%22use+it+or+lose+it%22&hl=en&lr=lang_en (accessed 12 September 2005).

Global gateway (2006) www.globalgateway.org/ (accessed 30 March 2006).

Hoffer, E., Wikipedia website, http://en.wikipedia.org/wiki/Eric_Hoffer (accessed 10 August 2006).

HM Government advice on health and safety, www.teachernet.gov.uk/wholeschool/ healthandsafety/visits/ (accessed 8 June 2006).

HM Government White Paper on Education, www.dfes.gov.uk/publications/school-swhitepaper/pdfs/DfES-Schools%20White%20Paper.pdf (accessed 21 March 2006).

International Primary Curriculum (IPC) (2006) www.internationalprimarycurriculum.com/press.php?id=0 (accessed 10 February 2006).

Layard, R. (2006) Report on depression, http://cep.lse.ac.uk/textonly/research/mental-health/DEPRESSION_REPORT_LAYARD.pdf (accessed 19 August 2006).

Maynard, T. (2004) Report on the effectiveness of Forest Schools in Wales, www2.swan.ac.uk/news_centre/news_item.asp?news_id=4630 (accessed 8 June 2006).

Morris, E. (2006) www.emotionalintelligence.co.uk/appliedei.htm (accessed 12 June 2006).

Murray, J. (2001) TV violence and brain mapping in children, *Psychiatric Times*, vol. 18, no.10, http://psychiatrictimes.com/p011070.html (accessed 19 August 2006).

National Literacy Trust (2005) www.literacytrust.org.uk/Database/stats/readchild.html#Young (accessed 28 August 2005).

OFSTED (2002) *The Curriculum in Successful Primary Schools*, www.ofsted.gov.uk/publications/index.cfm?fuseaction=pubs.displayfile&id=303&type=pdf (accessed 8 June 2006).

OFSTED (2003) Expecting the unexpected, www.ofsted.gov.uk/publications/docs/3377.DOC (accessed 8 June 2006).

One Org (2005) International campaign to make poverty history, www.makepoverty-history.org/schools/index.shtml (accessed 28 August 2005).

Pediatrics (2002) http://pediatrics.aappublications.org/cgi/content/full/109/6/1028 (accessed 12 June 2006).

Pew Internet and American Life project, (2005) http://medialit.med.sc.edu/mediause.htm (accessed 28 August 2005).

Project Zero (2006) http://pzweb.harvard.edu/ (accessed 8 June 2006).

QCA (2003) Respect for all: reflecting cultural diversity through the curriculum, www.qca.org.uk/8859.html (accessed 30 March 2006).

QCA (2005) *Creativity: Find It Promote It* (video May 2005) and website, www.ncaction.org.uk/creativity/index.htm (accessed 23 March 2006).

Race Relations Act (2000) www.opsi.gov.uk/acts/acts2000/20000034.htm (accessed 30 March 2006).

Reggio Emilia (2006) http://zerosei.comune.re.it/inter/index.htm (accessed 30 March 2006).

Room 13 Scotland (2005) website, www.room13scotland.com/ideology.html, (accessed 21 July 2005).

Rousseau, J. (1762) Translation of *Emile ou de l'education*, www.ilt.columbia.edu/pedagogies/rousseau/em_eng_bk1.html (accessed 17 October 2006).

RSA (2005) RSA's Global Challenges, by J. Glenn, August 2005, www.rsa.org.uk/journal/article.asp?articleID=574 (accessed 10 October 2005).

Sanchez, E. and Gruber (2005) *Rhythm is it* (film), www.rhythmisit.com/en/php/index_noflash.php (accessed 19 August 2006).

School Councils (2005) www.schoolcouncils.org/ (accessed 14 June 2006).

Scotsman (2006), Happiness and wealth article, http://216.239.59.104/search?q=cache:dNQiIlWIthsJ:money.scotsman.com/scotsman/articles/articledisplay.jsp%3Farticle_id%3D3014507%26section%3DBanking%26prependForce%3DSM_XML_+lottery+winners+happiness+2006&hl=en&gl=uk&ct=clnk&cd=5 (accessed 6 April 2006).

Smithers, A. and Robinson, P. (2001) *Teachers Leaving*, Centre for Employment Research University of Liverpool, report, London: NUT, http://publications. teachernet.gov.uk/eOrderingDownload/DfES10772004.pdf (accessed 12 December 2005).

Social and Emotional Aspects of Learning (SEAL) (2006) www.standards.dfes. gov.uk/primary/publications/banda/seal/pns_seal137805_guidance.pdf (accessed 21 March 2006).

Statistics on television-watching and young people(2005) www.ukfilmcouncil. org.uk/statistics/yearbook/?y=2004&c=9&skip=1 (accessed 11 August 2005).

Stephen Lawrence Inquiry (1999) (Macpherson Report), www.archive.official-documents.co.uk/document/cm42/4262/4262.htm (accessed 30 March 2006).

Thomas Coram School (2006) www.thomascoram.camden.sch.uk/ (accessed 6 February 2006).

Times Educational Supplement (2005) article on links with Ugandan schools, www. tes.co.uk/section/story/?story_id=2128257&window_type=print (accessed 25 November 2005).

UK Film Council (2004) www.ukfilmcouncil.org.uk/information/statistics/year-book/?y=2004&c=9&skip=1 (accessed 10 August 2006).

UN (1989) *Convention on the Rights of the Child*, www.unicef.org/crc/crc.htm (accessed 5 August 2005).

UN (2000) United Nation's millennium goals, www.un.org/millenniumgoals/ (accessed 14 April 2006).

UN (2006) Schools website 'Cyberschoolbus', www.un.org/cyberschoolbus/briefing/ labour/index.htm (accessed 12 June 2006).

UNICEF (2005) Children living in poverty: a review of child poverty definitions, measurements and policies, www.unicef.org/policyanalysis/files/child_poverty_ final_draft_4_05.pdf (accessed 29 August 2005).

USDE (2002) *No Child Left Behind*, US Education policy, www.ed.gov/nclb/landing. jhtml (accessed 12 June 2006).

WHO (2004) Health behaviour in school aged children study, international report 2001/2002, www.euro.who.int/Document/e82923.pdf (accessed 30 March 2006).

Wikipedia (2006) The case of Genie and language acquisition, http://216.239.59. 104/search?q=cache:6ZDk3ey-vRcJ:en.wikipedia.org/wiki/Language_acquisition+ Genie+language&hl=en&gl=uk&ct=clnk&cd=5 (accessed 12 June 2006).

Wilde, S., Wright, S., Hayward, G., Johnson, J. and Skerrett, R. (2006) *Nuffield Review Higher Education Focus Groups Preliminary Report, 09/02/06*, www.nuffield14-19 review.org.uk/files/news44-2.pdf (accessed 14 June 2006).

Index